PSYCHOLOGY PRACTITIONER GUIDEBOOKS

EDITORS

Arnold P. Goldstein, Syracuse University
Leonard Krasner, Stanford University & SUNY at Stony Brook
Sol L. Garfield, Washington University in St. Louis

POSTTRAUMATIC STRESS DISORDER

Titles of Related Interest

POSTTRAUMATIC STRESS DISORDER

A Behavioral Approach to Assessment and Treatment

Edited by
PHILIP A. SAIGH

Graduate School and University Center of the
City University of New York, NY

ALLYN AND BACON
Boston London Toronto Sydney Tokyo Singapore

Printed in the United States of America

10 9 8 7 6 5 4 3   96 95 94 93

ISBN 0-205-14553-7

Library of Congress Catologing-in-Publication Data

Posttraumatic stress disorder : a behavioral approach to assessment
    and treatment / edited by Philip A. Saigh.
      p.   cm. -- (Psychology practioner guidebooks)
    Includes indexes.
    1. Post-traumatic stress disorder. 2. Behavior therapy.
3. Cognitive therapy. I. Saigh, Philip A. II. Series.
    [DNLM: 1. Behavioral Therapy. 2. Stress Disorders, Post
-Traumatic. WM 170 P857]
RC552.P67P6678   1991
616.85'21--dc20
DNLM/DCL
for Library of Congress   91-1953
                                                                   CIP

For Samia Saigh

Contents

Foreword

Perhaps one of the most significant and constructive consequences of the war in Vietnam has been the professional and scientific study of those survivors of combat stress who suffer the condition now known as posttraumatic stress disorder. For over 200 years the medical literature has contained reports of the psychological and physiological distress of those so exposed. Interest in the acute symptoms, which resulted from life-threatening exposure, peaked during and after each successive war in every country. There came a recognition in the nineteenth century that significant suffering occurred in people exposed to major catastrophes as well as to the increasing number of major natural disasters that took place with industrialization and the expansion of rapid transport. Particularly with regard to industrial accidents, the persistence of symptoms over long periods of time brought both legal and professional controversy as to the etiology as well as the reality of enduring consequences of massive emotional threats to the individual. It was not until the end of the nineteenth century, in some parts of the medical community, that the symptom complex was thought to be the direct consequence of the massive psychological and emotional turmoil created by sudden catastrophic experiences. Indeed, it was only during the earlier decades of this century that the unique behavioral and symptomatic expression of what is now called posttraumatic stress disorder was acknowledged.

World War I deepened the conviction that the acute expressions of posttraumatic stress were the result of psychological threat and emotional turmoil. In both Allied and German armies, many combat soldiers who were seriously impaired behaviorally by their exposure to stress experienced resolution of their acute and major symptoms as the result of psychological treatment only—primarily through hypnosis or catharsis. An expansion of these therapeutic efforts brought narcosynthesis (the use of intravenous barbiturates), mainly as a therapeutic intervention during World War II.

Interest in the war neuroses, or traumatophobia, fell away after both world wars. But the studies of American World War I combat veterans by Kardiner and the growing knowledge of the seriously disabling psychological consequences to the Jewish survivors of the Nazi concentration camps and the surviving Allied prisoners of war from German and Japanese camps aroused a new interest in the etiology and treatment of the condition. The majority of therapeutic studies of these late consequences of massive psychological trauma were done by psychoanalysts. That work emphasized particularly the difficulty in establishing a therapeutic transference as well as the untreatability of the major symptoms of the disturbance. It led, however, to an appreciation of the potential uses of group therapies as a means of effecting a therapeutic milieu for some of the sufferers and of mitigating some of the expressions of social alienation.

Undoubtedly one of the major positive contributions of the disastrous American involvement in the Vietnam War was the arousal of interest in what is now denoted posttraumatic stress disorder. The condition is associated with social alienation, expressions of grief, rage and hostility, and severe social pathology, expressed in suicides, alcoholism, drug abuse, and manical breakdown and incapacity to maintain steady employment. An avalanche of professional papers, books, audiovisual presentations, and public discussions have been produced on this subject within the last decade. It was because of this interest, which aroused active political interest, that the U.S. Veterans Administration established its outreach centers to care for those veterans disabled by their experience in Southeast Asia.

Interest in the combat-induced state has spilled over, so that now many active studies have been reported on those victimized by assaults upon themselves in civil life. Within the U.S. Veterans Administration, the interest in the plight of the Vietnam veterans has rekindled interest in the longtime sufferers of World War II and the Korean conflict. Many of the latter have been found to have similar disorders and have been missed diagnostically over the years.

Among the treatment methods that have been tried in recent years are those based on learning theory—the behavioral approach. Dr. Saigh and his colleagues have done a service in putting this experience before us in this book. Every reader interested in this approach will find the material herein of value to them. This book fills a gap in our knowledge concerning treatment of posttraumatic stress disorder.

Lawrence C. Kolb, M.D.

Preface

Information pertaining to the effects of traumatic stress has been chronicled for centuries. Indeed, reports dating from the Great Fire of London attest to the unique symptoms of what the DSM-III Reactive Disorders Committee came to term as posttraumatic stress disorder (PTSD) in 1980. The formal recognition of the disorder definitely served to facilitate communication, research, and practice. A considerable amount of empirical research has been conducted by behaviorally oriented investigators since the disorder was included in the American Psychiatric Association's taxonomy of mental disorders. Despite the increased interest in the disorder, only a few books have dealt with the topic. In the main, these works have not provided an integrated approach to theory and practice. Moreover, these books have largely presented psychodynamic or atheoretical approaches that are antithetical to behavioral research and practice. In view of this and the availability of an expanded, empirically driven literature base, this book provides a behavioral approach to research and practice.

I owe a considerable debt of gratitude to John Fairbank for his perceptive chapter reviews and well-founded suggestions at various stages of the editorial process. I would also like to thank David Foy, Richard McNally, Jack Rachman and William Schlenger for the critical reviews they provided. Of course, the kind efforts of Lawrence Kolb and the chapter authors are appreciated. The editorial assistance of Sebastian Bonner and Chris Kaufman must also be acknowledged. Finally, the kind support of my wife and son is deeply appreciated.

Philip A. Saigh
New York

Chapter 1

History, Current Nosology, and Epidemiology

Philip A. Saigh

HISTORICAL OVERVIEW

Information regarding the effects of traumatic experiences has been chronicled for centuries. A vivid example is apparent in the 1666 diary of Samuel Pepys. Writing 6 months after he witnessed the Great Fire of London, Pepys observed that "it is strange to think how to this very day I cannot sleep a night without great terrors of the fire; and this very night could not sleep to almost two in the morning through thoughts of the fire" (quoted in Daly, 1983, p. 66). Somewhat later, Emil Kraepelin, the celebrated nineteenth-century nosologist, used the term *schreckneurose* ("fright neuroses") to denote a discrete clinical condition "composed of multiple nervous and psychic phenomena arising as a result of severe emotional upheaval or sudden fright which would build up great anxiety; it can therefore be observed after serious accidents and injuries, particularly fires, railway derailments or collisions" (Kraepelin, 1896, translated by Jablensky, 1985, p. 737).

During World War I, Frederick Mott (1919) and Ernest Southard (1919) extensively documented the neurological and psychological effects of war-related traumas. Viewed along these lines, Mott (1919) provided the following autobiographical account of a British lieutenant who was convalescing in England after having been trapped behind enemy lines:

> During the five days spent in the village of Roeux I was continually under our own shell fire and also continually liable to be discovered by the enemy, who was also occupying the village. Each night I attempted to get through

1

his lines without being observed, but failed. On the fourth day my sergeant was killed at my side by a shell. On the fifth day I was rescued by our troops while I was unconscious. During this time I had had nothing to drink or eat, with the exception of about a pint of water. At the present time I am subject to dreams in which I hear these shells bursting and whistling through the air. I continually see my sergeant, both alive and dead, and also my attempts to return are vividly pictured. I sometimes have in my dreams that feeling of intense hunger and thirst which I had in the village. When I awaken I feel as though all strength had left me and am in a cold sweat. For a time after awaking I fail to realize where I am, and the surroundings take on the form of the ruins in which I remained hidden for so long. Sometimes I do not think that I thoroughly awaken, as I seem to doze off, and there are the conflicting ideas that I am in the hospital, and again that I am in France. During the day, if I sit doing nothing in particular and I find myself dozing, my mind seems to immediately begin to fly back to France. (pp. 126–127)[1]

In a similar vein, Southard (1919) provided a detailed description of the war-induced startle response of a French corporal whose trench collapsed during a shelling incident. Although the corporal escaped physical injury, "his pulse was variable; at rest it stood at 60; if a table nearby was struck suddenly, it would go up to 120" (p. 309). Somewhat later, Myers' (1940) *Shell Shock in France, 1914–1919* made the distinction between "shell concussion" and "shell shock." Shell concussion was regarded as a neurological condition that was induced by a physical trauma, whereas shell shock was regarded as a psychic condition that was brought about by exposure to extreme stress.

In 1935, Prasad provided a general description of the emotional distress in India following a devastating earthquake. Adler (1943) went on to describe the "post-traumatic mental complications" of the survivors of Boston's Coconut Grove Fire. Adler's article is particularly relevant inasmuch as she made clear reference to the victim's trauma-related ideation, nightmares, insomnia, and avoidance behaviors.

With the advent of World War II, mental health practitioners (e.g., Grinker & Spiegel, 1945; Lewis, 1942; Raines & Kolb, 1943) evaluated and treated thousands of war-related psychiatric casualties. In their influential *Men Under Stress,* Grinker and Spiegel (1945) enumerated the symptoms of "returnees" (i.e., repatriated combatants) who suffered from "combat neuroses." These symptoms consisted of restlessness, aggression, depression, memory impairment, sympathetic overactivity, concentration impairment, alcoholism, nightmares, phobia, and suspicion. Somewhat later, Archibald, Long, Miller, and Tuddenham (1962) compared the symptoms of 57 World War II veterans with "chronic combat fatigue" to the symptoms of 24 veterans who had not been exposed to combat. Although the data collec-

---

[1]From Mott, F. W. (1919). *War Neuroses and Shell Shock,* (pp. 126–127). London: Oxford University Press. Copyright 1919 by Oxford University Press. Reprinted with permission.

tion took place 15 years after the armistice, the veterans with combat fatigue evinced higher estimates of psychiatric morbidity, as noted in Figure 1.1.

Although the aforementioned World War II reports attest to the psychiatric legacies of combat, similar patterns of morbidity were observed by mental health practitioners who evaluated and treated repatriated internees (Chadoff, 1963; Eitinger, 1962; Nandini, 1952; Wolf & Ripley, 1947; Nadler & Ben-Shushan, 1989). Shortly after the surrender of Japan, Wolf and Ripley (1947) described the emotional adjustment of 34 Allied prisoners who had been interned by the Japanese for approximately 3 years. In addition to inadequate rations, disease (e.g., malaria, beriberi, and dysentery), these individuals were subjected to forced labor, beatings, and more elaborate forms of torture. Of these cases, 22.9% presented with war-related nightmares and fears, blunted affect, memory impairment, anger, and depression. In a similar vein, Eitinger (1962) interviewed 100 Norwegian survivors of the Nazi concentration camps and observed that 85 cases presented with chronic fatigue, reduced concentration, and increased irritability. Eitinger also noted that most of these cases experienced "painful associations" that could occur in "any connection whatsoever, from seeing a person stretching his arms and associating this with his fellow prisoners

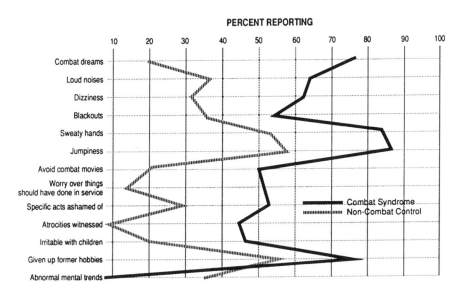

FIGURE 1.1. Psychiatric morbidity of combat veterans and noncombat controls. From H. C. Archibald, D. M. Long, C. Miller, & R. D. Tuddenham, (1962). Gross stress reaction in combat—A 15 year follow-up. *American Journal of Psychiatry, 119,* 317–322. Copyright 1962, the American Psychiatric Association. Reprinted by permission.

hung up by their arms under torture, to seeing an avenue of trees and visualizing long rows of gallows with swinging corpses" (p. 372).

Prompted by the prevalence of war-related psychiatric morbidity after World War II, the American Psychiatric Association's (APA) Committee on Nomenclature and Statistics included *gross stress reaction* as a psychiatric category in its *Diagnostic and Statistical Manual of Mental Disorders* (DSM-I) of 1952. According to the 1952 nosology, the diagnosis was justified in situations involving exposure to "severe physical demands or extreme stress, such as in combat or in civilian catastrophe" (p. 40). The DSM I went on to acknowledge (contrary to the prevailing psychodynamic view on psychosocial development) that "in many instances this diagnosis applies to previously more or less "normal" persons who experience intolerable stress" (p. 40). The DSM-I did not, however, provide operational criteria for the category.

Studies involving Korean war casualties (Edwards & Peterson, 1954; Glass, 1954; Glass, Ryan, Lubin, Reddy & Tucker, 1956; Lifton, 1954; Noble, Roudebush & Prince, 1952) presented a similar clinical composite. For example, Noble and Roudebush's (1952) assessment of 42 wounded combatants determined that 23 cases were experiencing "startle reactions, occasional combat dreams, slight stammering, and other evidences of tension that had arisen during their combat experiences" (p. 496).

The 1950s and 1960s were also associated with pioneering research involving civilians' reactions to natural and industrial disasters (cf. Quarantelli, 1985). Reasoning that information derived from civilian disasters may be used to gauge the effects of war-related disasters (e.g., a nuclear explosion), the National Academy of Sciences funded a number of investigations that sought to assess the adjustment of individuals who survived major fires, gas explosions, earthquakes, and the like. For example, Bloch, Silber, and Perry (1956) interviewed 88 children who survived a tornado that devastated much of Vicksburg, Mississippi, in 1953. The Bloch et al. (1956) report is particularly relevant inasmuch as it clearly indicated that traumatized children, much like traumatized adults, experience trauma-related nightmares, avoidance behaviors, startle reactions, irritability, and an increased sensitivity to traumatic stimuli. Subsequent studies involving the 1962 Alaska earthquake (Langdon & Parker, 1964), the sinking of the *Andrea Doria* (Friedman & Linn, 1957), and the Bristol floods (Bennet, 1968) served to highlight the unique distress of traumatized survivors.

In 1968, the APA's Committee on Nomenclature and Statistics reconvened and issued the DSM-II. Although the 1952 gross stress reaction category had achieved international recognition (Anderson, 1985), the classification was summarily omitted from the 1968 nosology. The APA went on to introduce the category of *transient situational disturbance* in the DSM-II. The 1968 appellation was reserved for "transient disorders of any severity (including those of psychotic proportions) that occur in individuals without any underlying mental disorders and that represent an acute reaction to overwhelming environmental stress" (American Psychiatric Association, 1968, p. 48). The DSM-II also listed a series of age-related subclassifications (i.e., adjustment reaction of childhood or adult life). As in the case of the DSM-I, the DSM-II did not provide operational diagnostic criteria for the classification.

In 1974, Burgess and Holmstrom published an influential paper on the "rape trauma syndrome." Their report was based on interviews conducted over a 1-year interval with 146 rape victims. Burgess and Holmstrom's analysis led to the conclusion that rape victims experience acute and long-term phases of distress. The acute phase was characterized by general physical soreness from the attack, tension headache, sleep disturbance, nightmares, gastrointestinal pains, genitourinary disturbances, fear, anger, and guilt. The long-term phase was associated with rape-related nightmares, ideation, avoidance (45.6% relocated), fears, and sexual dysfunction. Analogously, Kilpatrick, Veronen, and Resick (1979) provided a comparative analysis of postrape morbidity over time. In doing so, the authors administered the Modified Fear Survey (MFS; Veronen & Kilpatrick, 1979) to 46 rape victims and 35 controls. Assessments occurred 6 to 10 days following the rape and 1, 3, and 6 months thereafter. Data analysis determined that the aggregate MFS scores of the rape victims initially (i.e., at 6 to 10 days and at 1 month) significantly exceeded the aggregate MFS scores of the controls. Although the subsequent aggregate MFS comparisons were not significant, item-discrepancy estimates determined that the rape victims were significantly more fearful of discrete rape-related stimuli (e.g., strangers, being alone, emergency rooms, and nude men) across assessments.

Although preliminary reports regarding the mental health of American troops in Southeast Asia were quite favorable (Bloach, 1969; Bourne, 1970), Albert Glass (1973), the noted military psychiatrist, cautioned that the "reported low rates of neuropsychiatric casualties from Vietnam may be questioned until all categories of non-combat losses are stated" (p. 998). Subsequent reports regarding the adjustment of demobilized veterans (Horowitz & Solomon, 1975; Panzarella, Mantell, & Bridenbaugh, 1978; Shatan, 1978; Strayer & Ellenhorn, 1975) lent a good deal of credence to Glass's admonition. Viewed along these lines, Horowitz and Solomon (1975) used the term *delayed stress response syndrome* to describe the symptomatology of a considerable number of Vietnam veterans who were receiving psychiatric services at Veterans Administration hospitals. According to Horowitz and Solomon, the syndrome involved "nightmares, painful moods and emotional storms, direct or symbolic behavioral repetitions, and concomitant secondary signs such as impaired social relationships, aggressive and self-destructive behavior, and fear of loss of control over hostile impulses" (p. 72). Similar forms of morbidity were observed by Panzarella et al. (1978), who administered a symptom checklist to 143 military personnel (34 Vietnam veterans and 109 non-Vietnam veterans). Data analysis clearly revealed that the Vietnam veterans evinced more symptoms of "guilt, withdrawal, suspiciousness, feelings of being abused by others, apathy, anxiety, irritability, moodiness, depression, confusion, hostile impulses, anger episodes, tormenting memories, nightmares, insomnia, frustration over a banal existence, alienation, and flashback experiences" (p. 161).

Examined in toto, it is apparent that traumatized individuals may develop extensive and long-lasting emotional problems. It is also apparent that various appellations have been used over time to describe this form of morbidity. Regrettably, the use of different terms to describe the same phenomenon served to confuse and in some cases retard the progress of scientists and practitioners. Commenting on the nosological confusion, Kardiner (1969) lamented that despite the "vast store of data available . . . it is hard to find a province in psychiatry in which there is less discipline than this one. There is practically no continuity to be found anywhere, and the literature can only be characterized as anarchic. Every author has his own frame of reference—lengthy bibliographies notwithstanding" (p. 246). Clearly, this situation was counterproductive, and the need for a well-grounded (i.e., operational) and nationally recognized nosology was acutely apparent.

CURRENT NOSOLOGY

Prompted by the DSM-II's dearth of operational criteria, limited reliability, and modest coverage (only 108 classifications were listed) (Feighner, Robins, Guze, Woodruff, Winokur, & Munoz, 1972; Morey, Skinner, & Blashfield, 1986; Spitzer & Fleiss, 1974), the APA established a task force to update the 1968 taxonomy of mental disorders in 1975. Under the stewardship of Robert Spitzer, psychiatrists, psychologists, and social workers collaborated in preparing detailed symptomological profiles for 265 classifications. In the best sense of the Kraepelinian tradition, the various advisory committees provided information as to age of onset, associated features, course, predisposing factors, prevalence, sex ratio, and differential diagnosis. Viewed along these lines, the DSM-III (APA, 1980) Reactive Disorders Committee (Nancy Anderson, Robert Lifton, Chaim Shatan, Jack Smith, Robert Spitzer, and Lyman Wynne) drew on clinical experiences and the existing literature in formulating the diagnostic criteria for what was termed *posttraumatic stress disorder* (PTSD). According to the 1980 taxonomy, PTSD involved the "development of characteristic symptoms following a psychologically traumatic event that is generally outside the realm of human experience" (APA, 1980, p. 236). It was also indicated that the "stressor producing this syndrome would evoke significant symptoms of distress in most people, and is generally outside the range of such common experiences as simple bereavement, chronic illness, business losses or marital conflict" (p. 237). It is important to realize in this context that this clinical perspective served to facilitate the dissemination of scientific information among mental health practitioners inasmuch as it clearly recognized that puissant stressors (e.g., combat, rape, or natural disasters) could induce very similar patterns of psychopathology.

The 1980 nosology also provided specific diagnostic criteria for identifying the disorder. Examined in this context, Table 1.1 provides the criteria for formulating an Axis I DSM-III PTSD diagnosis.

Table 1.1. DSM-III Diagnostic Criteria for Posttraumatic Stress Disorder

A. Existence of a recognizable stressor that would evoke significant symptoms of distress in almost everyone.
B. Reexperiencing of the trauma as evidenced by at least one of the following:
    (1) recurrent and intrusive recollections of the event
    (2) recurrent dreams of the event
    (3) sudden acting or feeling as if the traumatic event were recurring because of an association with an environmental or ideational stimulus
C. Numbing of responsiveness to or reduced involvement with the external world, beginning some time after the trauma, as shown by at least one of the following:
    (1) markedly diminished interest in one or more significant activities
    (2) feeling of detachment or estrangement from others
    (3) constricted affect
D. At least two of the following symptoms that were not present before the trauma:
    (1) hyperalertness or exaggerated startle response
    (2) sleep disturbance
    (3) guilt about surviving when others have not, or about behavior required for survival
    (4) memory impairment or trouble concentrating
    (5) avoidance of activities that arouse recollection of the traumatic event
    (6) intensification of symptoms by exposure to events that symbolize or resemble the traumatic event

Subtypes

Posttraumatic Stress Disorder, Acute
A. Onset of symptoms within six months of the trauma.
B. Duration of symptoms less than six months.

Posttraumatic Stress Disorder, Chronic or Delayed
Either of the following, or both:
    (1) duration of symptoms six months or more (chronic)
    (2) onset of symptoms at least six months after the trauma (delayed)

Note: Criteria from the American Psychiatric Association: *Diagnostic and Statistical Manual of Mental Disorders, Third Edition.* Washington, DC, American Psychiatric Association, 1980. Reprinted by permission.

Following its publication in 1980, the DSM-III gained considerable recognition and came to serve as a lingua franca among mental health practitioners in the United States. Likewise, the PTSD classification gained considerable currency among mental health practitioners (see Figure 1.2). Despite the apparent success of the DSM-III, revisionary efforts were initiated in 1983. The DSM-III-R was subsequently published in 1987.

As in the case of the DSM-III PTSD classification, the 1987 nosology recognized the development of symptoms following "a psychologically distressing event that is outside the range of usual human experience" (p. 247). Unlike its predecessor, the DSM-III-R provides examples of different classes of trauma that could induce the disorder. Direct exposure to puissant stress characterized by "threats to one's life or physical integrity" (APA, 1987, p. 247) reflects one class of trauma. The second class of trauma involves observational experiences such as "sees another person who has been or is being seriously injured or killed as a result of an accident or physical violence" (APA, 1987, pp. 247–248). Finally, the DSM-III-R indicates that verbal mediation that entails "learning about a serious threat or harm to a close friend or relative (e.g., learning that one's child has been kidnapped or tortured," p. 248) constitutes the third class of trauma.

With respect to diagnostic criteria, the 30-member DSM-III-R PTSD subcommittee retained (with some elaboration) the criteria that were listed in the DSM-III, with a notable exception. The acute subtype was dropped. In lieu of this, examiners should indicate whether the onset was delayed

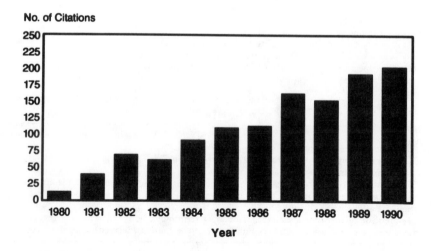

FIGURE 1.2. Medline PTSD citations over time.

for 6 months or more after the trauma. With these points in mind, Table 1.2 presents the criteria for establishing a DSM-III-R PTSD diagnosis.

Associated Features

The DSM-III-R indicates that symptoms of depression and anxiety are common and in some cases may be sufficiently severe to warrant additional diagnoses (e.g., simple phobia or major depression). Impulsive behavior

Table 1.2. DSM-III-R Diagnostic Criteria for Posttraumatic Stress Disorder

A. The person has experienced an event that is outside the range of usual human experience and that would be markedly distressing to almost anyone, e.g., serious threat to one's life or physical integrity; serious threat or harm to one's children, spouse, or other close relatives and friends; sudden destruction of one's home or community; or seeing another person who has recently been, or is being, seriously injured or killed as the result of an accident or physical violence.
B. The traumatic event is persistently reexperienced in at least one of the following ways:
    (1) recurrent and intrusive, distressing recollections of the event (in young children, repetitive play in which themes or aspects of the trauma are expressed)
    (2) recurrent distressing dreams of the event
    (3) sudden acting or feeling as if the traumatic event were recurring (includes a sense of reliving the experience, illusions, hallucinations, and dissociative [flashback] episodes, even those that occur upon awakening or when intoxicated)
    (4) intense psychological distress at exposure to events that symbolize or resemble an aspect of the traumatic event, including anniversaries of the trauma.
C. Persistent avoidance of stimuli associated with the trauma or numbing of general responsiveness (not present before the trauma), as indicated by at least three of the following:
    (1) efforts to avoid thoughts or feelings associated with the trauma
    (2) efforts to avoid activities or situations that arouse recollections of the trauma
    (3) inability to recall an important aspect of the trauma (psychogenic amnesia)
    (4) markedly diminished interest in significant activities (in young children, loss of recently acquired developmental skills such as toilet training or language skills)
    (5) feeling of detachment or estrangement from others
    (6) restricted range of affect, e.g., unable to have loving feelings
    (7) sense of foreshortened future, e.g., does not expect to have a career, marriage, or children, or a long life
D. Persistent symptoms of increased arousal (not present before the trauma), as indicated by at least two of the following:
    (1) difficulty falling or staying asleep
    (2) irritability or outbursts of anger
    (3) difficulty concentrating
    (4) hypervigilance
    (5) exaggerated startle response
    (6) physiologic reactivity upon exposure to events that symbolize or resemble an aspect of the traumatic event (e.g., a woman who was raped in an elevator breaks out in a sweat when entering any elevator).
E. Duration of disturbance (symptoms in B, C, and D) of at least one month.
Specify delayed onset if the onset of symptoms was at least six months after the trauma.

Note: Criteria from the American Psychiatric Association: *Diagnostic and Statistical Manual of Mental Disorders, Third Edition, Revised.* Washington, DC, American Psychiatric Association, 1987. Reprinted by permission.

(e.g., suddenly changing a place of residence) as well as symptoms of an organic mental disorder (e.g., poor memory, concentration impairment, headache, and vertigo) may also be evident. Finally, the DSM-III-R reports that individuals who were exposed to life-threatening traumas in the company of others may feel guilty about surviving (while others did not) or guilt regarding what they had to do to survive.

Validity

A well-validated nosology offers several important advantages (Morey, Skinner, & Blashfield, 1986). Initially, it may serve as a basis for accurate communication. Without this, practitioners would confuse their communications by using different terms to describe the same conditions, and identical terms to described different phenomena. In a similar vein, a well-validated nosology may facilitate research and theory formation. Finally, well-founded diagnoses that are based on a viable nosology should lead to the provision of a treatment of choice. With these points in mind, Quay (1986) offered that a psychiatric classification should be "empirically validated by determining its relationship to other variables. Of particular concern is differential validity; two putatively separate disorders ought not to be related in the same way to the same variable" (p. 37). In a similar vein, Van Praag (1990) observed that "there is nothing wrong with basing the first draft of an operational taxonomy on expert opinions. However, once having postulated a taxonomy, experts should be honorably discharged and replaced by researchers to study the merits of the system" (p. 149). From this information, it should be clear that the extant classification was intuitively established (i.e., field trials were not conducted) and that the notion that people may develop profound and chronic impairments due to stress exposures has not always been warmly embraced. General George Patton, for example, issued a memorandum on August 5, 1944, in which soldiers who claimed to be "nervously incapable of combat" were to be branded as "cowards." Four days later, General Patton proceeded to slap a hospitalized patient who had been diagnosed as having that condition (cf. Drayer & Glass, 1973, p. 26). More recently, Goodwin and Guze (1984) commented on the "almost total lack of evidence that posttraumatic stress disorder, delayed type, exists as a clinical entity" (p. 82).

In view of the aforementioned points, several comparative studies were conducted to test the validity of the classification. Roberts, Penk, Gearing, Robinowitz, Dolan, and Patterson (1982) divided a sample of Vietnam veterans into two subsamples (specifically, high or low incidence of PTSD symptoms). Roberts et al. (1982) subsequently observed that the veterans with high PTSD ratings evinced elevated scores on scales 0, 4, and 6 of the Minnesota Multiphasic Personality Inventory (MMPI). Fairbank, Keane, and Malloy (1983) tested the discriminant validity of the classification by administering a series of self-report inventories to three groups of Vietnam veterans. The first group was composed of veterans who were enrolled in a stress management program for PTSD patients. The second group consisted of patients with diverse psychiatric classifications (aside from PTSD), and the third group consisted of nonclinical controls. Fairbank and his colleagues observed that the PTSD patients presented higher ratings on all of the MMPI scales than the relevant comparison groups. In addition, it was apparent that the State Trait Anxiety Inventory (Spielberger, Gorsuch, & Lushene, 1970), Beck Depression Inventory (Beck, Ward, Mandelson, Mock, & Erbaugh, 1961), and Zung Depression Inventory (Zung, 1965) scores of the PTSD cases were significantly greater than the scores of the clinical and nonclinical controls.

Examined from a psychophysiological perspective, Blanchard, Kolb, Pallmeyer, and Gerardi (1982) created an experimental protocol to discriminate between Vietnam veterans with PTSD and a nonveteran control group. Both groups listened to recordings of combat sounds as their blood pressure, skin temperature, forehead muscle activity, and skin resistance were monitored. Blanchard et al. (1982) went on to observe that "only the PTSD group's heart rate, systolic blood pressure, skin temperature and forehead muscle activity consistently differed from the control group's" (p. 217). In a similar vein, Blanchard, Kolb, Gerardi, Ryan, and Pallmeyer (1986) compared a group of Vietnam veterans with PTSD to a group of Vietnam veterans without psychiatric morbidity. The heart rate of each group was monitored as a recording of "emotionally meaningful combat sounds including helicopters, AK47's firing, mortars and screaming wounded" was played (p. 597). As may be noted from Figure 1.3, the PTSD cases evinced more heartbeats per minute than the nontraumatized controls. Moreover, the PTSD cases experienced marked reactivity to combat sounds as compared to the controls.

Following the basic paradigm employed by Blanchard and his colleagues, Ornitz and Pynoos (1989) recorded startle responses (i.e., eyeblink reflex) to bursts of white noise among seven childhood PTSD cases and six nonclinical controls. To assess the nonstartling and facilitative modulation of startle response (DSM-III-R Criterion D5), startle response was modulated by nonstartling acoustic trials. Data analysis clearly revealed that the PTSD cases experienced a "significant loss of normal inhibitory modulation of startle response" (p. 866). Ornitz and Pynoos went on to propose that the traumatic experiences the subjects had encountered (i.e., a school shooting incident) induced a long-term brainstem dysfunction.

Adhering to a more biological model, Kudler, Davidson, Meador, Lipper, and Tim (1987) determined that PTSD patients, in contrast to de-

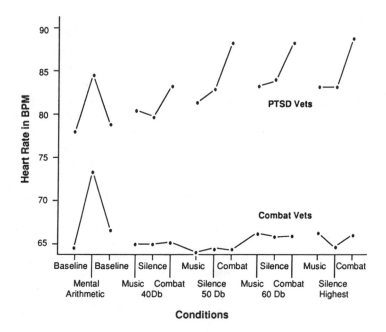

FIGURE 1.3. Mean heart rates of PTSD positives and negatives. From E. B. Blanchard, L. C. Kolb, R. J. Gerardi, P. Ryan, & T. P. Pallmeyer, (1986). Cardiac response to relevant stimuli as an adjunctive tool for diagnosing posttraumatic stress disorder in Vietnam veterans. *Behavior Therapy, 17,* 592–606. Copyright 1986 by the Association for Advancement of Behavior Therapy. Reprinted by permission of the publisher and the author.

pressed patients, rarely exhibited nonsuppression on the dexamethasone suppression test. Moreover, Kosten, Mason, Giller, Ostroff, and Harkness (1987) observed that the mean urinary norepinephrine and epinephrine levels of PTSD patients were elevated relative to the levels of patients with diverse DSM-III diagnoses (i.e., major depression, bipolar disorder-manic, paranoid schizophrenia, and undifferentiated schizophrenia).

Viewed from a child-clinical perspective, Saigh (1988a) administered the Revised Children's Manifest Anxiety Scale (RCMAS; Reynolds & Richmond, 1978), Children's Depression Inventory (CDI; Kovacs, 1981), Test Anxiety Inventory (TAI; Spielberger, 1980), and the Conners Teacher Rating Scale (CTRS; Conners, 1969) to three groups of adolescents. The first group presented with chronic PTSD, and the second group presented with test phobia. The third group consisted of nonclinical controls. Saigh reported that the PTSD cases evinced higher levels of morbidity on the RCMAS, CDI, and CTRS than the clinical and nonclinical controls. It was also apparent that the phobia cases had appreciably higher TAI scores than their counterparts. In a follow-up study, Saigh (1989a) administered the

RCMAS, CDI, and CTRS to three groups of children (i.e., PTSD, test phobia, and controls) whose ages ranged from 9 to 13 years. Saigh subsequently observed that the PTSD cases evinced markedly greater RCMAS, CDI, and CTRS scores than did their clinical and nonclinical peers. Analogously, the RCMAS and CDI scores of the phobic cases were appreciably greater than those of the control groups. On the other hand, the CTRS scores of the test phobia and control groups were not significantly different.

In an effort to test the DSM-III-R suggestion that PTSD may be induced through direct experience, observation, or information transmission, Saigh (in press) used the Children's Posttraumatic Stress Disorder Inventory (Saigh, 1989b) to identify 230 childhood PTSD cases. Of these, 58, 128, 13, and 31 had been traumatized through direct experience, observation, verbal mediation, or combinations thereof. In a similar vein, the Children's Posttraumatic Stress Disorder Inventory was used to identify 35 nonclinical controls. Both groups marked the RCMAS and CDI, and their conduct was rated against the CTRS criteria. Although there were no significant differences between the scores of the PTSD groups, all of the PTSD groups evinced significantly greater RCMAS, CDI, and CTRS scores than the nonclinical controls.

Although the aforementioned studies present a selected review of an expanding literature base, it is apparent that the differential levels of morbidity provide a good deal of support for the validity of PTSD as a unique psychiatric entity. Furthermore, the studies that were reviewed provide considerable evidence that the disorder may affect adults, adolescents, and children.

EPIDEMIOLOGY

Reliable information regarding the prevalence of a disorder among individuals who are at risk as well as the general population is of considerable import in understanding the nature and scope of a psychiatric classification (Saigh, 1988a). The accurate quantification of prevalence data is also essential for investigators and practitioners who are interested in issues relating to the etiology of the condition. Finally, viable epidemiological estimates are of considerable import to social policymakers who must formulate important decisions regarding the allocation of resources for prevention and treatment (Keane, Litz, & Blake, in press). With this in mind, it is interesting to note that despite the abundance of trauma-related investigations, epidemiologists have failed to reach a consensus about the prevalence of the disorder.

Rachman's (1978) salient analysis of the British psychiatric literature published during World War II clearly concluded that "the great majority of the people endured the air raids extraordinarily well, contrary to the universal expectation of mass panic. Exposure to repeated bombings did not produce a significant increase in psychiatric disorders. Although short-lived fear reactions were common, surprisingly few persistent phobic reactions emerged" (p. 182). In a similar vein, Kettner (1972) analyzed the service records of 1,086 Swedish UN troops that saw action in the Congo (now Zaire) during 1961 and observed that only 35 soldiers succumbed to "combat exhaustion." Four years after those events occurred, Kettner obtained the postmilitary records of 1,242 Swedes who were stationed in the Congo and who had not experienced combat. Kettner's analysis concluded that "the combat veterans did not differ from the noncombat veterans in total morbidity or psychiatric morbidity after their UN service" (p. 98). Analogously, Bourne's (1970) analysis of the medical records of American servicemen stationed in Vietnam concluded that "the most significant finding of the conflict has been that the number of psychiatric casualties has been amazingly low" (pp. 125–126).

Saigh (1984a, 1984b, 1985a, 1985b) described a series of serendipitous studies that charted the course of self-reported anxiety before and after the 1982 Israeli invasion of Lebanon. In conjunction with a test cross-validation study, Wolpe and Lang's (1964) Fear Survey Schedule, Spielberger, Gorsuch, and Lushene's (1968) State Trait Anxiety Inventory, and Saigh's (1982) Lebanese Fear Inventory (an index of war-related fears) were administered to 77 Lebanese junior high school students and 128 undergraduates at the American University of Beirut. On June 6, 1982 (57 days after the junior high school assessment and 6 days after the undergraduate assessment), Israel invaded Lebanon, and by June 14 Israeli units completely surrounded West Beirut (the areas where the junior high school and University are located). Although a considerable number of West Beirut's civilians evacuated to Christian East Beirut, the Lebanese mountains, or other countries, a substantial number of civilians remained in West Beirut. In addition to being exposed to intermittent shelling and strafing, these individuals experienced considerable environmental adversities (i.e., electricity and water were cut off at the height of the summer heat, and food, medicine, and petrol were in very short supply). Following the withdrawal of Israeli, Palestinian, and Syrian forces, the Lebanese government, with the aid of American, British, French, and Italian forces, was able to reassert its authority over West Beirut for the first time in 8 years. Although this tenure of authority was limited to 15 months, the assertion of Lebanese sovereignty was associated with a pronounced reduction in the level of hostility (i.e., abductions, shelling, and the like stopped).

Against this background, 64 junior high school students were interviewed regarding their experiences during the invasion. Of these, 16 indicated that they had been in West Beirut throughout the Israeli siege. The junior high school students went on to mark the self-report inventories 6 to 8 weeks after the withdrawal of foreign forces. Six months later, the junior high school students (46 evacuees and 16 nonevacuees) were retested. In a similar vein, 88 undergraduates (38 nonevacuees and 50 evacuees) were reassessed 6 months after the withdrawal of opposing forces. Data analysis of the junior high school and undergraduate scores determined that there were no significant differences between the preinvasion scores of the evacuees and nonevacuees. Surprisingly, it was also apparent that there were no significant differences between the postinvasion scores of the evacuees and nonevacuees. Moreover, the aggregate scores of the evacuees and nonevacuees on war-related stimuli as measured by the Lebanese Fear Inventory were significantly lower at postassessment. Saigh (1984a) subsequently concluded that "prolonged exposures to life threatening events that are subsequently mollified may not be associated with higher levels of delayed anxiety . . ." and that these levels of anxiety "may decrease following the withdrawal of t`ie stimuli that mediated them" (p. 682).

Commenting on earlier research (Taylor, Ross, & Quarantelli, 1976) involving the 1974 Xenia Ohio tornado, Quarantelli (1985) reported that the study found "an extremely low rate of severe mental illness, if any at all as a consequence of the tornado. On the contrary . . . a large percentage of people had *extremely positive reactions* to the disaster" (p. 192). Quarantelli also indicated that "only 1% of the population had considered suicide at any time" and that "only 3% reported any increase in drinking whereas 7% of the Xenians claimed that they consumed less alcohol" (p. 194). Clearly, the Rachman, Kettner, Bourne, Saigh, and Quarantelli reports strongly suggest that long-term reactivity to highly stressful events is extremely modest.

Despite the apparent consensus among the aforementioned reports, discordant estimates were reported by a different set of investigators. Kristal (1978), for example, compared 66 Israeli adolescents who resided in an agricultural settlement along the 1972 Israeli-Jordanian frontier to 77 matched cases who lived in an inland settlement. The former group resided from 1968 through 1971 in an environment of "ubiquitous threat and constant danger in the form of indiscriminate shelling and terrorist attacks" (p. 74). In contrast, the controls had not experienced war-related stress as described above. Eighteen to 20 months after the 1971 Arab-Israel cease fire, the subjects received dental exams and it was apparent that the shelled subjects had a higher incidence of bruxism (grinding of the teeth, a psychosomatic condition associated with stress). Kristal subsequently administered the Children's Manifest Anxiety Scale (CMAS; Castaneda, McCandless, Palermo, 1956) to both groups, and no significant differences were observed. At this point, both groups viewed a 12-minute film that simulated an ambush of an Israeli patrol, shelling, and civilians in turmoil. The subjects proceeded to mark the CMAS immediately after the film presentation. Data analysis determined that the anxiety estimates of the shelled adolescents significantly exceeded the estimates of the controls. Kristal went on to suggest that war-related stimuli (e.g., bomb shelters) in the border subjects' environment were stressful enough to evoke memories of earlier traumas and that this, coupled with uncertain peace prospects, were inducing bruxism. Kristal also suggested that the shelled adolescents developed a strong disposition to respond to war-related stimuli with elevated levels of situational anxiety.

In a similar vein, Lifton and Olson (1976) reported considerable morbidity after interviewing 22 survivors of the devastating flood in Buffalo Creek, West Virginia. Despite the fact that the interviews occurred 1 to 2 years after the flood, Lifton and Olson concluded that the disaster had a major impact on the "symbolization of life-continuity, and the persistence of psychic numbing had to do with the collective inability to overcome imagery of disintegration, separation, and stasis, or to achieve any new sense of purpose that might reactivate imagery of integrity, connection, or movement" (p. 17).

In a frequently cited war-related study, Egendorf, Kadushin, Laufer, Rothbart, and Sloan (1981) interviewed 1,089 Vietnam veterans and concluded that 16.6% of the overall sample and 29.6% of the interviewees with combat experience developed emotional problems after they repatriated. In a similar vein, Keane and Fairbank (1983) surveyed 1,380 mental health practitioners at 114 Veterans Administration Medical Centers across the United States and concluded that "the most consistent finding of the survey was the rating of Vietnam veterans as more poorly adjusted than veterans of previous wars" (p. 35).

Card (1983) described the pre- and post-Vietnam adjustment of 481 Vietnam veterans, 502 non-Vietnam veterans, and 487 nonveterans. All of Card's subjects completed a battery of cognitive, general information, personality, and vocational tests in 1963 (i.e., when they were 14 to 15 years old). Two to 12 years after the initial assessment, the Vietnam veterans experienced different degrees of war exposure (e.g., 12.7% never experienced combat and 4.87% experienced combat quite often). In 1974 (at the age of 29 to 30), the subjects marked a questionnaire that measured educational experiences, career plans, family life, health, community involvement, and discrete psychiatric symptoms (e.g., nightmares). Data analysis revealed that the Vietnam veterans reported a greater incidence and severity of physical problems than their classmates. Moreover, the Vietnam veterans reported more psychophysiological disturbances involving sleep-related problems, loss of control, blunted affect, hyperalertness, anxiety, and depression.

Kilpatrick, Best, Veronen, Amick, Villeponteaux, and Ruff (1985) interviewed 2,004 women in Charleston County, South Carolina, regarding crime experiences and subsequent mental health. The authors reported that 436 women indicated that they had been criminally victimized (e.g., raped, assaulted, or robbed) and that these victims reported significantly more nervous breakdowns, suicidal ideation, and attempted suicides than the nonvictimized subjects.

Examined conceptually, it is apparent that discordant estimates of morbidity have been reported. It should be realized, however, that these studies involved different stressors, ethnic groups, measures, and data collection procedures. As such, the epidemiological disparity may have been due to any or all of the aforementioned factors. It should also be noted that none of the aforementioned studies measured for PTSD per se. In view of this, a clearer conceptual synthesis may be obtained by considering studies that assessed PTSD through the administration of checklists or structured clinical interviews that reflect the DSM-III or DSM-III-R diagnostic criteria. Given that exposure to a discrete stressor is part of the diagnostic criteria for PTSD, a clearer epidemiological synthesis may also be obtained by reviewing the literature by major stressor category (i.e., war, disaster, and criminal victimization).

War-Related Studies

Helzer, Robins, and McEvoy (1987) used the DSM-III–based Diagnostic Interview Schedule (DIS; Robins et al., 1981) and observed a 1% lifetime prevalence of PTSD among 2,493 adults in the St. Louis area. It is interesting to note that Helzer and his colleagues also observed a 6.3% lifetime prevalence among a subsample ($n = 64$) of combat veterans. In a similar vein, Snow, Stellman, Stellman, and Sommer (1988) administered a PTSD symptom checklist that reflected the DSM-III PTSD criteria to 2,858 American legionnaires who had served in Southeast Asia. Data analysis determined that 429, or 15.0%, of the respondents met criteria for a current PTSD diagnosis. Analogously, the Centers for Disease Control (CDC) (1988) administered the DIS to 2,490 Vietnam veterans and 1,972 non-Vietnam veterans. At the time of this study, both groups were similar with respect to level of education, employment, income, marital status, and satisfaction with personal relationships. Despite these similarities, the Vietnam veterans evinced higher levels of depression (4.5% versus 2.3%), anxiety (4.9% versus 3.2%), and alcohol abuse (13.7% versus 9.2%) than the non-Vietnam veterans. The CDC also observed a 13% lifetime prevalence and 2.2% current prevalence of combat-related PTSD among the Vietnam cohort.

As part of an important epidemiological survey with etiological implications, Goldberg, True, Eisen, and Henderson (1990) administered a DSM-III-R symptom checklist to 715 monozygotic twin pairs who were discordant for military service in Southeast Asia. Although the survey by Goldberg et al. (1990) occurred 15 years after the Vietnam era, data analysis evinced a current prevalence of 16.8% among the twins who served in Southeast Asia as compared to a 5.0% prevalence among their co-twins who did not serve in Southeast Asia.

In the most comprehensive assessment of war-related PTSD to date (i.e., the National Vietnam Veterans Readjustment Study [NVVRS]), Kulka, Schlenger, Fairbank, Hough, Jordan, Marmar, and Weiss (1990) conducted face-to-face interviews with representative samples of veterans who served in Southeast Asia (1,173 males and 424 females), areas other than Southeast Asia (404 males and 296 females), and matched civilian controls (435 males and 210 females). Prevalence estimates were formulated on the basis of a multiple component assessment package that included the Structured Clinical Interview for the DSM-III-R (Spitzer & Williams, 1986), the Mississippi Scale for Combat-Related PTSD (Keane, Caddell, & Taylor, 1988), and the PTSD subscale of the MMPI (Keane, Malloy, & Fairbank, 1984). The analysis by Kulka et al. (1990) determined that 15.2% of the male and 8.5% of the female Southeast Asia veterans met criteria for a current PTSD diagnosis. These rates of morbidity markedly exceeded the rates observed among the non-Southeast Asia veterans (2.5% males and 1.1% females) or the civilian controls (1.2% males and 0.3% females). Given this data, Kulka and his colleagues estimated that 479,000 of the 3,140,000 men and 610 of the 7,200 women who served in Southeast Asia during the Vietnam era currently meet criteria for PTSD. Kulka et al. (1990) also observed a 30.6% lifetime PTSD prevalence among the male Southeast Asia veterans and a 26.9% lifetime prevalence among the female veterans. The NVVRS investigators went on to estimate that 960,000 men and 1,900 women who served in Southeast Asia had PTSD at some time in their lives.

Examined from a child clinical perspective, Kinzie and his colleagues (Kinzie et al., 1986; Kinzie et al., 1989) chronicled the psychiatric morbidity of a sample of Cambodian adolescents who immigrated to the United States following the fall of the abusive and violent Pol Pot regime (1975–1979). At the age of 8 to 12 years, these subjects suffered "catastrophic trauma caused by separation from their families, forced labor, starvation, personal injuries, and the witnessing of many deaths and executions" (Kinzie et al., 1986, p. 501). Kinzie et al. (1986) went on to administer the DIS to 40 adolescents (mean age = 17 years) approximately 2.5 years after their immigration to the United States. It was subsequently observed that 20 cases (50%) met DSM-III criteria for PTSD. Three years later (8 to 10 years after the traumatic events of Cambodia), Kinzie et al. (1989) were able to locate and reexamine 27 subjects. Of these, 8 (29.6%) met criteria for PTSD as indicated by DIS diagnoses. Eleven (40.8%) never met criteria, and the remaining 8 (29.6%) evinced a variable course of PTSD inasmuch as three (11.1%) persons who initially met criteria failed to do so at follow-up and five (18.5%) cases who initially did not meet criteria did so at follow-up.

Analogously, Saigh (1989a) administered the Children's Posttraumatic Stress Disorder Inventory to 840 Lebanese children (mean age = 10.7 years). These cases had been referred for assessment by Red Cross officials, physicians, or educators on the basis of having been exposed to puissant war-related stressors (e.g., being in a building that was shelled or witnessing the violent death of a relative). Although the assessments occurred from 1 to 2 years after the subjects had been exposed to traumatic war-related events, only 231 (27.5%) children met criteria for a current PTSD diagnosis.

Disaster Studies

The number of disaster studies that have measured for PTSD is very modest. Two recent investigations have, however, specifically tested for PTSD among tornado (Madakasira & O'Brien, 1987) and flood (Green, Lindy, Grace, Glesser, Leonard, Korol, & Winget, 1990) survivors. Viewed in this regard, Madakasira and O'Brien (1987) administered an expanded version of the Hopkins Symptom Checklist (HSC; Derogatis, Lipman, & Rickles, 1974) to 116 survivors of a tornado that ravaged Pitt County, South Carolina. The expanded version of the HSC was expressly modified to reflect the DSM-III criteria for PTSD. Although Madakasira and O'Brien's subjects marked the instrument 5 months after the disaster, 69 cases (59.5%) met DSM-III criteria for an acute PTSD classification.

Green, Lindy, Grace, Glesser, Leonard, Korol, and Winget (1990) went on to administer the DSM-III based SCID (Spitzer & Williams, 1986) to 120 adult survivors of the Buffalo Creek flood. Although Green et al.'s (1990) assessment occurred 14 years after the flood, 34 (28.3%) individuals met criteria for a current PTSD diagnosis. Interestingly, Green and her colleagues were able to make retrospective diagnoses on the basis of 1974 interview data. They subsequently determined that 53 (44.2%) of the subjects would have met DSM-III criteria for PTSD in 1974.

Criminal Victimization Studies

Kilpatrick, Saunders, Veronen, Best, and Von (1987) assessed the prevalence of crime-related PTSD among a representative sample of females in Charleston, South Carolina. In doing so, the DIS was administered to 391 women. Data analysis determined that 295 (75%) of the respondents had been victimized. Of these, 53% were the victims of sexual assault, 9.7% of aggravated assault, 5.6% robbery, and 45.3% burglary. Of the aggregate of crime victims, the DIS indicated that 27.8% met the criteria for PTSD at some time in their lives and that 7.5% currently met the criteria. A striking 57.1% of the rape victims met the lifetime prevalence criteria, and 16.5% of these individuals evinced sufficient symptomology to warrant a current diagnosis. It is also interesting to note that 28.2% of the subjects who were the victims of the "nonviolent" crime of burglary developed PTSD and that 6.8% of these cases were experiencing the disorder at the time of the assessments. McLeer, Deblinger, Atkins, Foa, and Ralphe (1988) administered a DSM-III-R PTSD symptom checklist to 31 children (mean age = 8.4 years). All of these children had been sexually abused on at least one occasion. Sexual abuse was defined as "sexual touching, with or without force, by anyone five or more years older than the child" (McLeer et al., 1988, p. 65). Data analysis determined that 15 (48.4%) children met DSM-III-R criteria for PTSD at the time of the assessments. Of these cases, 75% had been abused by natural fathers, 67% by strangers, and 25% by trusted adults. Interestingly, none of the subjects who had been abused by older children received a PTSD diagnosis.

Weisaeth (1989) administered a DSM-III-R symptom checklist to 13 Norwegian sailors who had been imprisoned and tortured in Libya. In the course of their 67-day ordeal, the crew was subjected to many traumatic experiences. Weisaeth reported that "one seaman was murdered, beaten to death. Before he died, he was taken to the ship so that his comrades could see him" (p. 65). In addition, the surviving crew experienced mock executions, unscheduled interrogations, threats of torture, extreme heat, infectious diarrhea, and a lack of medical services. Six months after their release, seven men (53.8% of the crew) met the criteria for PTSD.

Table 1.3 presents a summary of the prevalence data that were considered herein. On the basis of this information, it is apparent that discordant lifetime and current estimates have been observed. The discordance may be explained in part by recalling that a PTSD diagnosis requires exposure to trauma and that populations that systematically experienced extreme stress should evince more morbidity than general community-based populations. Thus, one would expect Kinzie's Cambodian refugees to have a higher prevalence of PTSD than Helzer's St. Louis ECA subjects. The disparity may also be explained by pointing out that investigations that used the DIS may have underestimated the prevalence of the disorder inasmuch as the sensitivity of this index is rather low (Davidson & Fairbank, 1990). In a similar vein, Davidson and Fairbank cogently argued that the variations between the CDC and NVVRS current prevalence estimates (2.2% vs. 15.2%) may also be due to the methods that were used to identify cases. Whereas the CDC diagnosed cases on the basis of DIS interviews conducted by lay interviewers, the NVVRS cases were identified on the basis of agreement over multiple measures of PTSD. These measures included the PTSD subscale of the MMPI, reports of symptoms to lay interviewers using the Mississippi Combat Scale for PTSD, and SCID diagnoses that were derived by highly trained expert clinicians. Finally, impressive variations were noted with respect to the type, duration, and intensity of precipitating stressors among the at-risk groups that were considered, and it is expected that these variations would have a bearing on the observed estimates.

Despite the variations in prevalence, it is clear that exposure to a psychologically distressing event that is beyond the realm of ordinary human experience is not sufficient to warrant the development of PTSD. It is of considerable interest to note that many individuals endure exceptionally traumatic experiences with few, if any, complications. On the other hand, others experience comparatively mild trauma and go on to develop severe PTSD. Obviously, these variations raise a host of etiological questions, and these concerns are addressed in the next chapter.

SUMMARY AND FUTURE DIRECTIONS

Information pertaining to the effects of traumatic stress has been chronicled for centuries. Reports dating from the Great Fire of London clearly document the unique symptoms of what the DSM-III Reactive Disorders Committee came to term as posttraumatic stress disorder. Despite considerable evidence to the contrary, the notion that people may develop profound and chronic impairments because of stress exposures has not always been warmly received. In view of this and the scientific need to empirically validate the classification as denoted in the American Psychiatric Association's taxonomy of mental disorders, several investigators examined the differential validity of the classification across a host of subjects and settings. These studies strongly support the validity of the classification as a unique psychiatric entity.

Unfortunately, it has been quite difficult to reach an epidemiological consensus regarding the prevalence of the disorder. A number of war-related, disaster, and criminal victimization studies attest to amazingly low levels of psychiatric morbidity. On the other hand, similar studies attest to much higher levels of pathology. The discordance may be explained in part by recalling that variations were noted among the populations that were sampled and the data collection procedures that were employed. Despite the epidemiological disparity, it is clear that exposure to a psycho-

Table 1.3. Current and Lifetime PTSD Estimates

Investigations	Subjects	Measures	PTSD (%) Current	Lifetime
Helzer et al., 1987	2,493 adults in St. Louis ECA	DIS		1.0
	Subsample of 64 combat veterans			6.3
Snow et al., 1988	2,858 American legionnaires	PTSD Symptom Checklist	15.0	
CDC, 1988	2,490 Vietnam veterans	DIS	2.2	13.0
Goldberg et al., 1990	715 monozygotic twins	PTSD Symptom Checklist		
	Vietnam veterans		16.8	
	Non-Vietnam veterans		5.0	
NVVRS, 1990	Southeast Asia veterans	SCID, MMPI, Mississippi PTSD		
	1,173 males	Combat Scale	15.2	30.6
	424 females		8.5	26.9
	Non-Southeast Asia veterans			
	404 males		2.5	
	296 females		1.1	
	Civilian controls			
	435 males		1.2	
	210 females		0.3	
Kinzie, et al., 1986	40 Cambodian adolescent refugees	DIS	50.0	
Kinzie, et al., 1989	27 Cambodian adolescent refugees	DIS	29.6	59.2
Saigh, 1989a	840 Lebanese children	Children's PTSD Inventory	27.5	
Madakasira & O'Brien, 1987	116 tornado victims	Adapted Hopkins Symptoms Checklist	59.5	
Green et al., 1990	120 flood victims	SCID	28.3	44.2
Kilpatrik et al., 1987	295 crime victims	DIS	7.5	27.8
McLeer et al., 1988	31 sexually abused children	PTSD Symptom Checklist	48.4	
Weiseath, 1989	13 tortured Norwegian sailors	PTSD Symptom Checklist	58.3	

logically traumatic event does not inevitably lead to the development of PTSD. Indeed, many individuals have endured exceptionally traumatic events with few, if any, long-term complications.

Without a doubt, the formal recognition of PTSD served to facilitate communication, research, and theory formation. As this work goes to press, a major field trial is in progress and a 31-member committee is preparing a revised set of PTSD diagnostic criteria for the DSM-IV. Although this committee has not concluded its work, it is anticipated that once formalized, the DSM-IV diagnostic criteria for PTSD will engender a new round of validation studies. It is also anticipated that these studies will further our understanding of the correlates of PTSD across a host of behavioral, self-report, psychophysiological, and biological indicators. In addition, it is expected that future epidemiological studies will go beyond the current cross-sectional approach and examine the effects of traumatization over time.

REFERENCES

Adler, A. (1943). Neuropsychiatric complications in victims of Boston's Coconut Grove disaster. *Journal of the American Medical Association, 123,* 1098–1101.

American Psychiatric Association. (1952). *Diagnostic and statistical manual of mental disorders.* Washington, DC: Author.

American Psychiatric Association. (1968). *Diagnostic and statistical manual of mental disorders* (2nd ed.). Washington, DC: Author.

American Psychiatric Association. (1980). *Diagnostic and statistical manual of mental disorders* (3rd ed.). Washington, DC: Author.

American Psychiatric Association. (1987). *Diagnostic and statistical manual of mental disorders* (3rd ed., Rev.). Washington, DC: Author.

Anderson, N. C. (1985). Posttraumatic stress disorder. In H. I. Kaplan & B. J. Sadock (Eds.), *Comprehensive textbook in psychiatry* (4th ed., pp. 918–924). Baltimore: William & Wilkins.

Archibald, H. C., Long, D. M., Miller, C., & Tuddenham, R. D. (1962). Gross stress reaction in combat—A 15 year follow-up. *American Journal of Psychiatry, 119,* 317–322.

Beck, A. T., Ward, C. H., Mandelson, M., Mock, J., & Erbaugh, J. (1961). An inventory for measuring depression. *Archives of General Psychiatry, 4,* 561–571.

Bennet, G. (1968). Bristol floods of 1968: Controlled survey effects on health of local community disaster. *British Medical Journal, 298,* 454–458.

Blanchard, E. B., Kolb, L. C., Gerardi, R. J., Ryan, P., & Pallmeyer, T. P. (1986). Cardiac response to relevant stimuli as an adjunctive tool for diagnosing posttraumatic stress disorder in Vietnam veterans. *Behavior Therapy, 17,* 592–606.

Blanchard, E. B., Kolb, L. C., Pallmeyer, T. P., & Gerardi, R. J. (1982). A psychological study of posttraumatic stress disorder in Vietnam veterans. *Psychiatric Quarterly, 54,* 220–229.

Bloach, H. S. (1969). Army clinical psychiatry in a combat unit. *American Journal of Psychiatry, 126,* 401–406.

Bloch, D. A., Silber, E., & Perry, S. E. (1956). Some factors in the emotional reaction of children to disaster. *American Journal of Psychiatry, 112,* 416–422.

Bourne, P. G. (1970). Military psychiatry and the Vietnam experience. *American Journal of Psychiatry, 127,* 481–488.

Burgess, A. W., & Holmstrom, L. L. (1974). Rape trauma syndrome. *American Journal of Psychiatry, 131,* 981–986.

Card, J. J. (1983). *Lives after Vietnam: The personal impact of military service.* Lexington, MA: Lexington Books.

Castaneda, R. M., McCandless, B. R., & Palermo, D. S. (1956). The children's form of the Manifest Anxiety Scale. *Child Development, 27,* 317–326.

Centers for Disease Control (1988). Health status of Vietnam veterans: Psychological characteristics. *Journal of the American Medical Association, 259,* 2701–2707.

Chadoff, P. (1963). Late effects of the concentration camp syndrome. *Archives of General Psychiatry, 8,* 323–333.

Conners, C. K. (1969). A teacher rating scale for use with children. *American Journal of Psychiatry, 126,* 884–888.

Daly, R. J. (1983). Samuel Pepys and posttraumatic stress disorder. *British Journal of Psychiatry, 143,* 64–68.

Davidson, J. R. T., & Fairbank, J. A. (1990). *Position paper on the epidemiology of PTSD.* Washington, DC: DSM-IV Subcommittee on PTSD, American Psychiatric Association.

Derogatis, L. R., Lipman, R. S., & Rickles, K. (1974). The Hopkins Symptom Checklist (HSCL): A self-report symptom inventory. *Behavioral Science, 19,* 1–15.

Drayer, C. S., & Glass, A. J. (1973). Italian campaign (9 September 1943–1 March 1944), Psychiatry established at the Army level. In W. S. Mulling (Ed.), *Neuropsychiatry in World War Two,* Vol. 2 (pp. 25–109). Washington, DC: Office of the Surgeon General, Department of the Army.

Edwards, R. M., & Peterson, D. B. (1954). Korea: Current psychiatric procedures and communication in the combat theater. *American Journal of Psychiatry, 110,* 721–724.

Egendorf, A., Kadushin, R. S., Laufer, R. S., Rothbart, G., & Sloan, L. (1981). *Legacies of Vietnam: Comparative adjustment of veterans and their peers.* New York: Center for Policy Research.

Eitinger, L. (1962). Concentration camp survivors in the postwar world. *American Journal of Orthopsychiatry, 32,* 367–375.

Fairbank, J. A., Keane, T. M., & Malloy, P. F. (1983). Some preliminary characteristics of Vietnam veterans with posstraumatic stress disorder. *Journal of Consulting and Clinical Psychology, 51,* 912–919.

Feighner, J. P., Robins, E., Guze, S. B., Woodruff, R. A., Winokur, G. W., & Munoz, R. (1972). Diagnostic criteria for use in psychiatry. *Archives of General Psychiatry, 26,* 57–63.

Friedman, P., & Linn, L. (1957). Some psychiatric notes on the *Andrea Doria* disaster. *American Journal of Psychiatry, 113,* 426–432.

Glass, A. J. (1954). Psychotherapy in the combat zone. *American Journal of Psychiatry, 110,* 725–731.

Glass, A. J. (1973). Lessons learned. In W. S. Mullins (Ed.), *Neuropsychiatry in World War Two,* Vol. 2 (pp. 989–1027). Washington, DC: Office of the Sugeon General, Department of the Army.

Glass, A. J., Ryan, F. J., Lubin, A., Reddy, C. V., & Tucker, A. C. (1956). *Psychiatric prediction and military effectiveness.* Walter Reed Army Institute of Research, Walter Reed Army Medical Center, Washington, DC.

Goldberg, J., True, W. R., Eisen, S. A., Henderson, W. G. (1990). A twin study of the effects of the Vietnam war on posttraumatic stress disorder. *Journal of the American Medical Association, 263,* 1227–1232.

Goodwin, D. W., & Guze, S. B. (1984). *Psychiatric diagnosis* (3rd ed.). New York: Oxford University Press.

Green, B. L., Lindy, J. D., Grace, M. C., Glesser, G. C., Leonard, A. C., Korol, M., & Winget, C. (1990). Buffalo Creek survivors in the second decade: Stability of stress symptoms. *American Journal of Orthopsychiatry, 60,* 43–54.

Grinker, R. R., & Spiegel, J. P. (1945). *Men under stress.* Philadelphia: Blakiston.

Grinker, R. R., & Spiegel, J. P. (1945). *War neurosis.* Philadelphia: Blakiston.

Helzer, J. E., Robins, L. N., & McEvoy, L. (1987). Posttraumatic stress disorder in the general population. *New England Journal of Medicine, 317,* 1630–1634.

Horowitz, M. D., & Solomon, G. F. (1975). A prediction of delayed stress response syndrome in Vietnam veterans. *Journal of Social Issues, 4,* 67–79.

Jablensky, A. (1985). Approaches to the definition and classification of anxiety and related disorders in European psychiatry. In A. H. Tuma & J. D. Maser (Eds.), *Anxiety and the anxiety disorders*. Hillsdale, NJ: Lawrence Erlbaum Associates.

Kardiner, A. (1969). Traumatic neuroses of war. In S. Arieti (Ed.), *American handbook of psychiatry* (pp. 246–257). New York: Basic Books.

Keane, T. M., Caddell, J. M., & Taylor, K. L. (1988). Mississippi Scale for Combat-Related Posttraumatic Stress Disorder: Three studies in reliability and validity. *Journal of Consulting and Clinical Psychology, 56*, 85–90.

Keane, T. M., & Fairbank, J. A. (1983). Survey analysis of combat-related stress disorder in Vietnam veterans. *American Journal of Psychiatry, 140*, 348–350.

Keane, T. M., Litz, B. T., & Blake, D. D. (1990). Posttraumatic stress disorder in adults. In M. Hersen & C. Last (Eds.). *Handbook of child and adult psychotherapy: A longitudinal perspective.* Elmsford, NY: Pergamon Press.

Keane, T. M., Malloy, P. F., & Fairbank, J. A. (1984). Empirical development of an MMPI subscale for the assessment of combat-related posttraumatic stress disorder. *Journal of Consulting and Clinical Psychology, 52*, 888–891.

Kettner, B. (1972). Combat strain and subsequent mental health. *Acta Psychiatrica Scandinavica, 22*, 5–107.

Kilpatrick, D. G., Best, C. L., Veronen, L. J., Amick, A. E., Villeponteaux, L. A., & Ruff, G. A. (1985). Mental health correlates of criminal victimization: A random community survey. *Journal of Consulting and Clinical Psychology, 53*, 866–873.

Kilpatrick, D. G., Saunders, B. E., Veronen, L. J., Best, C. L., & Von, J. M. (1987). Criminal victimization: Lifetime prevalence, reporting to police, and psychological impact. *Crime and Delinquency, 33*, 479–488.

Kilpatrick, D. G., Veronen, L. J., & Resick, P. A. (1979). Assessment of the aftermath of rape: Changing patterns of fear. *Journal of Behavioral Assessment, 1*, 133–147.

Kinzie, J. D., Sack, W. H., Angell, R. H., Clarke, G., & Ben, R. (1989). A three year follow-up of Cambodian young people traumatized as children. *Journal of the American Academy of Child and Adolescent Psychiatry, 28*, 501–504.

Kinzie, J. D., Sack, W. H., Angell, R. H., & Mason, S. M. (1986). The psychiatric effects of massive trauma on Cambodian children. *Journal of the American Academy of Child and Adolescent Psychiatry, 25*, 370–376.

Kosten, T. R., Mason, J. W., Giller, E. L., Ostroff, R. B., & Harkness, L. (1987). Sustained urinary norepinephrine and epinephrine elevation in post-traumatic stress disorder. *Psychoneuroendocrinology, 12*, 13–20

Kovacs, M. (1981). *The Children's Depression Inventory*. Pittsburgh: University of Pittsburgh Press.

Kraepelin, E. (1886). *Psychiatrie: Vol 5: Auflage*. Leipzig: Barth.

Kristal, L. (1978). Bruxism: An anxiety response to environmental stress. In C. D. Spielberger & I. G. Sarason (Eds.), *Stress and anxiety*, Vol 5, (pp. 45–58). New York: John Wiley & Sons.

Kudler, H., Davidson, J. Meador, K., Lipper, S., & Ely, T. (1987). The DST and posttraumatic stress disorder. *American Journal of Psychiatry, 144*, 1068–1071.

Kulka, R. C., Schlenger, W. E., Fairbank, J. A., Hough, R. L., Jordan, B. K., Marmar, C. R., & Weiss, D. S. (1990). *Trauma and the Vietnam generation: Report of findings from the National Vietnam Veterans Readjustment Study.* New York: Brunner/Mazel.

Langdon, J. R., & Parker, A. H. (1964). Psychiatric aspects of the March 27, 1964 earthquake. *Alaska Medicine, 6*, 33–35.

Lewis, A. (1942). Incidence of neurosis in England under war conditions. *Lancet, 2*, 175–183.

Lifton, R. J. (1954). Home by ship: Reaction patterns of American prisoners of war repatriated from North Korea. *American Journal of Psychiatry, 110*, 732–739.

Lifton, R. J., & Olson, E. (1976). The human meaning of total disaster: The Buffalo Creek experience. *Psychiatry, 20*, 1–17.

Madakasira, S., & O'Brien, K. F. (1987). Acute posttraumatic stress disorder in victims of a natural disaster. *Journal of Nervous and Mental Disease, 175,* 286–290.

McLeer, S. V., Deblinger, E., Atkins, M. S., Foa, E. B., & Ralphe, D. L. (1988). Post-traumatic stress disorder in sexually abused children. *Journal of the American Academy of Child and Adolescent Psychiatry, 27,* 650–654.

Morey, L. C., Skinner, H. A., & Blashfield, R. K. (1986). Trends in the classification of abnormal behavior. In A. R. Cimenero, K. S. Calhoun, & H. E. Adams (Eds.), *Handbook of behavioral assessment* (2nd ed.) (pp. 47–78). New York: John Wiley & Sons.

Mott, F. W. (1919). *War neuroses and shell shock.* London: Oxford University Press.

Myers, C. S. (1940). *Shell-shock in France: 1914–1918.* Cambridge: Cambridge University Press.

Nadler, A., & Ben-Shushan, D. (1989). Forty years later: Long-term consequences of massive traumatization as manifested by holocaust survivors from the city and kibbutz. *Journal of Consulting and Clinical Psychology, 57,* 287–293.

Nandini, J. E. (1952). Survival factors in American prisoners of war of the Japanese. *American Journal of Psychiatry, 109,* 241–248.

Noble, D., & Roudebush, M., & Prince, D. (1952). Studies of Korean War casualties. Part I: Psychiatric manifestations in wounded men. *American Journal of Psychiatry, 108,* 495–499.

Ornitz, E. M., & Pynoos, R. S. (1989). Startle modulation in children with posttraumatic stress disorder. *American Journal of Psychiatry, 146,* 866–870.

Panzarella, R. F., Mantell, D. M., & Bridenbaugh, R. H. (1978). Psychiatric syndromes, self-concepts, and Vietnam veterans. In C. R. Figley (Ed.), *Stress disorders among Vietnam veterans: Theory, research, and treatment* (pp. 148–172). New York: Brunner/Mazel.

Prasad, J. (1934). Psychology of rumors: A study of the great Indian earthquake of 1934. *British Journal of Psychology, 26,* 1–15.

Quarantelli, E. L. (1985). An assessment of conflicting values on mental health: The consequences of traumatic events. In C. R. Figley (Ed.), *Trauma and its wake* (pp. 173–218). New York: Brunner/Mazel.

Quay, H. C. (1986). Conduct disorders. In H. C. Quay & J. S. Werry (Eds.), *Psychopathological disorders of childhood* (3rd ed.). New York: John Wiley & Sons.

Rachman, S. (1978). *Fear and courage.* San Francisco: W. H. Freeman.

Raines, G. N., & Kolb, L. C. (July, 1943). Combat fatigue and war neurosis. *U.S. Navy Medical Bulletin, 923–926,* 1299–1309.

Reynolds, C., & Richmond, B. (1978). What I think and feel: A revised measure of children's manifest anxiety. *Journal of Abnormal Child Psychology, 6,* 271–280.

Roberts, W. R., Dolan, R., Penk, W. E., Gearing, M. L., Robinowitz, R. D., Patterson, E. T. (1982). Interpersonal problems of Vietnam veterans with symptoms of posttraumatic stress disorder. *Journal of Abnormal Psychology, 91,* 444–450.

Robins, L. N., Helzer, J. E., Croughan, J. L., Williams, J. B. W., Spitzer, R. L. (1981). *NIMH Diagnostic Interview Schedule: Version III.* Rockville, MD: NIMH, Public Health Service, Publication No. ADM-T-42-3 (5-8) (8-81).

Saigh, P. A. (1982). The Lebanese Fear Inventory: A normative report. *Journal of Clinical Psychology, 38,* 352–355.

Saigh, P. A. (1984a). Pre- and postinvasion anxiety in Lebanon. *Behavior Therapy, 15,* 185–190.

Saigh, P. A. (1984b). An experimental analysis of delayed post-traumatic stress. *Behaviour Research and Therapy, 22,* 679–682.

Saigh, P. A. (1985a). Adolescent anxiety following varying degrees of war stress in Lebanon. *Journal of Clinical Child Psychology, 14,* 210–215.

Saigh, P. A. (1985b). An experimental analysis of delayed posttraumatic stress among adolescents. *Journal of Genetic Psychology, 146,* 125–131.

Saigh, P. A. (1988a). Anxiety, depression, and assertion across alternating intervals of stress. *Journal of Abnormal Psychology, 97,* 338–341.

Saigh, P. A. (1988b). The validity of the DSM-III posttraumatic stress disorder classification as applied to adolescents. *Professional School Psychology, 3,* 283–290.

Saigh, P. A. (1989a). The validity of the DSM-III posttraumatic stress disorder classification as applied to children. *Journal of Abnormal Psychology, 98,* 189–192.

Saigh, P. A. (1989b). The development and validation of the Children's Posttraumatic Stress Disorder Inventory. *International Journal of Special Education, 4,* 75–84.

Saigh, P. A. (in press). On the development of posttraumatic stress disorder following four modes of traumatization. *Behaviour Research and Therapy.*

Shatan, C. F. (1978). Stress disorders among Vietnam veterans: The emotional context of combat continues. In C. R. Figley (Ed.), *Stress disorders among Vietnam veterans: Theory, research, and treatment* (pp. 43–56). New York: Brunner/Mazel.

Snow, B. R., Stellman, J. M., Stellman, S. D., & Sommer, J. F. (1988). Posttraumatic stress disorder among American Legionnaires in relation to combat experience in Vietnam: Associated and contributing factors. *Environmental Research, 47,* 175–192.

Southard, E. E., (1919). *Shell shock and neuropsychiatric problems.* Boston: Leonard.

Spielberger, C. D. (1980). *Test Anxiety Inventory.* Palo Alto, CA: Consulting Psychologists Press.

Spielberger, C. D., Gorsuch, R. L., & Lushene, R. E. (1968). *Manual for the State-Trait Anxiety Inventory* (self-evaluation questionnaire). Palo Alto, CA: Consulting Psychologists Press.

Spitzer, R. L., & Fleiss, J. L. (1974). A re-analysis of the reliability of psychiatric diagnosis. *British Journal of Psychiatry, 125,* 341–347.

Spitzer, R. L., & Williams, J. B. (1986). *Structured Clinical Interviews for the DSM-III: Non-Patient Version (SCID-NP-II-86).* New York: Biometrics Research Department, New York State Psychiatric Institute.

Strayer, R., & Ellenhorn, L. (1975). Vietnam veterans: A study exploring adjustment patterns and attitudes. *Journal of Social Issues, 31,* 81–93.

Taylor, V. A., Ross, G. A., & Quarantelli, E. L. (1976). *Delivery of mental health services in disasters: The Xenia tornado and some implications.* Newark, DE: Disaster Research Center.

Van Praag, H. M. (1990). The DSM-IV (depression) classification: To be or not to be. *Journal of Nervous and Mental Disease, 178,* 147–149.

Veronen, L. J., & Kilpatrick, D. G. Self-reported fears of rape victims: A preliminary investigation. *Behavior Modification,* 4(3):383–396, 1980.

Weisaeth, L. (1989). Torture of a Norwegian ship's crew. *Acta Psychiatrica Scandinavia Supplement, 80,* 63–72.

Wolf, S., & Ripley, H. (1947). Reactions among allied prisoners of war subjected to three years of imprisonment and torture by the Japanese. *American Journal of Psychiatry, 104,* 180–192.

Wolpe, J., & Lang, P. (1964). A fear survey schedule for use in behaviour therapy. *Behaviour Research and Therapy, 2,* 27–30.

Zung, W. (1965). A self-rating depression scale. *Archives of General Psychiatry, 12,* 63–70.

Chapter 2

Etiology of Posttraumatic Stress Disorder

David W. Foy
Sheryl S. Osato
Beth M. Houskamp
Debra A. Neumann

In the space of a few short years, the study of potential etiological factors in the development of posttraumatic stress disorder (PTSD) has progressed from simple nature vs. nurture studies to present-day studies in which the search for contributing factors is conducted in biological, psychological, and social domains. The advent of PTSD as a new diagnostic entity in 1980 stimulated expansive research efforts to validate it as a unique category. Initial research was often conceptualized without the benefit of existing literature in related areas to guide study design. More recently, however, studies seem to reflect two positive trends toward conceptualizing PTSD as yet another category of anxiety disorders for which a specific etiological agent is known. First, literature from World War I and World War II showing unequivocal relationships between intensity and duration of combat-related stress and measures of psychological distress is cited frequently, counteracting the well-known argument that PTSD is a phenomenon unique to the Vietnam War and its American participants. Second, studies reflecting a biopsychosocial approach to the study of PTSD etiological factors, as used for other major disorders, is more prevalent.

In view of the current trends, this chapter will focus on empirically derived variables and influential conceptual models as they relate to assessment and treatment of the disorder from a cognitive-behavioral perspective. Recent extensive reviews of etiological studies with combat veterans (Foy, Resnick, Sipprelle, & Carroll, 1987) and rape victims (Steketee & Foa, 1987) are available and will not be duplicated in this chapter.

EMPIRICALLY DERIVED ETIOLOGICAL FACTORS

Combat-Related Studies

Various etiological factors have been identified in the empirical literature on PTSD. These studies have examined pretrauma variables, such as family history, psychosocial adjustment, and physiological reactivity to stress; the nature of the trauma itself (i.e., the length and severity of the traumatic event) has been investigated, as well as subjects' immediate response to the event. While there is some literature on the role of social support in mediating PTSD symptoms (e.g., Carroll, Rueger, Foy & Donahoe, 1985), this variable is not conceptualized as an etiological factor per se. Accordingly, further discussion of this variable as a mediating factor in the development of PTSD will be presented later in the chapter.

Foy, Sipprelle, Rueger, and Carroll (1984) presented some of the first empirical data on variables that might contribute to the development of PTSD. Using a sample of combat veterans diagnosed as PTSD-positive and PTSD-negative, they evaluated premilitary variables such as level of education, occupational status, family functioning, and family history, and examined subjects' military records for evidence of court martials, dishonorable discharges, and the length and nature of the tour of duty. Most importantly, the length and severity of combat exposure was measured in this study. Postmilitary assessment was also included, and drug and alcohol abuse was assessed across all phases. After analyzing all of these variables, the authors found that combat exposure accounted for more of the variance in PTSD severity, relative to premilitary adjustment.

Foy et al. (1987) evaluated the family history of combat veterans who had high and low combat exposure, as well as PTSD-positive vs. PTSD-negative diagnoses. Their results indicated that while there was a higher rate of familial psychopathology in the PTSD-positive group, the role of family history was nonsignificant in veterans with high combat exposure. That is, a high percentage of veterans with high combat exposure developed PTSD regardless of whether they had a family history of mental illness. However, those veterans with lower levels of combat exposure and a positive history of familial psychopathology tended to develop PTSD more frequently than veterans with a negative family history. This particular study might underscore the interaction of predispositions to a disorder and the environmental factors necessary in the development of symptoms.

Davidson, Swartz, Storck, Rama Krishnan, and Hammett (1985) also conducted a study on the rates of familial psychopathology in the relatives of combat veterans. The veterans were compared to nonveterans who carried diagnoses of either major depression or generalized anxiety disorder. While the rates of family history of depression or anxiety were higher in the veterans' group relative to the depressed group, there were no significant differences between the veterans' group and the generalized anxiety group.

Cox, Hallam, O'Connor, and Rachman (1983) evaluated members of a bomb disarmament squad in Northern Ireland who had been decorated for bravery. These men were compared to men who had not been decorated, but who had the same job responsibilities and had received the same type of training. Heart rate changes and self-reported anxiety were assessed in a laboratory stress test, and results showed that the men in the decorated group had less cardiac reactivity to this type of stress than did men in the nondecorated groups. It was hypothesized that this lower physiological reactivity might represent constitutional differences in response to stress. While this study is confounded by the fact that the data were obtained retrospectively (and thus might represent a physiological adaptation to high levels of stress), further investigation of physiological reactivity in the development of PTSD appears to be warranted.

The level of combat exposure appears to be the most significant variable contributing to the development of combat-related PTSD. As noted previously, when compared to premilitary variables, combat exposure accounts for significantly more variance in PTSD symptom severity (Foy et al., 1984). Other evidence also comes from the family study cited above (Foy, et al., 1987), in which veterans with high levels of combat exposure developed PTSD, irrespective of family history of psychopathology. Finally, Penk, Robinowitz, Roberts, Patterson, Dolan, and Atkins (1981) evaluated premilitary variables (family environment), demographic variables, and combat exposure and found that combat exposure was more strongly related to PTSD symptomatology than the other variables studied. A recent meta-analysis of 67 Vietnam-related studies (Kaylor, King, & King, 1987) generally supported this basic etiological linkage as well.

While current studies generally supported extent of combat exposure as being a major etiological factor in the development of PTSD, further research needs to be done. The studies to date have generally identified etiological variables that have been empirically derived, and little attention has been given to theoretical models of the development of PTSD symptoms. There appears to be a greater need for study of hypotheses that test theoretically derived variables. Short of that approach, previously identified etiological variables might be analyzed in light of existing conceptual models of PTSD. For example, the identification of combat exposure as a critical etiological variable appears to support models incorporating classical conditioning quite well; if exposure (i.e., the traumatic event) is viewed as an unconditioned stimulus, one might predict that the acquisition of the unconditioned response would be positively correlated with the strength of the unconditioned stimulus. Finally, prospective, longitudinal studies will provide greater understanding of the development and nature of PTSD symptoms.

Approaches to the study of psychopathology can be distinguished according to the kinds of hypotheses they test. Etiological hypothesis testing involves examining relationships between specified variables and symptom measures of a particular disorder. Another type of hypothesis testing in studies of psychopathology involves treatment studies in which a therapeutic hypothesis is used. If a therapeutic approach with a known mechanism of action is effective with a particular disorder, then specific questions about the possible etiology of the disorder may be formulated. These questions could then be empirically addressed in subsequent studies on etiology. The following section reviews some of the current literature on the pharmacological treatment of PTSD in an attempt to develop hypotheses about the possible underlying neurochemical changes in this disorder.

Rosen and Bohon (1990) recently completed an extensive review of the PTSD pharmacological treatment literature in the combat veteran population. A number of different classes of medications had been used in treating this disorder, some with more demonstrated efficacy than others. According to Rosen and Bohon's review, one class of drugs that appeared ineffective in treating PTSD-related symptoms was antipsychotics (Bleich, Siegel, Garb, & Lerer, 1986).

Carbamazepine, an anticonvulsant, has been used in the treatment of PTSD symptoms. The use of this drug is based on the "kindling" hypothesis proposed by Goddard, McIntyre, and Leech (1969). This phenomenon was originally produced through the experimental application of a number of small, subclinical electrical shocks to the limbic area of the brain. Eventually, epileptic seizures occurred as a result of heightened sensitivity to the stimuli. However, even when the electrical shocks were discontinued, the brain remained in a state of heightened sensitivity to epileptogenic agents. It was later found that this phenomenon can also be produced by a variety of pharmacologic agents. Lipper, Davidson, Grady, Edinger, Hammett, Mahorney, and Cavenor (1986) conducted a study on the treatment efficacy of carbamazepine, and improvement was noted in 7 out of 10 subjects with PTSD. Specifically, decreases in flashbacks, nightmares, and intrusive recollections were reported. However, Toland, Goetz, Slawsky, and van Kammen (1987) found that carbamazepine was not as effective in reducing these PTSD symptoms when compared to desipramine.

Friedman (1988) recently hypothesized that benzodiazepines would be useful in treating PTSD because benzodiazepine receptor binding is greatly increased during the development of limbic kindling. Currently, there are no controlled treatment studies on the effectiveness of benzodiazepines in the treatment of PTSD. However, risk of addiction to these drugs in a population often showing substance abuse must be considered (e.g., Lion, Azcarate, & Koepke, 1975).

Lithium carbonate had been used in treating specific PTSD symptoms. Findings by Kitchner and Greenstein (1985) and Van der Kolk (1983) supported the use of this medication in improving symptoms such as rage, irritability, nightmares, intrusive thoughts, and chronic pain. From an etiological view, decreases of the serotonin metabolite 5-hydroxyindoleacetic acid (5-HIAA) measured in cerebrospinal fluid samples has been associated with increases in aggressive and impulsive behavior (Brown, Goodwin, Ballenger, Goyer, & Major, 1979). Since lithium carbonate has been shown to increase serotonin synthesis (Perez-Cruet, Tagliamonte, Tagliamonte, & Gessa, 1971), the use of this medication in treating specific PTSD symptoms would appear effective from both an empirical and conceptual viewpoint.

Antidepressants appear to have received the greatest support in the empirical literature for the treatment of PTSD symptoms. Falcon, Ryan, Chamberlain, and Curtis (1985) investigated the relative effectiveness of amitriptyline, desipramine, imipramine, and doxepin and found that subjects receiving each drug reported decreases in nightmares, flashbacks, startle response, and panic attacks. There were no differences between antidepressants in treatment efficacy.

MAO inhibitors have received varying degrees of support with regard to treatment efficacy. Positive findings were reported by Davidson, Walker, and Kilts (1987), who noted improvement in flashbacks, intrusive recollections, and constricted affect. However, Lerer, Bleich, Kotler, Garb, Hertzberg, and Levin (1987) assessed 12 PTSD-related symptoms and found clinically significant improvement on only one symptom—sleep disturbance.

In one of the few double-blind studies in this literature, Frank, Kosten, Giller, and Dan (1988) compared the treatment efficacy of imipramine, phenelzine, and a placebo. More positive outcomes were observed on a 5-point rating scale of improvement in the groups receiving antidepressants (combined in the analysis) when compared to the placebo group. The group receiving phenelzine showed a significant decline in scores on the Intrusion subscale of the Impact of Events Scale (Horowitz, Wilner, & Alvarez, 1979) when compared to the groups receiving imipramine and a placebo.

In evaluating the efficacy of this class of medications, it is interesting to note that some antidepressants increase serotonergic activity and thus might have the same type of therapeutic effect as lithium carbonate. However, Rosen and Bohon (1990) noted that it is not clear whether the effectiveness of antidepressants lies solely in reducing the impulsivity and aggressive behavior hypothesized earlier. Unfortunately, many of the studies cited do not include these symptoms as dependent measures and focus more on those symptoms related to diagnosis or depression-related symptoms and measures. Thus, while the use of these medications appears warranted on a conceptual basis for specific symptoms, this hypothesis has yet to be tested empirically.

Unfortunately, much of the PTSD pharmacological literature has suffered from a paucity of methodological rigor as well as from small sample sizes. There has also been a lack of treatment based on etiological theories of PTSD or rationally based pharmacotherapy. Furthermore, many pharmacological studies tend to neglect important variables implicated by "psychological explanations" (Kolb, 1988) in favor of a completely biological approach. There appears to be a need for integrating the psychological and biological approaches to clarify the brain-behavior relationships in PTSD.

Since our latest review of etiological factors in combat-related PTSD (Foy et al., 1987), important new findings have emerged from studies conducted by Zahava Solomon and her colleagues with Israeli veterans of the 1982 war with Lebanon. Approximately 15 separate reports of these findings were published in 1987 and 1988. Obviously, a detailed critique of this work is beyond the scope of this chapter. However, results of these studies are critically important in helping to formulate an up-to-date conceptual model of traumatic distress. Thus, a brief overview of this work will be provided.

The Israeli reports are drawn from extensive data collected on many combatants during and after their combat participation. This project represents the only large-scale, prospectively designed combat study conducted since the advent of PTSD as a discrete diagnostic entity in 1980. Accordingly, specific measures of PTSD conforming to DSM-III diagnostic criteria were used. While retrospective self-reporting was a primary method by which information was obtained, there is a distinct advantage of this work. Diagnosis of combat stress reactions during combat was made by trained mental health personnel after participants were referred by operational commanders for observed inability to function under combat demands. Thus, combatants' immediate stress reactions were independently evaluated against objective and operationalized criteria.

Findings from the work both confirm and extend findings from previous combat-related distress studies. For example, significant positive correlations were found between intense battle events and rates of combat stress reaction (Mikulincer, Solomon, & Benbenishty, 1988), replicating similar findings reported from World War II (e.g., Grinker & Spiegel, 1945). The pivotal role of combat stress reaction in the development of chronic trauma-related distress, including PTSD, was reported in several sources (Solomon & Mikulincer, 1988; Solomon, Weisenberg, Schwarzwald, & Mikulincer, 1987). Negative life events occurring in the 3 months prior to combat exposure were identified as possible contributing factors to the development of chronic distress. Specifically, disturbances in the individual's social relationships with family, friends, and workmates were more frequently reported by PTSD-positive subjects than by PTSD-negative subjects (Solomon, Mikulincer, & Flum, 1988). Similarly, subjects' attributional style in evaluating causation for combat-related adversity was also implicated in the development of PTSD. Increases in PTSD symptoms were associated with attribution of both good and bad events to more external and uncontrollable causes (Mikulincer & Solomon, 1988).

A final finding from the work of Solomon and her colleagues has relevance for our current consideration of etiological models for traumatic distress. There were high correlations found between several different measures of psychological distress in combat-related trauma. Measures of social functioning, the Global Severity Index of the SCL-90, and PTSD severity showed correlations in the .50 to .60 range (Mikulincer & Solomon, 1988). This would seem to indicate that these scores on these instruments reflect a general "psychological distress following trauma" rather than a narrow set of specific PTSD symptoms.

Rape-Related Studies

In parallel to research involving PTSD in combat populations, rape researchers have suggested that the symptom picture following rape also fits criteria for PTSD (Kilpatrick, Veronen, & Best, 1985). Recent research has shown that victims of rape suffer both short- and long-term psychological problems, such as depression (Atkeson, Calhoun, Resick, & Ellis, 1982), fear and anxiety (Kilpatrick et al., 1985), psychosomatic symptoms (Norris & Feldman-Summers, 1981), sexual dissatisfaction (Feldman-Summers, Gordon, & Meagher, 1979), intrusive thoughts (Roth, Dye, & Lebowitz, 1988), and an increase in general psychopathology (Stewart, Hughes, Frank, Anderson, Kendall, & West, 1987). Additional confirmation of PTSD as a diagnosis applicable to rape victims was provided by a recent study of PTSD in a nonclinical sample of crime victims. (Kilpatrick, Saunders, Amick-McMullen, Best, Veronen, & Resnick, 1989), in which PTSD was diagnosed in 28.6% of the rape victims who were assessed.

Several variables have been investigated as potentially influential in psychopathology in rape victims. Ruch and Hennessy (1982) examined the relationship of four factors to psychological trauma in a sample of 326 rape victims who were seen at a rape crisis center. Structured interview data were obtained on aspects of the sexual assault, victim demographics, preexisting life stress in victims, and victim social support. Factor analysis of this data identified two significant dimensions of sexual assault. The first dimension, "rape encounter," included intimidation used by an assailant, the resistance offered by a victim, and a resultant physical injury. A second dimension, "victim factors," was composed of preexisting life stress and social support.

Antecedent variables that have been investigated are victim demographic characteristics, such as age, ethnicity, marital status, socioeconomic status (SES), education level, and prerape adjustment and functioning. The only significant relationships found in this category have been between age and SES and psychopathology. Atkeson et al. (1982) found that age and SES were predictive of depressive symptomatology 12 months after the assault, with older and poorer women experiencing greater difficulties. These researchers also found that physical health problems and difficulties in sexual adjustment prior to the rape predicted depressive symptoms at 4 months postrape. Prior health problems were also related to increased psychopathology at 12 months postrape. Cohen and Roth (1987) found that rape victims with lower SES reported significantly more fears and general distress following the assault than victims with higher SES. Other studies have failed to find a significant short-term (Kilpatrick et al., 1985) or long-term (Santiago, McCall-Perez, Gorcey, & Beigel, 1985) relationship between demographic variables and psychological problems.

Several historical variables have been found to play a role in the development of rape-related distress. Ruch and Hennessy (1982) found prior sexual victimization to be a significant factor in postrape distress. Additionally, Santiago et al. (1985) found that prior victims of sexual assault showed greater depression and anxiety following rape than victims who had no prior history of assault. However, Frank and Anderson (1987) found that a prior sexual assault was not associated with a higher incidence of symptoms after the assault.

Studies have also shown that a prior psychiatric history may be related to increased postrape symptomatology. Frank, Turner, Stewart, Jacob, and West (1981) found that rape victims with a history of psychotropic drug therapy, suicidal ideation, and prior suicide attempts experienced greater depression, fears, and anxiety following rape. Atkeson et al. (1982) also found that a history of psychiatric treatment was predictive of increased depression 1 year after the assault. Frank and Anderson (1987) found that a postrape psychiatric diagnosis was related to diagnosis at the time of assault in rape victims.

The investigation of situational variables has focused on the role played by stressful life events within the year prior to the rape. Ruch and Hennessy (1982) found a bimodal distribution in their sample of rape victims. The two groups consisted of victims with moderate life stress in the past year and no history of prior sexual assault and of victims with severe life changes in the year prior to rape and a history of prior assault. Kilpatrick et al. (1985) investigated the relationship between intercurrent stressors and rape-related trauma. They found that low-distress victims had fewer life changes in the year preceding the rape. High distress was associated with the death of a close family member (other than spouse) and with a lower frequency of loving, intimate relationships with men in the year prior to the rape.

Several concurrent individual variables have been examined that involve a victim's perceptions of the rape event. Specifically, attributions made by the victim about the rape event were studied. Janoff-Bulman (1979) found that rape victims who blamed the rape on an aspect of their own behavior were less prone to depression after the rape than those victims who engaged in "characterological self-blame" by attributing the rape to an enduring personality flaw. It seems likely that these attributions interact with other etiological variables in poorly understood ways. In this regard, the relationship of a victim to her assailant may affect her perception of the threat in the rape event and attributions of blame that she (and others) make regarding it. Yet studies that have investigated differences in victims' distress between stranger vs. acquaintance perpetrators have not found differences in symptom patterns (Koss, Dinero, Seibel, & Cox, 1988).

Numerous studies have investigated the relationship between aspects of the trauma and subsequent distress. For example, Ellis, Atkeson, and Calhoun (1981) found that victims of "blitz" rape reported more fear, depression, fatigue, and difficulty relating socially to men than victims who had not experienced a sudden and violent assault. Norris and Feldman-Summers (1981) found a direct relationship between psychosomatic symptoms and severity of the assault in rape victims. Cohen and Roth (1987) also found a negative correlation between level of physical force used by an assailant and overall functioning of the victim after the assault. Other studies have produced negative findings regarding the relationship between aspects of the assault and distress (Atkeson et al., 1982; Kilpatrick et al., 1985; Santiago et al., 1985). More convincingly, however, Kilpatrick et al. (1989) recently reported that when the rape event included both physical injury to the victim and a threat upon her life, the PTSD rate was an astounding 78.6%. This would seem to indicate that as rape trauma increases, PTSD symptoms also increase. Indeed, most recently, Neumann, Gallers, and Foy (1989) also discovered a significant relationship between traumatic aspects of rape and PTSD rates in rape. In addition, they found that an increase in the number of exposure factors was positively related to an increase in PTSD symptom intensity.

Consequential variables refer to those characteristics of the immediate postassault milieu that potentiate or mitigate an unfavorable outcome. Although not directly etiological, these variables may play a significant role in symptom development and are clinically meaningful. Individual variables that have been considered in regard to rape are coping strategies and help-seeking behavior of the victim (Cohen & Roth, 1987), guilt as a concomitant of self-blame (Libow & Doty, 1979), and the acceptance of cultural rape myths (Burt, 1980). Initial response may be especially important. For example, initial distress indicated by the onset of substance abuse or increased use, deterioration in physical appearance and self-care and the presence of symptoms 6 to 21 days postrape was identified by Kilpatrick et al. (1984) as a better predictor of psychological functioning at 3 months postassault than demographic or history variables or aspects of the assault. The other variables in this category have either not been studied empirically or have yielded equivocal results.

Situational variables postrape that have been posited as related to outcome are interface with the police, medical, and legal systems (Cluss, Boughton, Frank, Stewart, & West, 1983), social support (Atkeson et al., 1982) and a change of residence or job postassault. Cluss et al. (1983) found that involvement in court proceedings resulted in higher self-esteem at 12 months postassault than was found in victims who chose not to prosecute. Norris and Feldman-Summers (1981) found that reporting the assault to the police or to a sexual assault crisis center had no relationship to the development of psychosomatic symptoms, sexual activity, and satisfaction or reclusiveness at an unspecified time postassault. Calhoun, Atkeson, and Resick (1982) found that at 12 months postrape, the prospect of testifying in court was the most fear-producing item of those assessed.

Support of family and friends has consistently been shown to play an important role in the postassault response of rape victims (Ruch & Hennessy, 1982). Norris and Feldman-Summers (1981) found that the presence of understanding male and female companionship was inversely related to reclusiveness following an assault. These findings are consistent with literature on the mediating effects of social support across types of psychopathology.

Comparison of Findings Across Trauma Types

When etiologically significant findings from studies of rape and combat are compared, several key similarities are found. First, the symptom picture presented following both types of trauma appears quite consistent with classic descriptions of intense posttrauma distress. Further, rates at which trauma-exposed individuals develop chronic PTSD appear comparable. A third commonality exists in the elements of the trauma that appear significant in the development of severe symptoms, these elements being overwhelming danger to self-preservation and physical injury.

Two tentative conclusions appear warranted at this point: Both types of trauma (rape and combat) are relevant for PTSD diagnostic purposes, and there is a common etiology for associated distress. While PTSD is unique in that the etiological agent is specified as part of the diagnostic criteria, intense trauma exposure by itself does not constitute both a necessary and sufficient condition for acute PTSD to occur in many instances. Obviously, not all individuals exposed to intense trauma develop PTSD in either combat or rape situations. Intense trauma exposure may be more appropriately viewed as etiological in the development of an immediate stress reaction in both combat and rape. In this case, exposure is both necessary and sufficient and thus presents a quite simple etiological hypothesis requiring no other variables in the causal chain to account for most cases. Furthermore, in both combat and rape-related PTSD, the immediate stress reaction seems to be etiologically significant in that most, if not all, individuals who subsequently develop PTSD had a debilitating immediate stress reaction. Thus, the most parsimonious etiological hypothesis for both trauma types is that acute PTSD results from intense trauma exposure followed by an immediate stress reaction. Other variables from biological, psychological, and social domains may be implicated in influencing this basic etiological linkage to produce more or fewer acute PTSD cases. Indeed, there is also consistency across rape and combat trauma study findings in identifying these factors, which can be classified as "risk" or "protective," depending upon the direction of their influence.

CONCEPTUAL MODELS OF PTSD

Why is it that some individuals exposed to extreme trauma develop debilitating symptoms while others do not? Among those individuals who exhibit stress reactions, why do some recover while others develop a chronic disorder? These are the types of questions that intrigue and perplex researchers and clinicians working with survivors of traumatic experiences. Accordingly, several conceptual formulations have been offered to help guide assessment, treatment, and research efforts. The following section presents a brief overview of four such models. Since other chapters in this book describe a PTSD model derived from Mowrer's two factor theory of avoidance learning and a recently proposed cognitive model based on Lang's bioinformational theory, these models will receive little attention here. More extensive treatment will be afforded to the two psychobiological models presented.

Psychological Models

Recently, researchers involved in studying PTSD have used Mowrer's (1947) two factor theory to conceptualize the etiology and symptoms of the disorder. According to this learning model, both instrumental and classical conditioning contribute to avoidance conditioning. The first factor in this theory is the classical conditioning of a fear response; a previously neutral stimulus is paired with a noxious unconditioned stimulus (UCS), resulting in a fear response (UCR). The neutral stimulus thus becomes a conditioned stimulus (CS) for eliciting the conditioned response of fear (CR). Through the process of higher order conditioning and stimulus generalization, the conditioned fear response may be attributed to additional neutral stimuli that are paired with the conditioned response or generalized to stimuli similar to the conditioned stimulus. The second factor of the two factor theory refers to the instrumental learning of avoidance responses to escape or decrease the fear elicited by the conditioned stimulus. Once escape or avoidance of the conditioned stimulus has been learned, the avoidance behavior is negatively reinforced by a reduction in the fear response.

Keane, Zimering, and Caddell (1985) and Kilpatrick, Veronen, and Resick (1982) utilized this two factor learning theory in conceptualizing the etiological mechanisms in PTSD. Keane et al. (1985) hypothesized that this learning theory accounted for the conditioned startle responses, avoidance behavior, and stimulus generalization found in combat veterans with PTSD. Kilpatrick et al. (1982) also used the two factor theory to account for the fear and anxiety in victims of sexual assault. Exposure to the life-threatening event of rape elicits intense fear, which is then also elicited by exposure to a variety of similar stimuli or by other stimuli associated with the traumatic event of sexual assault.

Foa and Kozak (1986) recently proposed a cognitive behavioral formulation of PTSD that includes the cognitive element of "meaning" of the traumatic event. This model utilizes the construct of fear structures developed by Lang (1979). He hypothesized that the cognitive network of fear structures contains three primary elements: information about the stimulus situation; information about physiological, cognitive, and behavioral responses to the stimulus; and the meaning of the connection between the stimulus and the response. Foa and Kozak (1986) proposed that the fear structure, consisting of cognitive and affective components, also involves the meaning of the event as dangerous. More recently, Foa, Steketee, and Rothbaum (1989) suggested that the etiological variable that distinguishes PTSD from other anxiety disorders is the attribution of dangerous meaning to stimuli that had previously been associated with safety.

Critical components of Foa and Kozak's model are the predictability and controllability of the traumatic event. The units of this fear structure provide the means for processing information related to the potential danger and therefore are the impetus for the avoidance response. In the formation of the fear structure, there is a negative association between the perceived predictability and controllability of the event and the PTSD symptoms experienced. That is, the less predictable and controllable the world appears as a result of the traumatic event, the greater the intensity of PTSD symptoms experienced.

Psychobiological Models

Recent studies have also focused on the physiological basis of PTSD using psychobiological models. Van der Kolk (1987) has proposed a neurobiological learning model based upon the animal model of inescapable shock (Maier & Seligman, 1976) to explain the etiological mechanisms of PTSD in humans. Inescapable shock in animals resulted in depletion of norepinephrine and dopamine levels. However, over an extended period of time, inescapable shock did not appear to have the expected effect of decreasing levels of norepinephrine and dopamine; rather, the levels of these neurotransmitters either remained constant or increased. In extending this model to humans, Van der Kolk (1985) proposed that the limbic system, particularly the locus ceruleus, is affected by the extended acute shock and that norepinephrine depletion becomes a conditioned response that leads to an increase in norepinephrine receptor hypersensitivity. The PTSD symptoms of numbing, constriction of affect, decline in motivation, and difficulties with occupational functioning (i.e., negative symptoms) reflect the norepinephrine depletion resulting from the inescapable stress of the trauma. The symptoms of hyperreactivity such as nightmares, startle responses, and intrusive thoughts (i.e., positive symptoms) reflect a chronic hypersensitivity of the norepinephrine receptors similar to that observed in animals confronted with extended and inescapable traumatic situations.

Van der Kolk (1987) also noted that animals have developed analgesia through increased activation of their brain opiate receptors following multiple exposures of unavoidable shock. Similarly, human beings may experience an endogenous opiate response when exposed to trauma, and the hyperreactive symptoms of PTSD could then be the result of withdrawal from excessive noradrenergic activity. Furthermore, the symptom of reexperiencing the traumatic event would reactivate the production of endogenous opiates, thereby providing a means for reducing the hyperreactive PTSD symptoms, such as startle responses, anxiety, hyperalertness, and sleep disturbance. Thus, the symptom of reexperiencing the traumatic event could lead to an addictive behavioral response.

Pharmacological treatment of PTSD, based on an inescapable shock model, implicates the use of drugs to decrease autonomic arousal. In particular, those psychotropics that would inhibit noradrenergic activity (clonidine and the beta blockers) and those that would increase the inhibitory effect of the GABAergic system (benzodiazepines) might be potentially effective in reducing the hyperreactive symptoms of PTSD (Van der Kolk, 1987).

Kolb (1988) noted that the inescapable shock model overlooked the avoidance behavior often seen in PTSD and that it also failed to account for the chronic forms of PTSD. He therefore proposed an alternative conditioned emotional response (CER) model. He identified an elicited acute fear in response to a perceived life-threatening situation as the central element in the development of PTSD. The intense and repeated exposure to such a stimulus, either the actual stimulus or one perceived to be similar to it, leads to psychophysiological responses, including hyperreactive symptoms, nightmares, and panic attacks. In chronic forms of the disorder, the cognitive processes functioning as defenses fail whenever a person is exposed to the original stimulus or one similar to the original.

In the CER model of PTSD, Kolb proposed that the breakdown of the cognitive protective mechanisms and the symptomatology identified with PTSD result from excessive stimulation of the neuronal networks in the limbic system. Confronted with intense and prolonged stimulation, the cortical neural structures suffer fatigue and subsequent impairment, similar to the process by which long-term exposure to loud noise results in impairment to the neural network of the auditory system. The intensity and duration of exposure to the stimulus determine the degree of impairment of the neural functioning and also the degree to which the neuronal networks may recover functioning subsequent to removal from the fear-eliciting situation.

Kolb suggested that if PTSD symptomatology reflects an impairment of the neuronal cortical network, then neurological theory may be utilized as a model for conceptualizing the etiology and symptomatology of PTSD. Classical neurological theory (Jackson, 1958) proposed four aspects of impairment observed when the underlying neuronal network had been affected: symptoms of loss of function, symptoms of lessened inhibition, with resulting excessive stimulation of cortical structures, and reactive and substitutive symptoms that reflected the cortical structure's ongoing attempts at repair. In Kolb's CER model, symptoms of loss include the inability to discriminate between nonthreatening and threatening stimuli, impairment of control of aggressive impulses, and impairment of capacity for concentration. The symptoms due to lessened inhibition include intrusive thoughts, repetitive dreams, and hyperreactive symptoms. The reactive symptoms reflecting the neuronal network's ongoing repair are the affective components of PTSD, such as depression, anxiety, terror, and the accompanying panic attacks and severe dissociative states. Finally, the symptoms reflective of the substitutive repair work of the underlying cortical structure are the remaining personality factors and coping mechanisms developed when confronted with the traumatic event and subsequent psychophysiological symptoms.

Currently, Kolb's model is a heuristic one and has not yet been examined from an empirical basis. It is useful, however, in explaining possible underlying neuronal mechanisms in the development of PTSD-related symptoms.

While these models of PTSD represent an advance over earlier "residual stress" and "stress evaporation" formulations, none can adequately account for all symptoms currently included in the DSM-III-R criteria for PTSD. Thus, a truly comprehensive theory of PTSD does not yet exist. For the present, we need both psychological and biological formulations to understand the variety of fear-related behaviors and profound changes in neurophysiological functioning that characterize this disorder.

Proposed PTSD Etiological Hypothesis

Based on our understanding of the current trauma literature, we propose a back-to-basics approach for advancing empirical work with trauma victims. Rather than further theorizing along cognitive, behavioral, or psychobiological lines, tempting though it may be, we have returned to a familiar, widely used, and well-researched life events model that is empirical as opposed to theoretical in nature. The core unit of focus is the predictable relationship between an adverse life event and resultant psychological distress. Our elaboration of this model into a testable hypothesis on the etiology of PTSD is shown in Figure 2.1. We propose that overwhelming trauma in conjunction with an immediate stress reaction (conditioned emotional response) constitute the necessary and sufficient conditions for acute PTSD symptoms to occur. Trauma can occur from three routes. Direct personal experience and observational experience, such as witnessing the death or near-death of another person, comprise the two most obvious mechanisms. However, recent work with PTSD in war-traumatized children demonstrated that "vicarious" experience, such as learning about the death of a loved one, can also elicit PTSD reactions (Saigh, 1989).

Whether symptoms persist for 1 month or more or are present in episodic fashion is a more complex issue involving distinction between variables involved in onset vs. maintenance of PTSD symptoms. In the case of chronic PTSD symptoms, additional mediating variables probably interact as "risk" or "resiliency" factors with the primary etiological factor, trauma.

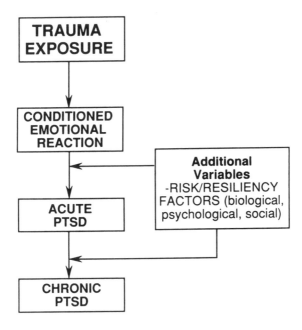

FIGURE 2.1. Proposed PTSD etiological hypothesis.

The ways in which these additional mediating variables interact with the etiological event include three primary possibilities. First, the additional factor could present the individual with vulnerability through experiencing distress beyond the actual potential of the trauma by itself. Thus, as a "vulnerability" factor, the additional mediating variable has no ability to produce distress by itself, but rather interacts with the traumatic event to heighten PTSD reactivity. The same relationship, in reverse, would hold for a resiliency or "protective" factor.

A second type of interactive relationship involves an additional mediating variable that is independently capable of producing distress. An "independent causes" relationship exists when distress is increased by the presence of an independent factor that adds to resultant distress but does not interact with the traumatic event.

Finally, a third type of possible interaction between an additional variable and the traumatic event is potentiation. Capable of producing distress itself, a potentiating variable interacts with the traumatic event to heighten the resultant PTSD reaction beyond the simple additive effects of the two variables. Thus, the potentiating variable is both an independent cause and is interactive with the etiological event. Mutual potentiation occurs when distress produced by the potentiating variable is heightened by interaction with the traumatic event. Hierarchical regression analysis provides a statistical model by which the nature of the interactive relationships between the etiological event and these additional mediating variables can be established (Cooke, 1985).

IMPLICATIONS FOR FUTURE WORK

Assessment and Treatment

Both combat and rape studies show critical elements of trauma exposure that have direct clinical assessment implications. In both trauma areas, there seem to be threshold levels of exposure beyond which the probability of an acute PTSD reaction is very high. For combat veterans, threshold level involves death exposure, either through personal involvement in the killing of enemy combatants or through the loss of close buddies. For sexual assault, an actual completion of the rape experience, as opposed to other forms of nonpenetrating assaultive activities, seems to constitute such a threshold. More severe exposure factors for both kinds of trauma include physical injury in the experience and exposure to other thematically related trauma events. For example, the probability of a PTSD reaction in combat veterans is increased if the veterans were involved in deaths of noncombatants. Similarly, the probability is increased in rape victims when there is a history of previous sexual assault. For assessment purposes, the implication is that careful attention must be paid to both qualitative and quantitative aspects of the traumatic experience to understand presenting trauma exposure-distress relationships. Heterogeneity of traumatic experiences must be assumed to fully evaluate victims' psychological reactions and treatment needs.

Treatment implications derive from the same basic exposure-distress relationship. First, if physical survival was the immediate goal during the traumatic experience, psychological survival assumes primacy next. For many victims, avoidance of traumatic cues or memories is equated with survival in a psychological sense. Conversely, our knowledge of PTSD etiology strongly implies that reexposure and desensitization to traumatic cues and memories are required for the individual to regain self-determination in making life choices. Unlike many other psychiatric diagnoses that are primarily descriptive of a particular symptom pattern, PTSD is an etiological diagnosis for which the causal agent is known. However, for treatment purposes, the traumatic experience needs to be viewed as complex and composed of multiple elements, each of which requires processing by the victim for mastery of the experience, both affectively and cognitively.

The significance of additional mediating variables in assessment and treatment implications is less clear. If meaningful differences in PTSD risk are associated with high vs. low trauma exposure, then it would seem that other potential mediating factors would be more influential etiologically under low exposure conditions. If so, other sources of vulnerability, independent causes of distress, or PTSD potentiating factors will require therapeutic attention as well. In the case of high exposure, resiliency factors such as supportive significant others and low-stress life conditions may assume importance in mobilizing available resources to reduce PTSD symptoms and help the individual regain life control.

Recent studies by Solomon and her colleagues call into question the validity and usefulness of the diagnostic criteria for PTSD currently in use as the sole appropriate measure for trauma-related distress. In clinical samples of combat-related PTSD subjects, there is a concurrent diagnosis of alcohol or polydrug abuse in more than 60% of all cases. High rates of depression and other anxiety disorders are also frequently reported. Thus it seems that the current view of PTSD as "conditioned anxiety" defined by a narrow set of specific unique characteristics may require reappraisal.

Research

Research implications include the following:

1. Traumatic exposure needs to be treated as a continuous variable so that meaningful differences between equally exposed individuals can be evaluated (i.e., in terms of PTSD positive or negative status, symptom presentation, and course).

2. Universal elements of trauma exposure across trauma types need to be empirically derived. This would allow for true "cross-trauma" studies to be conducted with equivalence of traumatic experience established through empirical means.

3. Neurophysiological dependent measures need to be included in future trauma studies. Psychobiological conceptual models of PTSD and potential drug treatments deserve serious consideration by those of us more familiar with psychosocial models and methods. It is necessary, however, that biological hypotheses about PTSD be tested in a broader psychosocial context.

4. Statistical methods need to be used that identify the nature of interactions between the etiological variable and other mediating variables.

SUMMARY

This chapter reviewed empirically derived psychological factors implicated in the development of combat-related and rape-related PTSD, including findings from recently published studies on Israeli combat veterans. Psychopharmacological studies testing the efficacy of different classes of psychoactive drugs in reducing PTSD symptoms were also reviewed. A comparison was made between findings from rape and combat studies, identifying similarities in components of the traumatic exposure, and in mediating variables that have been found to modify the traumatic event-acute PTSD etiological relationship.

Current popular conceptual models applied to PTSD were also reviewed. Models were evaluated in terms of ability to account for PTSD symptoms currently included in the DSM-III-R criteria for PTSD. It was concluded that no existing model adequately accounted for all PTSD symptoms. We proposed our own PTSD etiological hypothesis as a means of testing current models and specific variables and their possible interaction with trauma in the etiology of acute PTSD. Vulnerability-resiliency, independent causes, and potentiation were presented as three means by which interactions could occur. Finally, we suggested implications of PTSD etiological findings for clinical assessment and treatment, as well as for future research.

REFERENCES

Atkeson, B. M., Calhoun, K. S., Resick, P. A., & Ellis, E. M. (1982). Victims of rape: Repeated assessment of depressive symptoms. *Journal of Consulting and Clinical Psychology, 50,* 96–102.

Bleich, A., Siegel, B., Garb, R., & Lerer, B. (1986). Post-traumatic stress disorder following combat exposure: Clinical features and psychopharmacological treatment. *British Journal of Psychiatry, 149,* 365–369.

Brown, G. L., Goodwin, F. K., Ballenger, J. C., Goyer, P. F., & Major, L. F. (1979). Aggression in humans correlates with cerebrospinal fluid amine metabolites. *Psychiatry Research, 1,* 131–139.

Burt, M. R. (1980). Cultural myths and support for rape. *Journal of Personality and Social Psychology, 38,* 217–230.

Calhoun, K. S., Atkeson, B. M., & Resick, P. A. (1982). A longitudinal examination of fear reactions in victims of rape. *Journal of Counseling Psychology, 29,* 655–661.

Carroll, E. M., Rueger, D. B., Foy, D. W., & Donahoe, C. P. (1985). Vietnam combat veterans with posttraumatic stress disorder: Analysis of marital and cohabitating adjustment. *Journal of Abnormal Psychology, 94,* 329–337.

Cluss, P. A., Boughton, B., Frank, E., Stewart, B. D., & West, D. (1983). The rape victims: Psychological correlates of participation in the legal process. *Criminal Justice and Behavior, 10,* 342–357.

Cohen, L. J., & Roth, S. (1987). The psychological aftermath of rape: Long-term effects and individual differences in recovery. *Journal of Social and Clinical Psychology, 5,* 525–534.

Cooke, D. J. (1985). Psychosocial vulnerability to life events during the Climacteric. *British Journal of Psychiatry, 147,* 71–75.

Cox, D., Hallam, R., O'Connor, K., & Rachman, S. (1983). An experimental analyses of fearlessness and courage. *British Journal of Psychiatry, 74,* 107–117.

Davidson, J., Swartz, M., Storck, M., Rama Krishnan, R., & Hammett, E. (1985). A diagnostic and family study of post-traumatic stress disorder. *American Journal of Psychiatry, 42,* 90–93.

Davidson, J., Walker, J. I., & Kilts, C. (1987). A pilot study of phenelzine in posttraumatic stress disorder. *British Journal of Psychiatry, 50,* 252–255.

Ellis, E. M., Atkeson, B. M., & Calhoun, K. S. (1981). An assessment of long term reaction to rape. *Journal of Abnormal Psychology, 19(3),* 263–266.

Falcon, S., Ryan, C., Chamberlain, K., & Curtis, G. (1985). Tricyclics: Possible treatment for posttraumatic stress disorder. *Journal of Clinical Psychiatry, 46,* 385–389.

Feldman-Summers, S., Gordon, P. E., & Meagher, J. R. (1979). The impact of rape on sexual satisfaction. *Journal of Psychology, 88,* 101–105.

Foa, E. B., & Kozak, M. J. (1986). Emotional processing of fear: Exposure to corrective information. *Psychological Bulletin, 99,* 20–35.

Foa, E. B., Steketee, G., & Rothbaum, B. O. (1989). Behavioral/cognitive conceptualizations of post-traumatic stress disorder. *Behavior Therapy, 20,* 155–176.

Foy, D. W., Resnick, H. S., Sipprelle, R. C., & Carroll, E. M. (1987). Premilitary, military, and postmilitary factors in the development of combat-related posttraumatic stress disorder. *The Behavior Therapist, 10(1),* 3–9.

Foy, D. W., Sipprelle, R. C., Rueger, D. B., & Carroll, E. M. (1984). Etiology of posttraumatic stress disorder in Vietnam veterans: Analysis of premilitary, military, and combat exposure influences. *Journal of Consulting and Clinical Psychology, 52,* 79–87.

Frank, J. B., Kosten, T. R., Giller, E. L., & Dan, E. (1988). A randomized clinical trial of phenelzine and imipramine for posttraumatic stress disorder. *American Journal of Psychiatry, 145,* 1289–1281.

Frank, E., & Anderson, V. P. (1987). Psychiatric disorders in rape victims. *Comprehensive Psychiatry, 28,* 77–82.

Frank, E., Turner, S. M., Stewart, B. D., Jacob, M., & West, D. (1981). Past psychiatric symptoms and the response of sexual assault. *Comprehensive Psychiatry, 22,* 479–487.

Friedman, M. J. (1988). Toward rational pharmacotherapy for post-traumatic stress disorder: An interim report. *American Journal of Psychiatry, 145,* 281–284.

Goddard, G. V., McIntyre, D. C., & Leech, C. K. (1969). A permanent change in brain functioning resulting from daily electrical stimulation. *Experimental Neurology, 25,* 295–330.

Grinker, R. R., & Spiegel, J. P. (1945). *Men under stress.* Philadelphia: Blakistan.

Horowitz, M. J., Wilner, N., & Alvarez, W. (1979). Impact of Events Scale: A measure of subjective stress. *Psychosomatic Medicine, 41,* 209–218.

Jackson, J. H. (1958). Selected writing, Vol. II. In J. Taylor, (Ed.), *Evolution and dissolution of the nervous system.* New York: Basic Books.

Janoff-Bulman, R. (1979). Characterological versus behavioral self-blame: Inquiries into depression and rape. *Journal of Personality and Social Psychology, 37,* 1789–1809.

Kaylor, J. A., King, D. W., King, L. A. (1987). Psychological effects of military service in Vietnam: A meta-analysis. *Psychological Bulletin, 102,* 257–271.

Keane, T. M., Zimering, R. T., & Caddell, J. M. (1985). A behavioral formulation of posttraumatic stress disorder in Vietnam veterans. *Behavioral Therapist, 8,* 9–12.

Kilpatrick, D. G., Saunders, B. E., Amick-McMullen, A., Best, C. L., Veronen, L. J., & Resnick, H. S. (1989). Factors affecting the development of crime-related post-traumatic stress disorder: A multivariate approach. *Behavior Therapy, 20,* 199–214.

Kilpatrick, D. G., Veronen, L. J., & Best, C. L. (1985). Factors predicting psychological distress among rape victims. In C. R. Figley (Ed.), *Trauma and its wake: The study and treatment of posttraumatic stress disorder.* New York: Brunner/Mazel.

Kilpatrick, D. G., Veronen, L. J., & Resick, P. A. (1982). Psychological sequelae to rape: Assessment and treatment strategies. In D. M. Doleys, R. L. Meredith, & A. R. Ciminero, (Eds.), *Behavioral medicine: Assessment and treatment strategies.* New York: Plenum Publishing.

Kitchner, I., & Greenstein, R. (1985). Low dose lithium carbonate in the treatment of post traumatic stress disorder: Brief communication. *Military Medicine, 150,* 378–381.

Kolb, L. C. (1988). A critical survey of hypotheses regarding post-traumatic stress disorders in light of recent findings. *Journal of Traumatic Stress, 1(3),* 291–304.

Koss, M. P., Dinero, T. E., Seibel, C., & Cox, S. (1988). Stranger, acquaintance, and date rape: Is there a difference in the victims' experience? *Psychology of Women Quarterly, 12,* 1–24.

Lang, P. J. (1979). A bioinformational theory of emotional imagery. *Psychophysiology, 16,* 495–512.

Lerer, B., Bleich, A., Kotler, M., Garb, R., Hertzberg, M., & Levin, B. (1987). Posttraumatic stress disorder in Israeli combat veterans. *Archives of General Psychiatry, 44,* 976–981.

Libow, J. A., & Doty, D. W. (1979). An exploratory approach to self-blame and self-derogation by rape victims. *American Journal of Orthopsychiatry, 49,* 670–679.

Lion, J. R., Azcarate, C. L., & Koepke, H. H. (1975). "Paradoxical rage reactions" during psychotropic medication. *Diseases of the Nervous System, 36,* 557–558.

Lipper, S., Davidson, J. R., Grady, T. A., Edinger, J. D., Hammet, E. B., Mahorney, S. L., & Cavenar, J. O. (1986). Preliminary study of carbamazepine in post-traumatic stress disorder. *Psychosomatics, 27,* 849–854.

Maier, S. F., & Seligman, M. E. P. (1976). Learned helplessness: Theory and evidence. *Journal of Experimental Psychology: General, 105,* 3–45.

Mikulincer, M., & Solomon, Z. (1988). Attributional style and combat-related posttraumatic stress disorder. *Journal of Abnormal Psychology, 97(3),* 308–313.

Mikulincer, M., Solomon, Z., & Benbenishty (1988). Battle events, acute combat stress reaction, and long-term psychological sequelae of war. *Journal of Anxiety Disorders, 2(2),* 121–133.

Mowrer, O. H. (1947). On the dual nature of learning: A reinterpretation of "conditioning" and "problem solving." *Harvard Educational Review, 17,* 102–148.

Neumann, D. A., Gallers, J., & Foy, D. W. (1989). The relationship between traumatic violence and PTSD symptoms in rape victims. Unpublished masters thesis at Fuller Theological Seminary, Graduate School of Psychology, Pasadena, CA.

Norris, J., & Feldman-Summers, S. (1981). Factors related to the psychological impact of rape on the victim. *Journal of Abnormal Psychology, 90,* 562–567.

Penk, W. E., Robinowitz, R., Roberts, W. R., Patterson, E. T., Dolan, M. P., & Atkins, H. G. (1981). Adjustment differences among male substance abusers varying in degree of combat experience in Vietnam. *Journal of Consulting and Clinical Psychology, 49,* 426–437.

Perez-Cruet, J., Tagliamonte, A., Tagliamonte, P., & Gessa, G. L. (1971). Stimulation of serotonin synthesis by lithium. *Journal of Pharmacology and Experimental Therapeutics, 178,* 325–330.

Rosen, J., & Bohon, S. (1990). Pharmacotherapy of post-traumatic stress disorder. In M. Hersen & A. Bellack (Eds.), *Handbook of comparative treatments.* New York: John Wiley & Sons.

Roth, S., Dye, E., & Lebowitz, L. (1988). Group therapy for sexual assault victims. *Psychotherapy, 25,* 82–93.

Ruch, L. O., & Hennessy, M. (1982). Sexual assault: Victim and attack dimensions. *Journal of Victimology, 7,* 94–105.

Saigh, P. A. (August, 1989). The development of posttraumatic stress disorder pursuant to different modes of traumatization. Paper presented at the American Psychological Association Convention, New Orleans, LA.

Santiago, J. M., McCall-Perez, F., Gorcey, M., & Beigel, A. (1985). Long-term psychological effects of rape in 35 rape victims. *American Journal of Psychiatry, 142,* 1338–1340.

Solomon, Z., & Mikulincer, M. (1988). Psychological sequelae of war: Two year follow-up of Israeli combat stress reaction casualties. *Jounal of Nervous and Mental Disease, 176(5),* 264–269.

Solomon, Z., Mikulincer, M., & Flum, H. (1988). Negative life events, coping responses, and combat-related psychopathology: A prospective study. *Journal of Abnormal Psychology, 97(3),* 302–307.

Solomon, Z., Weisenberg, M., Schwarzwald, J., & Mikulincer, M. (1987). Posttraumatic stress disorder among frontline soldiers with combat stress reaction: The 1982 Israeli experience. *American Journal of Psychiatry, 144(4),* 448–454.

Steketee, G., & Foa, E. B. (1987). Rape victims: Post-traumatic stress responses and their treatment: A review of the literature. *Journal of Anxiety Disorders, 1,* 69–86.

Stewart, B. D., Hughes, C., Frank, E., Anderson, B., Kendall, K., & West, D. (1987). The aftermath of rape: Profiles of immediate and delayed treatment seekers. *Journal of Nervous and Mental Disorders, 175,* 90–94.

Toland, A. M., Goetz, K. L., Slawsky, R. C., & Van Kammen, D. P. (1987). Comparative therapeutic efficacy of desipramine and carbamazepine in posttraumatic stress disorder. Presented at the Annual Meeting of the American Psychological Association, New York, NY.

Van der Kolk, B. A. (1983). Psychopharmacological issues in posttraumatic stress disorder. *Hospital and Community Psychiatry, 34,* 683–691.

Van der Kolk, B. A. (1987). *Psychological trauma.* Washington, DC: American Psychiatric Press.

Van der Kolk, B. A., Greenberg, M., Boyd, H., & Krystal, J. (1985). Inescapable shock, neurotransmitters, and addiction to trauma: Toward a psychobiology of posttraumatic stress. *Biological Psychiatry, 20,* 314–325.

Chapter 3

Assessment of Posttraumatic Stress Disorder

Brett T. Litz
Walter E. Penk
Robert J. Gerardi
Terence M. Keane

The psychological assessment of individuals who have been traumatized by extreme stressors is a challenging and multidimensional process. It includes not only a delineation of symptoms, but also an evaluation of the nature of people's traumatic experience, their unique mode of adaptation, and their methods of coping with the often-debilitating symptoms of posttraumatic stress disorder (PTSD). The assessment is also a valuable time for the patient. It is during the initial assessment that many individuals will, for the first time, discuss their trauma with a helping professional who is capable of providing a conceptualization about the development and course of his or her unique manifestation of PTSD. The assessment of PTSD can also be considered as a collaborative endeavor between clinician and patient that requires sensitivity and empathy and provides the necessary context to facilitate the positive expectancies and motivation required for the strenuous treatment tasks ahead.

Due to the diversity of stressful events over a person's life span and the myriad ways in which people cope with traumatic events, which by definition overwhelm them, the assessment of PTSD is a complex enterprise. The clinician is required to gather a great deal of information about stressful life events in the past and about the parameters of a person's past and current adjustment. This is accomplished by obtaining multiple sources of assessment data that increase the validity of diagnostic classification and treatment planning (Keane, Wolfe, & Taylor, 1987).

In this chapter we describe in detail three methods of obtaining assessment data: the structured clinical interview, psychometric inventories, and psychophysiological measurement. The goal of the assessment of PTSD is to gather data regarding (a) differential diagnosis and classification of PTSD and co-occurring or previously existing DSM disorders, (b) a functional analysis of the person's interpersonal behavior (e.g., social withdrawal), (c) an assessment of the nature of a patient's intrapersonal experiences, which often serve as targets for treatment (e.g., nightmares, intrusive trauma-related memory reactivations), (d) the delineation and prioritization of targets for treatment, and (e) decision making about appropriate treatment strategies (e.g., stress management techniques and exposure therapies). We have designed this chapter to provide the clinician with a detailed literature review about empirically validated instruments and effective assessment strategies that have utility in achieving these objectives.

We describe methods of classifying PTSD utilizing structured clinical interview formats and then offer practical guidelines for the clinician when interviewing prospective PTSD patients. This is followed by a detailed description of available psychometric instruments that measure PTSD symptoms. We then discuss psychophysiological methods that can be used as an adjunct to interview and paper-and-pencil measures in the diagnosis of PTSD. Finally, we provide the reader with several heuristics that can guide clinical decision making and the behavioral treatment planning of PTSD.

CLINICAL EVALUATION
METHODS

While considerable progress has been made in the psychological assessment of PTSD (Fairbank, Keane, & Malloy, 1983; Keane, Malloy, & Fairbank, 1984), there is currently no gold standard for diagnosing the disorder. Rather, a multimethod approach, incorporating information obtained from a variety of sources, has been advocated to establish a PTSD diagnosis (Lyons, Gerardi, Wolfe, & Keane, 1989; Kulka, Schlenger, Fairbank, Hough, Jordan, Marmar, & Weiss, 1988). The cornerstone of such an approach is the clinical interview. The clinician's task in diagnosing a patient with PTSD is to establish a link between traumatic experiences and subsequent PTSD symptomatology, to classify coexisting diagnoses, and to determine other, associated disturbances that are troubling for the individual.

Structured Diagnostic Interviews

Several structured clinical interviews have been used in the diagnosis of PTSD. Perhaps the most widely used of these instruments is the *Structured Clinical Interview for DSM-III-R* (SCID; Spitzer & Williams, 1985). The SCID was developed for use by trained mental health professionals familiar with the DSM-III-R. The interview is divided into several sections, each of which assesses for a particular Axis I disorder. Each section of the SCID begins with an introductory statement that helps to orient the patient to a particular area of inquiry. A series of symptom-specific questions are then provided that allow the interviewer to confirm or reject that diagnostic category. The interviewer is also asked to make a judgment about the quality of the patient's self-report. Each patient response is rated as "true" (clearly representative of a particular symptom), "false" (not reported), "subthreshold" (nearly representative of a symptom), or providing "inadequate information" (insufficient data).

Several features recommend the SCID. The format of the interview is easy to follow. Suggested phrasing of questions is provided along with the DSM-III-R criteria for establishing both Axis I and Axis II diagnoses. There is also a branching built into the interview such that, if a patient denies a given key or necessary symptom (e.g., extended periods of sadness for the depression section), the interviewer can move to the next section. In this way, not every question of every section needs to be asked, saving considerable time. In addition, the clinician is encouraged to ask as many questions as necessary to determine the presence or absence of a given symptom. This feature distinguished the SCID from other diagnostic interviews. Finally, Spitzer and his colleagues provide seminars and videotaped instructions to train clinicians in the use of the SCID. (Data are presented on the reliability and validity of the PTSD sections of the SCID in the psychometric considerations section of this chapter.)

The *Diagnostic Interview Schedule* (DIS; Robins, Helzer, Croughan et al., 1981) is a lay-administered, structured interview that assesses DSM-III-R diagnostic categories, including PTSD. When the DIS was utilized in a recent epidemiological study, it estimated the prevalence of civilian-trauma-related PTSD to be 1 percent, and combat-related PTSD to be 3½ percent in the general population (Helzer, Robins, & McEvoy, 1987). Regarding the DIS's capacity to classify combat-related PTSD, the results of the National Vietnam Veterans Readjustment Study (NVVRS) indicated that the DIS underestimated the prevalence of PTSD in Vietnam veterans (Kulka et al., 1988; Keane & Penk, 1989). Consequently, the DIS should be used with caution when applied to the diagnosis of PTSD until modifications are made.

The *Jackson Interview for Combat-Related PTSD* is a semistructured interview developed to diagnose combat-related PTSD and collateral difficulties (Keane, Fairbank, Caddell, Zimering, & Bender, 1985). In addition to assessing specific symptoms of PTSD, the Jackson Interview evaluates an individual's premilitary, military, and postmilitary functioning across the life span. This developmental approach permits clinicians to examine *changes* (or at least differences) in psychosocial functioning before and after the trauma.

From their premilitary history, veterans are asked about family and peer relationships, school performance and behavior, and physical health. The military history includes branch of service, years of service, duties, and frequency and intensity of combat experienced based upon the *Combat Exposure Scale* (Keane, Fairbank, Caddell, Zimering, Taylor, & Mora, 1989). The postmilitary history includes questions about job performance and family and interpersonal relationships. Veterans are also asked about the occurrence of traumatic events, significant losses, legal infractions, drug and alcohol use, and frequency and severity of specific DSM-III-R PTSD symptoms across the three time frames. These are obtained and recorded as therapist ratings.

Another structured interview that has received some empirical support in the area of PTSD diagnosis is the *Anxiety Disorders Interview Schedule* (ADIS; DiNardo, O'Brien, Barlow, Waddell, & Blanchard, 1983). The ADIS was developed to aid in the differential diagnosis of anxiety disorders. It includes sections for ruling out psychosis, major depression, and substance abuse disorders. The ADIS also contains the Hamilton Anxiety and Depression Inventories. In a recent study (Blanchard, Gerardi, Kolb, & Barlow, 1986), Vietnam veterans were independently interviewed by two clinicians using the ADIS. Interrater agreement on the diagnosis of PTSD chronic or delayed, PTSD in remission, or no PTSD was 93% (kappa = .857).

Examined from a child clinical perspective, the *Children's PTSD Inventory* (CPTSDI; Saigh, 1989a) was constructed on the basis of the DSM-III (APA, 1980) criteria for formulating a PTSD diagnosis. The instrument consists of four subtests that are scored on a dichotomous basis (i.e., 1 for the presence and 0 for the absence of symptoms). The first subtest assesses traumatization through experiential, vicarious, or verbal mediation. The second subtest assesses unwanted anxiety-evoking recollections, and the third subtest assesses general affect. Finally, the fourth subtest assesses for divergent symptoms that were apparent before the trauma. Examined psychometrically, English, French, and Arabic versions of the Children's PTSD Inventory have been validated as based on the responses of Lebanese children. Viewed in this context, the test-retest reliability of the instrument in terms of kappa coefficients ranges from .77 to .88. The validity of the instrument as based on examiner-criterion agreements ranges from .78 to .81.

In sum, no single best clinical interview instrument recommends itself in the diagnosis of PTSD. However, there are several structured clinical interviews that, in the hands of a trained clinician, can yield reliable diagnoses (Kulka et al., 1988). Clearly, the population with which one is working will have some bearing on the choice of an instrument. For example, the Jackson Interview would be useful in evaluating PTSD in veterans but would need adaptation for use with civilians, whereas the SCID, DIS, ADIS, or CPTSDI may be easily applied. Unfortunately, the SCID and ADIS are limited in that they ask questions strictly about symptoms required for diagnostic classification and omit information regarding the stressful experience that led to symptom development. They would be valuable for diagnosis but less valuable for treatment planning.

We advocate the use of structured clinical interviews chiefly because they provide a framework by which the clinician can obtain reliable data for the targeted disorder and other concurrent psychological conditions (however, this approach is not universally recommended [Arnold, 1985; Atkinson, Sparr, Sheff, White, & Fitzsimmons, 1984]). There are several advantages for the clinician. They combine a standardized assessment method with the skills and decision making of a trained clinician. The use of structured interviews also evaluates a broad spectrum of symptoms ensuring the clinician of a comprehensive understanding of the patient's condition. This allows for enhanced reliability and at the same time creates a clinical context whereby the interviewer can explore with the patient the psychological impact of various symptoms and life events. Thus, despite the structure imposed on the clinician, the experienced clinician can bring flexibility to the interview situation.

It should be stressed that these instruments are tools intended to help structure the clinical inquiry. Structured interviews do not readily lend themselves to the kinds of functional analyses of controlling factors responsible for PTSD symptoms. They are not substitutes for skillful and detailed investigation into a person's unique problem areas. The SCID, for example, is a measurement tool for dichotomously classifying patients' adjustment problems both historically and posttrauma; it does not yield a dimensional picture of patients' traumas or their unique forms of coping over time. Finally, no structured interviews to date have response set measures built into them. Thus, the clinician must be well trained to offset distortions from over- and underreporting of symptoms. The instrument should be administered only by a specially trained clinician.

Moreover, clinical interviewing is never limited to diagnosis and classification. A traumatized person, for example, will typically present him- or herself with an array of problem areas. Some of these problems will reflect the nomothetic and defining symptoms of PTSD, which can be readily evaluated using any of the structured instruments described above, while others will reveal the person-specific constellation of collateral difficulties that require exploration. These latter problems are likely to reflect either a patient's idiographic response to the experience of posttrauma events (e.g., self-medication; Keane, Gerardi, Lyons, & Wolfe, 1988), some exacerbation of a longstanding coping deficit, or a prior chronic, or comorbid manifestation of psychopathology (see Bromet, Schulberg, & Dunn, 1982; Kilpatrick, Best, Veronen, Amick, & Vileponteaux, 1985; Kulka et al., 1988; Solomon, Mikulincer, & Avitzur, 1988; Steketee & Foa, 1987), or an environmental deficiency of some kind (e.g., inadequate social support, see Keane, Scott, Chavoya, Lamparski, & Fairbank, 1985; Solomon & Mikulincer, 1987; Stretch, 1985; Wirtz & Harrell, 1987).

The clinician's task is further complicated in the interview in that PTSD patients will seek psychological assistance at varying points in time after their trauma, often after an extended period of effective functioning (see Keane, Litz, & Blake, 1990). Typically, some kind of life crisis situation precipitates the patient's desire for treatment. These crises initially may seem unrelated to the trauma (e.g., a dissolving marriage, loss of a loved one, loss of a job, retirement). However, after a detailed interview, the stressful life experience that prompted help-seeking is likely to have an important thematic connection to a previous traumatic event and thus serves to reactivate a network of painful memories that trigger PTSD symptomatology (Litz & Keane, 1989).

For example, a World War II combat veteran recently sought treatment after many years of effective functioning. The patient was complaining of problems with sleeping and depressive symptoms after he viewed on television the accidental gun-turret explosion aboard the battleship United States Iowa. The patient had served on a similar battleship in World War II and had witnessed a similar incident. Upon evaluation, it was clear that the patient met diagnostic criteria for PTSD.

The following guidelines are recommended as ways of increasing the reliability and validity of structured clinical interviews. These suggestions should also serve to increase a clinician's sensitivity toward traumatized patients while ascertaining information about important collateral problems.

CLINICAL INTERVIEWING
GUIDELINES

Delineate the Influences of Pre- and Posttrauma History

Although converging data suggest that the nature and extent of a person's trauma predominantly account for the emergence of PTSD (Foy, Carroll, & Donahoe, 1987; Kulka et al., 1988), many associated problem areas can reflect either chronic pretrauma difficulties or some other form of learned, maladaptive, posttrauma behavior. It is essential for any PTSD interview to include specific questions about a person's early learning history as well as inquiries into any posttrauma complications (Keane et al., 1985). The goal here is to differentiate significant contributing events in each period of time that may interact in the development of both PTSD and associated maladaptive behaviors. The tracing of the temporal parameters of collateral problem areas can lead to more effective treatment planning. In determining which experiences have affected the course of an individual's disorder over time, the clinician has the additional responsibility to determine the strengths that a person brings to the clinical setting. These strengths, once identified, can be useful in treatment planning as well.

Essential areas to address in an interview for each time period (pre- and posttrauma) are: (a) Is there any history of extreme or overwhelming levels of stress, especially physical or sexual abuse? While backgrounds of abuse are frequently observed in clinic patients (Herman, Perry, & van der Kolk, 1989), it is clear that people who seek help for PTSD may have been exposed to multiple traumatic events in their lives. Information about specific events as well as how those stressors were subjectively appraised is important to gather. The use of the DSM-III-R "severity of psychosocial stressors scale" (Axis IV) is one empirical method of quantifying the extent of stressful life events (e.g., Saigh, 1989a). Questions about how previous extreme stressors were appraised and managed can provide data about a person's specific coping style. (b) What was (is) the family/home environment like? (e.g., was there any history of mental illness or substance abuse in the family? How did role models cope with stress?) (c) Is there any history of academic, social, or occupational impairment or deficits? (e.g., any antisocial behaviors?) (d) Is there any history of drug or alcohol abuse or dependence? (e) Is there any history of head injury or cognitive impairment? (f) What have been the person's relative cognitive and behavioral strengths? (e.g., what part of a person's behavioral repertoire can be augmented or enhanced in treatment?) This is particularly important information to be identified in reference to the PTSD patient who is also depressed and socially isolated. The prompting or promoting of behaviors and activities that had formerly been mood enhancing and pleasurable can aid in the treatment of depressive affect (cf. Lewinsohn, Munoz, Youngren, & Zeiss, 1986).

Monitor Cognitive Factors

It has been noted in both clinical and research contexts that individuals with PTSD are likely to perceive and interpret their environments in characteristic and often distorted ways. It appears that attention is drawn selectively to potential threat stimuli, which in turn act as retrieval cues activating frightening trauma-related memories. Researchers have also suggested that PTSD patients are likely to exaggerate the probability of threat in their environments and experience higher levels of psychophysiological reactivity in various life situations that prompts them to look for evidence of threat in order to confirm their expectations of fear and to construct an explanation or attribution for their arousal (see Chemtob, Roitblat, Hamada, Carlson, & Twentyman, 1989; Foa, Steketee, & Olasov Rothbaum, 1989; Litz & Keane, 1989). These cognitive processes in turn facilitate the behavioral avoidance and withdrawal often seen in PTSD (e.g., Penk, Peck, Robinowitz, Bell, & Little, 1988).

Thus, each traumatized individual, depending on the nature and extent of his or her learning history, possesses a distinctive network of trauma-related memories. This network primes the cognitive processing of environmental information and biases it toward its threatening potential, which in turn, contributes to the expressed symptom picture in PTSD. Furthermore, this affects a person's ability to cope with future stressors. Finding any confirming evidence of threat also reinforces this distorted model of thinking and relating to the person's environment. These person variables are important to identify in the assessment of PTSD (Keane et al., 1989). A useful scheme that can guide clinicians' thinking about cognitive factors in posttrauma adjustment can be extrapolated from Walter Mischel's work (1973; see Evans & Litz, 1987). These are *construction competencies* (e.g., a person's general knowledge base, problem-solving abilities [Nezu & Carnevale, 1987]); *encoding strategies* (how stressful situations are appraised, or misperceived as personally threatening; see Chemtob et al., 1989; and Litz & Keane, 1989, for a discussion of information-processing factors in the development and maintenance of PTSD); *expectancies* (both outcome and self-efficacy confidence judgments in specific high-fear situations); *values and preferences* (e.g., judgments of the valence of key reinforcing and aversive stimuli; see Foa et al., 1989, for a discussion of these factors in the development of PTSD), and *self-regulatory systems and plans* (coping style, e.g., Solomon, Mikulincer, & Avitzur, 1988; arousal management ability; characteristic self-statements).

Attention given to cognitive factors in the assessment and conceptualization of individual PTSD cases is particularly useful for those therapists who take a stress inoculation approach to the treatment of PTSD (e.g., Kilpatrick, Veronen, & Resick, 1982; Veronen & Kilpatrick, 1983). Through the active self-monitoring of characteristic modes of responding and modification of the coping repertoires (e.g., getting a patient to change self-statements and cognitive appraisals regarding trauma-related information), idiosyncratic cognitive responses in high-risk situations (e.g., a lunch date for a victim of a rape) can be specifically targeted in treatment.

Expect Comorbidity

Epidemiological and clinical research (chiefly with combat veterans) suggests that PTSD co-occurs with some other Axis I disorder in approximately 60 to 100% of cases (Helzer et al., 1987; Keane & Wolfe, in press; Kulka et al., 1988; Sierles, Chen, McFarland, & Taylor, 1983; Sierles, Chen, Messing, Besyner, & Taylor, 1986). The single most common co-occurring diagnosis is some form of substance abuse or dependence that often serves to quell intrusive cognitive experiences, promote sleep, or alleviate arousal states (Keane et al., 1988). Other common disorders include major depression, dysthymia, generalized anxiety disorder, and panic disorder.

The use of a structured clinical interview that assesses Axis I and Axis II disorders is a recommended tool for the assessment of comorbidity in PTSD. The structured interview phase of the PTSD evaluation is also an opportunity for the clinician to get a broader picture of a person regarding his or her current problems, any etiological and controlling factors responsible for those problems (e.g., family history), and previous coping or treatment efforts (e.g., the efficacy of prior psychological or pharmacological interventions, a history of suicidal or other self-destructive behavior, any history of treatment noncompliance).

Evaluate Ethnic and Cultural Factors

The most comprehensive epidemiological study of PTSD to date has been the NVVRS (Kulka et al., 1988). These researchers found some striking differences in the prevalence of PTSD among the different ethnic groups that served in combat: caucasians, 14%; blacks, 21%, and Hispanics, 28%. Although much research remains to be done on the factors that might account for these differences, this preliminary information should begin to influence the development of assessment and treatment programs specifically geared to these minority populations.

While many treatment programs for minorities are being developed, the majority of treatment for these populations is provided in nonspecialized programs by nonminority clinicians. Several general principles must be considered in the successful evaluation and treatment of a minority person who has been traumatized. First, it is important for the clinician to explore whether the minority patient finds it difficult to talk to a clinician who does not share the same cultural background. We have found that this strategy gives permission to the patient to openly address any concerns about communication in the assessment. Second, a patient with a different cultural and ethnic background is likely to feel unable to relate well to or trust a clinician who does not share the same background. This latter factor is always present to some degree in all traumatized populations, but it is likely to impinge on the assessment process to a greater extent for minorities who are interviewed by a nonminority individual. Third, it is likely that a patient from a different culture will use a personal idiom, especially in expressing emotionally significant events. The clinician can enlist the support of the patient in helping him or her to understand the nuances of the self-report and self-representation. It is also helpful to use words that are comfortable for the patient from a different background to increase ease of understanding in a nonpatronizing way.

Fourth, a person from a nonwhite background may have learned a reporting style that is different from the "representative" sample of individuals who make up standardization samples on psychological tests. Cultural differences, for example, are critical to examine when using the MMPI (Dahlstrom, Lachar, & Dahlstrom, 1986). This necessity led Butcher and his colleagues to develop culture-specific norms for the MMPI-2 (Butcher, Dahlstrom, Graham, Tellegen, & Kaemmer, 1989). Individuals from different cultures are likely to underreport or overreport their symptoms, which has implications for diagnosis and treatment planning.

Assess the Needs of Significant Others

Couples' and family problems are common among traumatized individuals (Carroll, Rueger, Foy, & Donahoe, 1985; Resick, Calhoun, Atkeson, & Ellis, 1981; Roberts, Penk, Gearing, Robinowitz, Dolan, & Patterson, 1982). It is important to include significant others, whenever possible, in the assessment of PTSD patients. We have found that the following assessment goals can be accomplished when a significant other or family member is invited to be part of a PTSD evaluation: (a) corroboration of patient's self-reported PTSD symptoms; (b) assessment of the treatment needs of family members; (c) provision of information and education about the psychological aftereffects of traumatization (e.g., an explanation about the symptoms of PTSD, the role the trauma plays in the victim's [and his or her family's] life, and the reason why PTSD symptoms are likely to be expressed in certain situations); (d) reduction in any blaming or misplaced responsibility for certain problems in the home (e.g, parenting deficits); and (e) training of family members or significant others in supporting and coping with treatment efforts.

Evaluate Ongoing Litigation

Litigation frequently surrounds the events that lead to PTSD. Questions about patient's attempts to get compensation for their trauma or victimization experiences should be part of a PTSD interview. The clinician can provide a useful service by helping the patient to separate out compensation and treatment issues and make clear their role as treatment providers. A discussion of these secondary gain issues in the beginning stages of the assessment can also improve the reliability of self-report data. For a more thorough discussion of the impact of compensation seeking on assessment data, the reader is referred to Atkinson, Henderson, Sparr, and Deale (1982); Fairbank, McCaffrey, and Keane (1985); Gerardi, Blanchard, and Kolb (1989); Hyer, Fallon, Harrison, and Boudewyns (1987); Lynn & Belza (1984); and Sparr and Pankratz (1983).

Realize that PTSD Assessments Can Be Stressful

Divulging painful, often-avoided material is threatening for patients. Some patients express concerns about going "crazy" or losing control or acting violently. Moreover, there is frequently some manifestation of difficulty in trusting others as well.

Sensitivity to the stress that the assessment process can provoke for patients is especially important for those patients at risk for alcohol or drug abuse. It is important to monitor the emotional reactions of patients during the PTSD assessment process as well as to monitor the patient's urge to use substances to reduce aversive affect. The clinician will at times need to decide, along with the patient, whether it would be prudent to suspend the assessment until the patient has learned some relapse-prevention skills or provide the patient with some arousal-reducing strategies during the assessment (e.g., muscle relaxation, deep breathing, allowing the patient time to recuperate after an assessment session). Pacing the assessment process to suit the needs of the individual patient is an important task for the clinician.

The above guidelines are specifically tailored to the interview situation. They will apply equally well, however, to the administration of psychological tests that have been designed to assess PTSD.

PSYCHOMETRIC CONSIDERATIONS

This section reviews psychometric developments in assessing PTSD. Because most work in psychometric development has centered, until recently, on evaluating men who fought in Vietnam, the presentation focuses upon PTSD that is combat related. Knowledge gained from such landmark studies as Legacies of Vietnam (Egendorf, Kadushin, Laufer, Rothbart, & Sloan, 1981) and the NVVRS (Kulka et al., 1988) serve as benchmarks for guiding future psychometric development in measuring PTSD, particularly PTSD produced by exposure to civilian trauma. The review is organized to answer two questions:

1. What progress has been made in developing psychometrically based instruments for reliably and validly measuring PTSD, and how can current psychometric instruments be used in everyday practice?
2. What problems need to be resolved to improve measurement of PTSD, and how do such strategies and tactics influence the current practice of assessing PTSD?

In answering these two general questions, with a view toward improving psychological assessment, it is necessary to consider the psychometrics of PTSD measurement within the following context.

First, although psychometrics have not always been highly regarded in behavioral assessment, behaviorally oriented clinicians, in practice, do indeed use findings from traditional assessment measures, particularly when psychometric scores reflect observable behaviors or when scores are competency based. Thus, many behaviorially oriented clinicians do not eschew opportunities to integrate psychometric results with other ways of learning about patients.

Second, psychometric development of PTSD measures will lag behind clinical progress in diagnosing PTSD simply because it is far less complicated to clinically describe a phenomenon than it is to develop reliable and valid measures. Practical ways to overcome the limitations of descriptive criteria and incomplete psychometric measures of PTSD are to administer many measures in many forms over many occasions (cf. Keane et al., 1987).

Third, it is not surprising to learn that many clinicians are impatient with psychometrics. Some simply do not believe that psychometric measures of any disorder are important in devising treatment plans. Others would rather act from clinical intuition quickly formed rather than proceed through the tedium of obtaining psychometric measures. However, the implications of misdiagnosis or misclassification for secondary gain considerations alone should encourage careful assessment. PTSD is a disorder for which financial compensation often results (as occurs in veterans compensation, civil litigation, or in product liability cases). Diagnostic accuracy is essential, not only to avoid inappropriately burdening society with unnecessary depletion of its limited resources, but also to ensure that patients are given accurate information about their psychological condition.

Fourth, assessment of any psychological disorder requires obtaining information from many different sources as well as using many different kinds of measures. This does not mean that psychometrics are any less or any more important than behavioral or other forms of information. Rather, what it does mean is that clinicians can use psychometric results for help in classifying disorders and for planning treatment.

Fifth, even though there are many strengths in the psychometric developments in measuring PTSD, this review of PTSD measures in clinical practice is written very early in the development of psychometrics in PTSD. At the outset, it must be appreciated that more research is needed. The decade of the eighties began with the promulgation of descriptive criteria for classifying PTSD (i.e., DSM-III, 1980, with DSM-III-R to follow in 1987). Most PTSD measurement was based upon adaptation of existing assessment procedures that were developed to evaluate other disorders. By the end of the 1980s, however, the picture had changed markedly: Behavioral and psychometrically based assessment procedures were constructed that precisely evaluated PTSD.

Finally, it is likely that the next battleground for establishing the validity of PTSD as a disorder will also shift in the eighties from the clinic and the hospital to the courts. Already there are many challenges to the psychometrics of PTSD in the scientific literature that can be answered only by rigorously implementing a system of classifying instruments according to their predictive validity and clinical utility (Dawes, Faust, & Meehl, 1989; Faust, 1984; Gerardi, Keane, and Penk, 1989; Swets, 1988).

Progress in Developing Psychometrically Based PTSD Measures

The development of PTSD measures has moved quickly from the promulgation of descriptive criteria in DSM-III (1980) to the development of several reliable and valid measures of PTSD. The most that any clinician had for measuring PTSD at the beginning of the 1980s was a few checklists, such as Figley's (1978) Vietnam Veteran's Questionnaire; Wilson and Krauss's (1985) Vietnam Stress Inventory; the Legacies of Vietnam scales (Egendorf et al., 1981). All of these instruments received some refinement over the decade, as reported in the prospective-like study of Card (1983) using the Figley scales, and in research from the Forgotten Warrior's Project (e.g., Wilson & Krauss, 1985).

However, none of the studies met essential criteria for adequately developing sound psychometric measures of PTSD. One such set of criteria for the development of reliable and valid assessment measures can be found in Denny, Robinowitz, and Penk (1987). In addition to the standard features of reliability and validity associated with test development, clinical research studies also need to supply diagnostic accuracy measures (e.g., hit rates, sensitivity and specificity statistics, with PTSD base rates among populations where PTSD diagnoses are being classified). All of these criteria must be met in any research so that trauma-PTSD links are solidly forged and not attributable to factors other than the trauma hypothesized to cause PTSD symptoms.

Few psychometrically based PTSD measures have been derived under rigorous conditions in which all of the foregoing criteria have been met and in which possibly confounding influences have been ruled out when developing PTSD measures. This section on psychometrics will focus on those PTSD measures developed under the most rigorous psychometric conditions.

The more robust adult measures of PTSD were cross-validated in the Pre-Test Validation phase of the NVVRS (Kulka et al., 1989). Table 3.1 is a table of diagnostic accuracy that permits comparison, since all of the instruments were administered to the same subjects. (Thus, this table from the NVVRS represents the only available comparison of the major (adult) psychometrically based PTSD measures administered to the same subjects.)

Impact of Event Scale. The Impact of Event Scale (IES; Horowitz, Wilner, & Alvarez, 1979) is a 15-item scale on which subjects rate the impact of a traumatic (or stressful) event. The scale is administered by having the respondent specify an event that was traumatic (or stressful), thereby leaving the respondent free to select and nominate the event that is being rated. Then the patient rates seven items that represent episodes of intrusion (e.g., "I thought about it when I didn't mean to") and eight items demonstrating avoidance symptoms (e.g., "I tried to remove it from memory").

The IES has acceptable test-retest reliability (.87) and internal consistency (e.g., Cronbach's alpha, .78 for the intrusion score and .82 for the avoidance items, with a split-half reliability correlation of 0.86). As shown

Table 3.1. Relative Diagnostic Accuracy of PTSD Measures

Measure	Percentage Correctly Classified[a]	Kappa[b]	Sensi- tivity[c]	Speci- ficity[d]
Mississippi PTSD Scale for Combat-Related PTSD (Keane et al., 1988)	88.9	.753	94.0	79.7
NVVRS PTSD Diagnostic Interview (Kulka et al., 1988), DIS-based, sum of positive items	87.5	.714	95.5	72.6
PTSD Checklist (based on DSM-III-R)	84.9	.672	88.3	78.9
NVVRS PTSD DIS-like Scale, using DSM-III-R, 1987, decision rules	83.5	.639	87.2	72.6
MMPI PTSD Scale (Keane et al., 1984)	81.5	.605	90.1	68.8
Impact of Event Scale (Horowitz et al., 1979)	81.6	.565	91.7	61.8

[a]Percentage Correctly Classified is the percentage of the entire sample (true cases and true noncases) that are correctly classified by the survey measure.
[b]Kappa is a measure of the extent of agreement between two assessments corrected for the effects of chance. (Kappas above .75 are considered to indicate excellent agreement; those between .40 and .75, fair to good agreement; and those below .40, poor agreement).
[c]Sensitivity is the percentage of "true" cases that are classified as cases by the survey measure.
[d]Specificity is the percentage of "true" noncases that are classified as noncases by the survey measure.

in Table 3.1, the IES achieved good diagnostic accuracy. But, although it is able to correctly classify "true" cases of PTSD with excellent sensitivity, it is appreciably less proficient in identifying noncases of PTSD.

What also recommends the IES is that it is one of the few PTSD scales with acceptable psychometric properties in which the standardization samples were women and in which the standardization samples had experienced civilian (noncombat) traumas. The scale has also been validated on combat veterans (Kulka et al., 1988; Schwarzwald, Solomon, Weisenberg, Mikulincer, 1987; Weisenberg, Solomon, Schwarzwald, & Mikulincer, 1987).

What is less attractive about the IES is that it does not yield definitive cutting scores to specify the presence or absence of PTSD. Moreover, the IES contains few items about the fourth set of PTSD criteria: psychophysiological reactivity and arousal. Another problematic aspect of the IES is that test administration does not specify how to distinguish between traumatic levels of stressful life events and other forms of non-life-threatening stress. This deficiency can be compensated for if the examiner carefully interviews to determine whether an event meets the first criterion of PTSD as being beyond the range of ordinary human experience and being life-threatening. Perhaps the major limitation of the IES is that it does not contain any psychometrically controlled response set indicators. Again, this is not a fatal flaw, but a weakness that is readily overcome by adding psychometrically based validity indicators from other well-established tests such as the MMPI.

Structured Interviews—The SCID and DIS. Both of these instruments have already been described in preceding sections. However, it must be noted that the test developers who constructed these interviews followed well-established psychometric procedures in regard to test development. A brief note is indicated regarding their utility in diagnosing PTSD, recalling that each is a global measure yielding presence-absence PTSD classification and current and lifetime distinctions (although, in the NVVRS, Kulka et al. [1988], have now driven the SCID in the direction of a "partial" PTSD classification that goes beyond the dichotomy developed originally by Spitzer & Williams, 1985).

Kulka et al. (1988), after finding that the DIS was promising in their pretest validation study, discovered that the DIS-type instrument did not perform well in the NVVRS study. When compared to clinician's interviews, kappa for the DIS dropped into the poor range (.26). Whereas its specificity was excellent (97.9% correct identification of noncases), its sensitivity was poor (21.5% correct identification of PTSD cases). Kulka et al. (1988) have cautioned clinical researchers about the continued use of DIS-type instruments, although their cautionary remarks have not been extended to other psychiatric categories.

Whereas a DIS-type interview did not work well, at least for the NVVRS in studying combat-related PTSD (Kulka et al., 1988), the SCID lived up to its pretest validation promise in the larger National Vietnam Veterans Readjustment Study. The SCID also proved to be a diagnostically accurate instrument across ethnic groups (i.e., white, black, and Hispanic).

Thus, the SCID emerges as the preferred structured interview to be used in diagnosing PTSD. The SCID surveys all the elements comprising PTSD criteria. Its kappa coefficient was quite robust as based on comparisons between expert clinician classification and SCID NVVRS interviews (i.e., .93). The SCID also yields classification of other Axis I disorders. Recently, a section for classifying Axis II disorders was added to the interview format (but its reliability and validity are still under evaluation). Table 3.2 presents NVVRS sensitivity and specificity information about the SCID for the clinical subsample (i.e., those who met PTSD criteria in the field interviews) of the NVVRS. One significant finding from the NVVRS was that diagnostic accuracy was superior when several PTSD measures were used in combination. Such data underscore the basic recommendation advocated in this chapter—namely, using several diagnostic measures together yields greater diagnostic sensitivity and specificity.

MMPI PTSD Subscales. Two scales have been developed from an existing psychometrically sound instrument, the Minnesota Multiphasic Personality Inventory (MMPI; Hathaway & McKinley, 1951). One is the Keane et al. (1984) MMPI PTSD subscale, and the other is the Schlenger & Kulka (1989) PTSD subscale for the recently revised MMPI, or MMPI-2, as it is being called (Butcher et al., 1989). Both scales are derived from instruments that have built-in validity indicators, a feature that enables the examiner to determine whether or not scores are indeed valid (a feature that has not been built into the DIS, SCID, IES, or any other instrument for classifying PTSD). Moreover, reliability of the MMPI in general, and for the PTSD subscales, is excellent.

The Keane et al. (1984) MMPI PTSD subscale items were retained in the revision of the MMPI to create MMPI-2. Whereas the Keane MMPI PTSD subscale can be calculated from either the original MMPI or the new MMPI-2, the Schlenger-Kulka MMPI PTSD is obtainable only from the MMPI-2. The Keane scale contains 49 items; the Schlenger-Kulka scale contains 102 items. Neither scale is readily distorted by the face-valid, transparent nature of their items, since both scales were devised using empirical methods (i.e., the classic contrasted-group approach). It is unlikely that most test-takers would be able to say which of the 566 MMPI items comprises either scale.

The Keane et al. (1984) MMPI PTSD subscale was developed by identifying items that differentiated psychiatric patients with PTSD from psychiatric patients without PTSD (a cutoff score of 30 had been able to sucessfully identify PTSD patients in 82% of the cases examined in the original validation study). The Schlenger-Kulka (1989) scale was developed from the non-treatment-seeking combat veterans randomly identified in the stratified sample that comprised the NVVRS. As a consequence, one would expect that the Keane scale would perform more accurately with psychiatric clinical samples, and the Schlenger-Kulka scale would perform better with non-treatment-seeking groups. Actually, in practice, the Keane et al. (1984) has worked well with a wide range of samples in the many cross-validating efforts that have been published (see Penk, Keane, Robinowitz, Fowler, Bell, & Finkelstein, 1988, for an updated review of PTSD assessment using the MMPI, as well as Denny, Robinowitz, & Penk, 1987).

If there are any limitations in the MMPI PTSD subscales (after the many improvements in rewriting, restandardizing, and renorming the MMPI-2), they will probably arise from the unspecified role of civilian (noncombat) traumas and their impact in scale development. Other limitations may arise from demographic differences among subjects—such as uncontrolled ethnic and gender differences that, as yet, may not have been taken into account in MMPI PTSD scale development (or in any other PTSD scales that have been developed for other instruments). Perhaps the most complicated question to answer will be the contributions of comorbidity to MMPI PTSD scale development—specifically, the differential role of co-occurring disorders that are documented as meeting criteria before or after onset of PTSD (especially substance abuse). Many of these questions can be answered as data analysis proceeds apace from the comprehensive results produced by the NVVRS.

A major advantage of using PTSD scales from the MMPI (and now MMPI-2) is that the MMPI has been translated into more than 100 languages. This multilingual feature of the MMPI recommends it as highly desirable and will enable investigators to study PTSD resulting from comparable civilian traumas across many cultures. The MMPI is an untapped and underutilized diagnostic procedure for studies of civilian trauma across many languages and many cultures.

MMPI configurational analysis (one example of which is the F, 2, 8 configuration first proposed by Keane et al., 1984) is still used but is not attracting as much attention as has MMPI PTSD scale development. One problem facing PTSD classification based upon MMPI configuration profile analysis (where classification is based upon original validity and clinical scales) is that no prototypical or modal MMPI profile has emerged characterizing the disorder. As examiners amass a large number of MMPI (or other instrument) profiles, one quickly finds from profile classification that no one profile appears any more frequently than any other (see Penk et al., 1988, for a fairly even distribution of frequencies across 20 major categories of MMPI codetypes, using the Gilberstadt-Duker, 1965, form of profile analysis.). As of this writing, MMPI configurational profile analysis does not appear promising—until, perhaps, cluster analyses have been conducted where potentially confounding influences in profiles have been ruled out or neutralized. Work in this area of PTSD analysis portends greater attention to the influence of comorbidities.

Mississippi Scale for Combat-Related PTSD. A useful psychometric instrument developed for measuring war-related PTSD is the Mississippi Scale for Combat-Related PTSD (Keane, Caddell, & Taylor, 1988). This is a 35-item scale on which subjects rate each of the items on a 5-point Likert scale. Items were generated by clinicians who had extensive experience in treating patients with PTSD. In the original standardization studies, the Mississippi Scale had an internal consistency coefficient of .94. Factor analysis of the 35 items yielded six factors—one for intrusive memories and depressive symptomatology, a second for interpersonal adjustment problems, a third representing lability of affect and memory, the fourth and fifth for registering ruminative features of PTSD, and the sixth factor for sleep problems. Validation studies have suggested a cutoff score of 107 to be used when identifying combat-related PTSD patients; this cutoff score yielded a hit rate of 90%, with a sensitivity of .93 and a specificity of .89. Alternate forms of the Mississippi scale have been developed, quite successfully, for use with female veterans and for civilians.

One limitation of the Mississippi measure of PTSD is the failure to contain response validity indicators. Test-givers are recommending that clinicians and researchers use the Mississippi Scale with some kind of validity indicators and most certainly with some sort of cross-checking through interview or through review of records. The Mississippi can be readily improved by adding response set scales; currently, it is a face-valid measure that clinicians and researchers should interpret only when one is certain that the person responding has experienced life-threatening, traumatic events and when one has assessed possibilities of secondary gain in symptom reporting.

Table 3.2 presents NVVRS results of the better-performing tests in the diagnostic comparison trials and shows that several instruments used together are diagnostically more accurate than any one of the better instruments.

These findings, among the first to permit comparison of different PTSD measures administered to the same patients, provide a comparison of diagnostic accuracy of measures used separately and in combination. The findings are based upon 252 patients identified as meeting PTSD criteria in the epidemiological survey of a stratified sampling of more than 3,000 combat male veterans. The recommended battery of psychometric-based instruments consists of the SCID, the Mississippi Scale, and the Keane et al. (1984), along with the Schlenger & Kulka (1988) MMPI PTSD scales. The clinician should also use some scale that quantifies the nature of the traumatic experience. These are discussed next.

Combat Exposure Scales. Recently, some progress has been made in the quantification and measurement of the traumatic event itself. This development was prompted by converging evidence that the nature and extent of the trauma account for the greatest variance in etiological models of combat-related PTSD (Foy et al., 1987; Penk et al., 1981). By today's standards, early primitive scales were developed by Figley (1978), Laufer et al. (1981), Boulanger and Kadushin (1986), and Wilson and Krauss (1985). These early scales have been the source for many items used in later, more psychometrically sound scales. Foy et al. (1987) have published results of a Combat Exposure Scale (which was cross-validated using Card's [1983] *Lives after Vietnam* data—see Foy and Card, 1987). This was followed by the development of a Combat Exposure Scale for use in psychiatric settings

Table 3.2. Comparison of Separate and Combined NVVRS PTSD Diagnoses

Instrument	Sensitivity	Specificity	Kappa
Mississippi PTSD Scales	82.4	86.4	.644
SCID PTSD	81.2	97.6	.821
MMPI PTSD	81.6	87.7	.649
Any two of the above instruments combined	92.1	94.1	.832

(Keane et al., 1989), a scale with excellent internal stability and test-retest reliability.

None of these scales has built-in validity indicators, but any one may be used in conjunction with response set measures, such as the validity scales of the MMPI. Because these are self-report measures, answers to items may be influenced by respondents' biased recollection of the past or some hidden motive about present circumstances (a cry for help or compensation seeking). Assessment tactics should strive to delineate objective aspects of the traumatic stressor as well as a person's appraisal of it (see Gleser, Green, & Winget, 1981; and Wilson, Smith, & Johnson, 1985; for a conceptual scheme depicting dimensions of traumatic stress). Furthermore, independent verification of the traumatic event is a needed addition to the traumatized person's report about the traumatic event and their reactions to it.

The concept that trauma must be differentiated into component parts has guided the thinking and practice of many clinicians and researchers who are all striving toward the unfulfilled dream of eventually being able to create a taxonomy of trauma with quantifiable stress reactions (e.g., Brett & Ostroff, 1985; Gleser et al., 1981; Keane, 1989). Another excellent step has been taken in this direction by Kulka and Schlenger, with their recent creation of a 98-item War Zone Stressor Scale, differentiated for males and females, and featuring such factors as Exposure to Combat, Exposure to Abusive Violence and Related Conflicts, Deprivation, Loss of Meaning and Control, and Prisoner of War subscales. These subscales justify the need to design research that breaks down the global dichotomies of our thinking about trauma and PTSD until we can differentiate the relevant dimensions comprising the disorder.

FUTURE DEVELOPMENTS IN PTSD PSYCHOMETRICS

We will now briefly consider psychometrics of PTSD from the perspective from which problems must be resolved in order to improve the assessment of PTSD in the future.

First and foremost, clinical researchers must extend psychometrics from combat-related PTSD to civilian (noncombat) PTSD. The latest epidemiological data suggest that PTSD is about as prevalent as schizophrenia in the general population (1%, or approximately 2,400,000 cases at any point in time; Helzer et al., 1987). Intuitively, most clinicians understand that trauma caused by early sexual abuse evokes different reactions and different coping than a car accident; surviving a tornado is different from being tortured as a political prisoner. Trends in the research completed to date indicate that each class of trauma demands its own form of special assessment. Thus it is crucial that the practicing clinician have some form of readily available psychometric device or devices that can measure PTSD from a variety of events.

Work on developing instruments to assess civilian-related PTSD is well underway (e.g., Black, Penk, Robinowitz, Dolan, Bell, Rubenstein, & Skinner, 1984). Even though the prevalence of noncombat trauma is high, few of the civilian trauma studies have approached the scope or sophistication of combat trauma studies. Nor have investigators studying psychometric measurement of civilian trauma evaluated their assessment instruments by reference to principles of diagnostic accuracy advocated here (i.e., obtaining measures of sensitivity and specificity).

The practicing clinician has two basic strategies in regard to psychometric evaluation of civilian-related PTSD. One is the use of a general-purpose, global and dichotomous measure like the SCID (suggesting presence or absence of PTSD). The other is an adjunctive measure specifically tailored for a particular form of trauma. In practice, we recommend using both approaches—that is, to begin by surveying the incidence of trauma followed by an examination of details of both the stimulus conditions as well as the person's coping response.

General PTSD instruments are just beginning to be developed. Saigh (1989) is developing an Adult Trauma Inventory that, like the IES, can be used as a general-purpose instrument for assessing civilian trauma-related PTSD. Black et al. (1984) are developing a checklist of civilian traumatic events that could be used by clinicians in varied mental health settings.

Progress has also been made in specific trauma inventories as well. Kilpatrick, Amick, Lipovsky, and Resick (1989) are developing instruments for use in criminal victimization-related PTSD, as well as adapting existing instruments such as the SCL-90 and the Fear Survey Schedule (Resick, Veronen, Kilpatrick, Calhoun, & Atkeson, 1986). They have devised an Incident Classification Interview that gathers data about the key aspects of a crime episode, akin to a trauma exposure scale. These researchers have also developed a checklist for assessing one particular kind of crime—rape (Kilpatrick, Veronen, & Best, 1985). In addition, Davidson, Fleming, and Baum (1987) have summarized the many instruments that can be used to evaluate the reactions of victims to disasters created by human failure (e.g., Three Mile Island). Green, Grace, Lindy, Titchner, and Lindy (1983) have also presented some instrumentation for assessing reactions to catastrophic environmental events. Finally, a civilian form of the Mississippi Scale was developed for use in the NNVRS.

Second, as illustrated in the instance of developing refined measures of Combat Exposure scales, psychological assessment of PTSD in the 1990s will need to feature even greater differentiated measures of specific PTSD dimensions, with increasing attention to the separate areas of avoidance symptoms, intrusive reexperiencing symptoms and psychophysiological reactivity. From a clinical perspective, it appears that PTSD is both a chronic and a phasic disorder consisting of both positive and negative symptoms (Keane, 1989). Thus, psychometric instruments in the future should be sensitive to changes in the quality of PTSD symptoms over time. Such differentiation of measures may eventually produce a multidimensional PTSD profile (or "multiphasic" profile, if shifts in symptoms across time and events can be empirically demonstrated). Multidimensional analysis of PTSD will then permit developing a typology of PTSD. By producing a multidimensional PTSD profile, the clinical therapist may then be able to write a treatment plan that prioritizes a hierarchical list of preferred problems for treatment. Such plans may preclude the current "shotgun" approach to treating traumatized persons.

PSYCHOPHYSIOLOGICAL METHODS OF ASSESSMENT

Psychophysiological methods have played a major role in our understanding of anxiety disorders in general (Lang, 1977b) and PTSD in particular. Physiological reactivity is a salient diagnostic feature of PTSD, and assessment of this phenomenon presents the rare opportunity to obtain information on a disorder that is not reliant solely upon the self-report of the patient. The basic paradigm entails the presentation of trauma-relevant stimuli (and some neutral or control stimuli) concurrent with the measurement of multimodal response channels: the physiological response (e.g., heart rate); the self-report of arousal, often measured in Subjective Units of Distress (SUDS); and an instrumental or behavioral response (e.g., termination/avoidance of the assessment procedure once it has begun).

Despite the importance of such physiological measurement in PTSD, most clinicians are not in a position to obtain these data. For many clinicians, equipment costs and expertise required to operate and maintain the equipment make obtaining physiological measures prohibitive. Despite these apparent impediments, it may be possible for clinicians in some settings to obtain some physiological data at little cost. Blanchard et el. (1986) have suggested the use of heart rate alone, which can be obtained in any hospital setting with a simple EKG machine. Research has shown that several methods of stimulus presentation may be used (auditory, audiovisual, narrative descriptions of the traumatic event) in the assessment of PTSD. In the absence of any psychophysiological assessment capabilities, the clinician may, with the patient's consent, obtain physiological information (heart rate, systolic and diastolic blood pressure) from medical records. There is some evidence that individuals with PTSD may be chronically hyperaroused (or hyperreactive), even in situations unrelated to traumatic events (Gerardi, Keane, Cahoon, & Klauminzer, 1989).

Numerous psychophysiological laboratory studies have been conducted with veterans with combat-related PTSD, and different paradigms have emerged. These studies are presented in detail in the following sections. It is noteworthy that despite the variety of stimuli presented (auditory, audiovisual, imaginal), the paradigm employed, and the types of control groups used, veterans with PTSD are consistently found to be more physiologically reactive to trauma-related cues.

Blanchard et al. (1982) compared 11 Vietnam veterans diagnosed with PTSD with 11 age- and sex-matched nonveterans. Subjects listened to an audiotape consisting of five trials of 30 seconds of music, 30 seconds of silence, and 30 seconds of combat sounds. The volume was increased on each trial. Results indicated that veterans experienced significantly greater increases in heart rate, systolic and diastolic blood pressure, and forehead EMG relative to nonveterans. A discriminant analysis using heart rate alone correctly classified 21 of the 22 subjects (95.5%). These effects have been replicated in several subsequent studies.

Pallmeyer, Blanchard, and Kolb (1986) assessed 12 Vietnam veterans with PTSD, 10 Vietnam veterans with no psychiatric disorder, 5 Vietnam veterans with other psychiatric disorders, 5 Vietnam era veterans with no psychiatric disorders and no combat experience, and 8 nonveterans with specific phobias. Once again, the veterans with PTSD appeared to be the most reactive to the combat stimuli. On the basis of heart rate alone, 75% of the veterans with PTSD and 100% of the combat veterans without PTSD were correctly classified. When all subjects were included in the analysis, 67% of the PTSD veterans and 86% of all the others were correctly classified. Finally, these authors examined subjects' heart rate reactivity to combat stimuli relative to their responses to a mental arithmetic task. At a cutoff of −3.5 beats per minute (bpm) (i.e., response to mental arithmetic is ≥3.5 bpm higher than the maximum response to combat sounds), 83.3% of PTSD veterans and 89.3% of all other subjects were correctly classified.

In a second replication, Blanchard et al. (1986) assessed 57 Vietnam veterans with PTSD and 34 Vietnam veterans with no mental disorder. Using subjects' single largest heart rate response (the change in heart rate from music to combat sounds on the same trial) and a cutoff score of 7 bpm, 88% of veterans with PTSD and 70% of veterans without PTSD were correctly classified. The authors then calculated a difference score by subtracting the heart rate response to mental arithmetic from the single largest heart rate response to the combat sounds. Using a cutoff greater than zero, this single index correctly classified 73% of subjects with PTSD and 88% of subjects without PTSD.

In a separate research laboratory, Malloy, Fairbank, and Keane (1983) compared the heart rate and skin resistance responses of 10 Vietnam veterans with PTSD, 10 Vietnam-era inpatient psychiatric controls, and 10 normal Vietnam veteran controls. Subjects were exposed to audiovisual cues consisting of nine neutral scenes and nine combat scenes. A discriminant function analysis of four physiological measures (mean heart rate, mean skin resistance level, mean number of skin resistance responses, and mean skin resistance magnitude) correctly classified 80% of the total sample. When self-report (SUDS ratings) and behavioral (amount of tape viewed) data were included, 100% of the subjects were correctly classified as PTSD or non-PTSD.

In an excellent study designed to individually tailor the combat stimuli to the experiences of the subject, Pitman, Orr, Forgul, and de Jong (1987) exposed 15 Vietnam veterans with PTSD and 18 Vietnam veterans without PTSD to a series of 30-second audiotaped scripts. The scripts consisted of individualized descriptions of the two most stressful combat experiences recalled by each subject. The authors measured heart rate, skin conductance, and EMG from the left corrugator, lateral frontalis, and zygomatic facial muscles. Correct classifications of subjects based on psychophysiological responses to the scripts were as follows: heart rate, 64%; skin conductance, 73%; and EMG, 67%. All measures combined correctly classified 100% of the PTSD subjects but only 61% of the non-PTSD subjects.

Pitman et al.'s (1987) study determined that imaginal exposure to scripts depicting idiographic trauma cues can elicit a reliable psychophysiological response in PTSD patients. Their data suggest that a practicing clinician does not have to have specially validated and generic trauma cues to present to patients to conduct a psychophysiological assessment. Clinicians can save time and resources by simply generating individualized scripts based on the person's traumatic experience(s), regardless of the type of trauma. In addition, since Blanchard et al.'s (1986) data suggest that heart rate reactivity is the single best predictor of PTSD, a practicing clinician interested in assessing psychophysiological responsivity in PTSD may choose to employ a single channel monitor.

Finally, it should be noted that the direct measurement of psychophysiological reactivity can be used as a method of testing hypotheses about malingering in PTSD patients. But can psychophysiological reactivity in PTSD be faked? To address this question, Gerardi, Blanchard, and Kolb (1989) examined the ability of veterans to fake their responses during a psychophysiological assessment. Subjects with PTSD were asked to control or decrease their physiological responses, and subjects without the disorder were asked to increase their physiological responses to the combat sounds. Results indicated that veterans with PTSD could not significantly alter their psychophysiological responses. However, the non-PTSD group was actually quite good at increasing their physiological responses during the combat sounds. Using heart rate accelerations alone and the 7 bpm cutoff score recommended by Blanchard et al. (1986), only two of nine veterans were correctly classified as non-PTSD. However, when baseline heart rate and heart rate change scores were considered together, six out of nine (66.7%) veterans attempting to fake PTSD and 83% of all subjects were then correctly classified.

The data that have emerged from the various laboratories described above validated psychophysiological measurement as an accurate diagnostic tool in the assessment of PTSD. Consistent findings of situationally specific fear responses to trauma-related cues have also served to confirm the cognitive-behavioral conceptualization of PTSD as a learned, trauma-related response pattern (Keane, Zimering, & Caddell, 1985). An assessment finding of psychophysiological reactivity to generalized trauma-related cues can be utilized by the behavioral clinician as data that suggest that some form of exposure treatment may be indicated to reduce this conditioned emotional response. It is to these decision-making factors in the behavioral assessment of PTSD that we now turn.

CLINICAL DECISION MAKING

The assessment of PTSD can be characterized then, not only by the types of interview-based, psychometric, and psychophysiological information obtained from a patient, but also by the decision-making strategies of the therapist (see Evans & Litz, 1987; Evans & Wilson, 1983; Kanfer, 1985). The behavioral assessor's task is to base his or her clinical judgments about a given patient on a theoretical model of PTSD that incorporates empirically derived cognitive-behavioral principles (Fairbank & Nicholson, 1987; Foa et al., 1989; Keane et al., 1985; Levis, 1980; Litz & Keane, 1989). In this regard, diagnostic, psychometric, and psychophysiological data are useful inasmuch as they aid in hypothesizing about the functional nature and controlling characteristics of a PTSD patient's unique difficulties, in helping to identify targets and strategies for treatment, and in monitoring meaningful clinical change (cf. Nelson & Barlow, 1981). Those clinical decision-making factors that affect treatment planning are discussed next.

Prioritizing Targets for Change

A clinical diagnosis of PTSD, based on DSM-III-R criteria, can direct the clinician toward nomothetic areas to be addressed in treatment. Comprehensive psychological treatments of PTSD usually entail multiple techniques and strategies that target specific clusters of symptoms (Keane et al., 1985). Reexperiencing symptoms may be treated with direct therapeutic exposure of traumatically conditioned cues in imagery; avoidance symptoms are primarily treated by gradually encouraging the person to increase the range of his or her interpersonal contacts and activities coupled with the application of learned coping skills. Hyperarousal symptoms are primarily addressed by training in stress management skills. However, for many patients with PTSD, there is typically some preponderance of either *positive symptoms* (reexperiencing coupled with psychophysiological hyperreactivity symptom clusters) or *negative symptoms* (avoidance behaviors, numbness, withdrawal) that can guide the choice of initial treatment strategies (cf. Keane, 1989).

Since some kind of direct therapeutic exposure or processing of trauma-related information in imagery is indicated for PTSD patients with severe positive symptoms, it is crucial to systematically assess the nature and extent of a person's trauma in a manner that can guide the course of such treatment (Fairbank & Brown, 1987; Keane et al., 1985; Keane, Fairbank, Caddell, & Zimering, 1989). Foa and Kozak (1986), in their expansion of Lang's (1977a, 1985) conceptualization of the fear network model, provide a useful scheme for assessing the nature of traumatic memories. They argue that a fear network is comprised of information about stimulus cues that elicit fear (e.g., sights, smells, sounds associated with the trauma), information about cognitive, motor, and psychophysiological responses engendered during the traumatic stressor (e.g., co-occurring thoughts, actions, affects), and information that defines the meaning of the stimulus cues and responses for the person (e.g., "Everything in life is unfair and unpredictable; I'm going to go crazy and lose control if I allow myself to think about what happened to me"). Thus it is important for the clinician to gather information about these three categories of conditioned stimuli, for they will guide the direct therapeutic exposure of traumatic memories.

In those PTSD cases in which the assessment yielded a symptom picture with a preponderance of negative symptoms (social isolation, anhedonia), a clinician might begin treatment by focusing on efforts to increase interpersonal risk taking and to fashion success experiences through in vivo exercises coupled with a skills training program. Increases in social contacts and the greater expression of affect may lead a patient to recall more details of the trauma that may then be addressed through exposure treatment.

When Is Exposure Treatment Indicated?

As mentioned previously, the systematic therapeutic processing of traumatic events utilizing systematic desensitization, flooding in imagery, or implosive therapy has been hypothesized as a viable treatment for certain PTSD cases (Keane et al., 1985; Keane et al., 1989). Until recently, the research that has supported this thesis has been primarily case studies (Fairbank & Keane, 1982; Keane & Kaloupek, 1982; Rychtarik, Silverman, Van Landingham, & Prue, 1984; Saigh, 1986). However, Keane et al. (1989) completed a randomized clinical trial that indicated that exposure treatments can lead to considerable improvement for many PTSD patients. A recent replication by Cooper and Clum (1989) provided further substantiation of this approach. Exposure treatments, however, are rigorous and require a good deal of resources on the part of the patient and the therapist. Thus, deciding whether exposure treatment is indicated for a given patient-therapist combination is a critical task in the assessment of PTSD.

Several conditions are necessary for a therapist to consider exposure treatments. First, the patient must meet the boundary conditions of the technique (e.g., ability to imagine; see Boudewyns & Shipley, 1983; Levis, 1980). Second, the patient must be able to tolerate the intense levels of arousal associated with exposure treatment, as well as the possible increase in PTSD symptoms that occurs in the short run. In regard to the first factor, a PTSD patient should report reexperiencing symptoms and exhibit some level of anxious arousal in response to reminders of their trauma. PTSD patients appropriate for exposure treatments should be able to follow the therapist's instructions as well as clearly imagine various stimuli.

When deciding whether a PTSD patient can handle the intense levels of arousal generated during exposure treatment, the therapist should be concerned about the potential for dropouts. We have found it to be important for the patient to be in relatively good health (especially no cardiovascular disease), have a stable living environment (or some consistent and available social supports during extratherapy hours), and not be involved in substance abuse.

While no empirical data support the necessity of the above conditions for the use of direct therapeutic exposure, these decision rules are conventions that have been derived from clinical experience. One preliminary study, however, sought to delineate the manner in which expert behavioral clinicians working in the area of PTSD made decisions about the appropriateness of exposure treatments for particular types of patient presentations (Litz, Blake, Gerardi, & Keane, 1990). They found that 42% of the PTSD cases that expert clinicians treated over the years were *not* treated with exposure therapy. The following factors were used to preclude exposure treatments for these behavior therapists: 91% judged that severe levels of psychological impairment and comorbidity, such as poor cognitive functioning or severe depression, ruled out the use of exposure treatment. Concurrent personality disorder or substance abuse disorder (27% agreement), treatment noncompliance (27% agreement), unresolved life crises

(18% agreement), and poor physical health (18% agreement) were judged as additional rule-out factors.

SUMMARY AND FUTURE DIRECTIONS

This chapter has described state-of-the-art methods for evaluating the psychological status of individuals who have suffered through severe forms of stress. We have advocated the use of multiple sources of assessment data (interview, psychometric, and psychophysiological) to increase diagnostic validity as well as to aid in the accurate understanding of PTSD patients' unique form of adaptation over time. We have also provided clinical guidelines and decision-making heuristics that will help the clinician in gathering assessment data and assisting in behavioral treatment planning.

Many theoretical, empirical, and practical assessment issues remain for PTSD researchers to explore. Several of these issues were raised in the preceding sections (e.g., the need for the development of specific PTSD assessment instruments related to civilian trauma; greater attention to the special needs of minorities in the assessment of PTSD). As final comments, we add a brief discussion of future research needs in the assessment of PTSD.

One pressing need in the assessment of PTSD is for measures that assess the severity of PTSD symptoms and their impact on social adjustment. To date, the majority of instruments that have been developed to assess PTSD have used a total score to reflect PTSD symptomatology globally and categorically (e.g., the SCID, the Mississippi Scale). What is needed is structured interview-formatted and paper-and-pencil instruments that measure the subjective intensity of specific symptoms of PTSD as well as measures of the extent to which symptoms interfere in an individual's functioning, in both qualitative and quantitative terms (e.g., CAPS; Blake, Weather, Nagy, Kaloupek, Klauminzer, Charney, & Keane, 1990). Such measures will foster the gathering of data that will likely influence future definitional models of PTSD (e.g., DSM IV), and our understanding of the underlying processes of the disorder.

For example, correlating the nature of traumatic experiences and symptom severity and impact over time may lead to subtyping of the disorder (e.g., positive vs. negative symptom clusters or subtypes are likely to have distinct effects on a traumatized person's adaptation), or to the conceptual development of clinical models that describe specific types of PTSD syndromes that relate to specific types or degrees of traumatization (criminal victimization vs. natural disaster, etc.), or the analysis of the variable nature of certain PTSD symptoms and the stable course of others. If clinicians can empirically assess the severity and impact of PTSD symptoms, they will be better able to plan treatments that would be geared toward a patient's specific manifestation of PTSD as well as the potential maladaptive effect those symptoms have on the environment (e.g., family conflict that stems from a patient's avoidance symptoms).

Another major area that needs to be explored in the future is the utility of the newly revised and restandardized MMPI in the assessment of PTSD (MMPI-2; Butcher, Dahlstrom, Graham, Tellegan, & Kaemmer, 1989). This is a particularly important issue to be explored empirically because of the proven utility of the original MMPI and its PTSD scale in the assessment of PTSD. Although preliminary research has suggested that the MMPI-2 is highly comparable to the original MMPI in its applicability to the assessment of combat-related PTSD (Litz, Penk, Walsh, Hyer, Blake, Marx, Keane, and Bitman, 1991), much remains to be explored. For example, does the MMPI-2 PTSD subscale have as high a degree of utility as the original MMPI in the diagnosis of PTSD (in combat-related and civilian-related cases)? Is the MMPI-2 any more helpful in determining the validity of self-report due to the addition of new scales that are purported to assess consistency, diligence, underreporting, or exaggeration in test-taking behavior (thus reflecting on the usefulness or validity of a patient's self-report in the diagnosis of PTSD).

Finally, measurement strategies are needed that will facilitate data collection on the course of PTSD and the psychosocial effects of PTSD as it occurs in different developmental phases. The development of generic PTSD assessment instruments and also methods to assist clinicians in disentangling the effects of an extremely stressful discrete event from a lifetime of chronic stressors will be a challenging and formidable task for future research. Success in these areas will promote both theoretical and clinical advances in the field.

REFERENCES

American Psychiatric Association (1980). *Diagnostic and statistical manual of mental disorders (3rd ed.)*. Washington, DC, American Psychiatric Association.

American Psychiatric Association (1987). *Diagnostic and statistical manual of mental disorders (3rd ed.)—Revised*. Washington, DC, American Psychiatric Association.

Arnold, A. (1985). Diagnosis of PTSD in Vietnam veterans. In A. Sonnenberg, A. Blank, & J. Talbott (Eds.), *The trauma of war: Stress and recovery in Vietnam veterans* (pp. 101–123). Washington, DC: American Psychiatric Association.

Atkinson, R. M., Henderson, R. G., Sparr, L. F., & Deale, S. (1982). Assessment of Vietnam veterans for posttraumatic stress disorder in Veterans Administration disability claims. *American Journal of Psychiatry, 139,* 1118–1121.

Atkinson, R. M., Sparr, L. F., Sheff, A. G., White, R. A. F., & Fitzsimmons, J. T. (1984).

Diagnosis of posttraumatic stress disorder in Vietnam veterans: Preliminary findings. *American Journal of Psychiatry, 141,* 694–696.

Black, J. L., Penk, W., Robinowitz, R., Dolan, M., Bell, W., Rubenstein, J., & Skinner, J. (1984). *Checklist for stressful and traumatic events, CSTE.* Paper presented at the annual meeting of the American Psychological Association, Los Angeles, 1984.

Blake, D. D., Weather, F. W., Nagy, L. M., Kaloupek, D. G., Klauminzer, G., Charney, D., & Keane, T. K. (1990). A clinician rating scale for assessing current and lifetime PTSD: The CAPS-1. *The Behavior Therapist. 18,* 187–188.

Blanchard, E. B., Gerardi, R. J., Kolb, L. C., & Barlow, D. H. (1986). The utility of the Anxiety Disorders Interview Schedule (ADIS) in the diagnosis of post traumatic stress disorder in Vietnam veterans. *Behaviour Research and Therapy, 24,* 577–580.

Blanchard, E. B., Kolb, L. C., Pallmeyer, T. B., & Gerardi, R. J. (1982). The development of a psychophysiological assessment procedure for post-traumatic stress disorder in Vietnam veterans. *Psychiatric Quarterly, 54,* 220–229.

Boudewyns, P. A., & Shipley, R. H. (1983). *Flooding and implosive therapy.* New York: Plenum Publishing.

Boulanger, G., & Kadushin, C. (1986). *The Vietnam veteran redefined: Fact and fiction.* Hillsdale, NJ: Lawrence Erlbaum Associates.

Brett, E. A., & Ostroff, R. (1985). Imagery and posttraumatic stress disorder: An overview. *American Journal of Psychiatry, 142,* 417–424.

Bromet, E., Schulberg, H. C., & Dunn, L. (1982). Reactions of psychiatric patients to the Three Mile Island nuclear accident. *Archives of General Psychiatry, 39,* 725–730.

Butcher, J. N., Dahlstrom, W. G., Graham, J. R., Tellegen, A., & Kaemmer, B. (1989). *Manual for the restandardized Minnesota Multiphasic Personality Inventory: MMPI-2. An administrative administrative and interpretive guide.* Minneapolis: University of Minnesota Press.

Card, J. J. (1983). *Lives after Vietnam: The personal impact of military service.* Lexington, MA: Lexington Books.

Carroll, E., Rueger, D., Foy, D., & Donahoe, C. (1985) Vietnam combat veterans with post-traumatic stress disorder: An analysis of marital and cohabitating adjustment. *Journal of Abnormal Psychology, 94,* 329–337.

Chemtob, C., Roitblat, H., Hamada, R., Carlson, J., & Twentyman, C. (1989). A cognitive action theory of post-traumatic stress disorder. *Journal of Anxiety Disorders, 2,* 253–275.

Cooper, N. A., & Clum, G. A. (1989). Imaginal flooding as a supplementary treatment for PTSD in combat veterans: A controlled study. *Behavior Therapy, 20,* 381–391.

Dahlstrom, W. G., Lachar, G., & Dalhstrom, L. (1986). *MMPI patterns of American minorities.* Minneapolis: University of Minnesota Press.

Davidson, L. M., Fleming, R., & Baum, A. (1987). Chronic stress, catecholamines, and sleep disturbances at Three Mile Island. *Journal of Human Stress, 13,* 75–83.

Dawes, R. M., Faust, D., & Meehl, P. E. (1989). Clinical versus actuarial judgement. *Science, 243,* 1668–1674.

Denny, N., Robinowitz, R., & Penk, W., (1987). Conducting applied research on Vietnam combat-related post-traumatic stress disorder. *Journal of Clinical Psychology, 43,* 56–66.

DiNardo, P. A., O'Brien, G. T., Barlow, D. H., Waddell, M. T., & Blanchard, E. B. (1983). Reliability of DSM-III anxiety disorders categories using a new structured interview. *Archives of General Psychiatry, 40,* 1070–1074.

Egendorf, A., Kadushin, C., Laufer, R. S., Rothbart, G., & Sloan, L. (1981). *Legacies of Vietnam: comparative adjustment of veterans and their peers.* Washington, DC: U.S. Government Printing Office.

Evans, I. M., & Litz, B. T. (1987). Behavioral assessment: A new theoretical foundation for clinical measurement and evaluation. In H. J. Eysenck & I. Martin (Eds.), *Theoretical foundations of behavior therapy* (p. 331–351). New York: Plenum Publishing.

Evans, I. M., & Wilson, F. E. (1983). Behavioral assessment as decision-making: A theoretical analysis. In M. Rosenbaum, C. M. Franks, & Y. Jaffe (Eds.), *Perspectives on behavior therapy in the eighties* (pp. 35–53). New York: Springer.

Fairbank, J. A., & Brown, T. A. (1987). Current behavioral approaches to the treatment of posttraumatic stress disorder. *Behavior Therapist, 10,* 57–64.

Fairbank, J. A., & Keane, T. M. (1982). Flooding for combat-related stress disorders: Assessment of anxiety reduction across traumatic memories. *Behavior Therapy, 13,* 499–510.

Fairbank, J. A., Keane, T. M., & Malloy, P. F. (1983). Some preliminary data on the psychological characteristics of Vietnam veterans with posttraumatic stress disorders. *Journal of Consulting and Clinical Psychology, 51,* 912–919.

Fairbank, J. A., McCaffrey R. J., & Keane, T. M. (1985). Psychometric detection of fabricated symptoms of posttraumatic stress disorder. *American Journal of Psychiatry, 142,* 501–503.

Fairbank, J. A., & Nicholson, R. A. (1987). Theoretical and empirical issues in the treatment of post-traumatic stress disorder in Vietnam veterans. *Journal of Clinical Psychology, 43,* 44–55.

Faust, D. (1984). *The limits of scientific reasoning.* Minneapolis: University of Minnesota Press.

Figley, C. R. (1978). The Vietnam veteran survey (VVS). In J. Card (Ed.), *Lives after Vietnam* (pp. 161–180). Lexington, MA: Lexington Books.

Foa, E. B., & Kozak, M. J. (1986). Emotional processing of fear: Exposure to corrective information. *Psychological Bulletin, 99,* 20–35.

Foa, E. B., Steketee, G., & Olasov-Rothbaum, B. O. (1989). Behavioral/cognitive conceptualizations of stress disorder. *Behavior Therapy, 20,* 155–176.

Foy, D. W., & Card, J. J. (1987). Combat-related post-traumatic stress disorder etiology: Replicated findings in a national sample of Vietnam-era men. *Journal of Clinical Psychology, 43,* 28–31.

Foy, D. W., Carroll, E. M., & Donahoe, C. P. (1987). Etiological factors in the development of PTSD in clinical samples of Vietnam combat veterans. *Journal of Clinical Psychology, 43,* 17–27.

Gerardi, R.J., Blanchard, E. B., & Kolb, L. C. (1989). Ability of Vietnam veterans to dissimulate a psychophysiological assessment for post-traumatic stress disorder. *Behavior Therapy, 20,* 229–243.

Gerardi, R. J., Keane, T. M., Cahoon, B. J., & Klauminzer, G. W. (November 1989). *Physiological arousal in Vietnam veterans: Hyperarousal or hyperreactivity?* Presented at the Association for the Advancement of Behavior Therapy Convention, Washington, DC.

Gerardi, R., Keane, T. M., & Penk, W. E. (1989). Utility: Sensitivity and specificity in developing diagnostic tests of combat-related PTSD. *Journal of Clinical Psychology, 45,* 6–18.

Gilberstadt, H., & Duker, J. (1965). *A handbook for clinical and actuarial MMPI interpretation.* Philadelphia, PA: W B Saunders.

Gleser, G. C., Green, B. L., & Winget, C. (1981). *Buffalo Creek revisited: Prolonged psychosocial effects of disaster.* New York: Simon & Schuster.

Green, B. L., Grace, M. C., Lindy, J. D., Titchner, J. L., & Lindy, J. G. (1983). Levels of functional impairment following a civilian disaster: The Beverly Hills Supper Club fire. *Journal of Consulting and Clinical Psychology, 51,* 573–580.

Hathaway, S. R., & McKinley, J. C. (1951). *Minnesota multiphasic personality inventory: Manual for administration and scoring.* New York: Psychological Corporation.

Helzer, J. E., Robins, L. N., & McEvoy, L. (1987). Post-traumatic stress disorder in the general population: Findings of the Epidemiological Catchment Area Survey. *The New England Journal of Medicine, 317,* 1630–1634.

Herman, J. L., Perry, J. C., & van der Kolk, B. A. (1989). Childhood trauma in borderline personality disorder. *American Journal of Psychiatry, 146,* 490–495.

Horowitz, M., Wilner, N., & Alvarez, W. (1979). Impact of event scale: A measure of subjective stress. *Psychosomatic Medicine, 41,* 209–218.

Hyer, L., Fallon, J. H., Jr., Harrison, W. R., & Boudewyns, P. A. (1987). MMPI overreporting by Vietnam combat veterans. *Journal of Clinical Psychology, 43,* 79–83.

Kanfer, F. H. (1985). Target selection for clinical change programs. *Behavioral Assessment, 7,* 7–20.

Keane, T. M. (1989). Post-traumatic stress disorder: Current status and future directions. *Behavior Therapy, 20,* 149–153.

Keane, T. M., Caddell, J. M., & Taylor, K. L. (1988). Mississippi scale for combat-related PTSD: Three studies in reliability and validity. *Journal of Consulting and Clinical Psychology, 56,* 85–90.

Keane, T. M., Fairbank, J. A., Caddell, J. M., Zimering, R. T., Bender, M. E. (1985). A behavioral approach to assessing and treating post-traumatic stress disorder in Vietnam veterans. In C. R. Figley (Ed.), *Trauma and its wake,* (p. 257–294). New York: Brunner/Mazel.

Keane, T. M., Fairbank, J. A., Caddell, J. M., Zimering, R. T., Taylor, K. L., & Mora, C. A. (1989). Clinical evaluation of a measure to assess combat exposure. *Psychological Assessment: A Journal of Consulting and Clinical Psychology, 1,* 53–55.

Keane, T. M., Gerardi, R. J., Lyons, J. A., Wolfe, J. (1988). The interrelationship of substance abuse and posttraumatic stress disorder. In M. Galanter (Ed.), *Recent developments in alcoholism,* (pp. 27–48). New York: Plenum Publishing.

Keane, T. M., & Kaloupek, D. G. (1982). Imaginal flooding in the treatment of a post-traumatic stress disorder. *Journal of Consulting and Clinical Psychology, 50,* 138–140.

Keane, T. M., Litz, B. T., & Blake, D. D. (1990). Post-traumatic stress disorder in adults. In M. Hersen & C. G. Last (Eds.), *Handbook of child and adult psychopathology: A longitudinal perspective.* Elmsford, NY: Pergamon Press.

Keane, T. M., Malloy, P. F., & Fairbank, J. A. (1984). Empirical development of an MMPI subscale for the assessment of combat-related posttraumatic stress disorder. *Journal of Consulting and Clinical Psychology, 52,* 888–891.

Keane, T. M., & Penk, W. E. (1988). The prevalence of post-traumatic stress disorder. Letter to the Editor, *New England Journal of Medicine, 318,* 1690–1691.

Keane, T. M., Scott, W. O., Chavoya, G. A., Lamparski, D. M., & Fairbank, J. A. (1985). Social support in Vietnam veterans with posttraumatic stress disorder: A comparative analysis. *Journal of Consulting and Clinical Psychology, 53,* 95–102.

Keane, T. M., & Wolfe, J. (1990). Comorbidity in post-traumatic stress disorder: An analysis of community and clinical studies. *Journal of Applied Social Psychology, 20,* 1776–1788

Keane, T. M., Wolfe, J., & Taylor, K. C. (1987). Post-traumatic stress disorder: Evidence for diagnostic validity and methods of psychological assessment. *Journal of Clinical Psychology, 43,* 32–43.

Keane, T. M., Zimering, R. T., & Caddell, J. M. (1985). A behavioral formulation of post-traumatic stress disorder in Vietnam veterans. *The Behavior Therapist, 8,* 9–12.

Kilpatrick, D. G., Amick, A., Lipovsky, J. A., & Resick, H. S. (1989). *Can self-reported inventories discriminate cases of crime-related post-traumatic stress disorder?* Paper presented at the Association for the Advancement of Behavior Therapy, New York.

Kilpatrick, D. G., Best, C. L., Veronen, L. J., Amick, A. E., Vileponteaux, L. A., & Ruff, C. A. (1985). Mental health correlates of criminal victimization: A random community survey. *Journal of Consulting and Clinical Psychology, 53,* 866–873.

Kilpatrick, D. G., Veronen, L. J., and Best, C. L. (1985). Factors predicting psychological distress among rape victims. In C. R. Figley (Ed.), *Trauma and its wake: The study and treatment of post-traumatic stress disorder.* New York: Brunner/Mazel.

Kilpatrick, D. G., Veronen, L. J., and Resick, P. A. (1982). Psychological sequelae to rape: Assessment and treatment strategies. In D. M. Doleys & R. L. Meredith (Eds.), *Behavioral medicine: Assessment and treatment strategies.* New York: Plenum Publishing.

Kulka, R. A., Schlenger, W. E., Fairbank, J. A., Hough, R. L., Jordan, B. K., Marmar, C. R.,

& Weiss, D. S. (1988). *National Vietnam veterans readjustment study (NVVRS): Description, current status, and initial PTSD prevalence estimates.* Washington, DC: Veterans Administration.

Lang, P. J. (1977a). Imagery in therapy: An information processing analysis of fear. *Behavior Therapy, 8,* 862–886.

Lang, P. J. (1977b). The psychophysiology of anxiety. In H. Akiskal (Ed.), *Psychiatric diagnosis: Exploration of biological criteria.* New York: Spectrum.

Lang, P. J. (1985). The cognitive psychophysiology of emotion: Fear and anxiety. In A. H. Tuma & J. D. Maser (Eds.), *Anxiety and the Anxiety Disorder.* Hillsdale, NY: Lawrence Erlbaum.

Laufer, R., Yager, T., Grey-Wouters, E., et al. (1981). Post-war trauma: Social and psychological problems of Vietnam veterans in the aftermath of the Vietnam war. In A. Egendorf, C. Kadushin, R. S. Laufer, et al. (Eds.), *Legacies of Vietnam,* Vol. III. Washington, DC: US Government Printing Office.

Levis, D.J. (1980). Implementing the technique of implosive therapy. In A. Goldstein & E. B. Foa (Eds.), *Handbook of behavioral interventions: A clinical guide.* New York: John Wiley & Sons.

Lewinsohn, P. M., Munoz, R. F., Youngren, M. A., Zeiss, A. (1986). *Control your depression.* New York: Prentice-Hall.

Litz, B. T., Blake, D. D., Gerardi, R. J., & Keane, T. M. (1990). Decision making guidelines for the use of direct therapeutic exposure in the treatment of post-traumatic stress disorder. *The Behavior Therapist, 13* (4), 91–93.

Litz, B. T., & Keane, T. M. (1989). Information processing in anxiety disorders: Application to the understanding of post-traumatic stress disorder. *Clinical Psychology Review, 9,* 243–257.

Litz, B. T., Penk, W. E., Walsh, S., Hyer, L., Blake, D. D., Marx, B., Keane, T. K., & Bitman, D. (1991). Similarities and differences between Minnesota Multiphasic Personality Inventory (MMPI) and MMPI-2 applications to the assessment of post-traumatic stress disorder. *Journal of Personality Assessment.*

Lynn, E. J., & Belza, M. (1984). Factitious PTSD: The veterans who never got to Vietnam. *Hospital and Community Psychiatry, 35,* 697–701.

Lyons, J. A., Gerardi, R. J., Wolfe, J., & Keane, T. M. (1989). Multiaxial assessment of PTSD: Phenomenological, psychometric, and psychophysiological considerations. *Journal of Traumatic Stress Studies, 1,* 373–394.

Malloy, P. F., Fairbank, J. A., & Keane, T. M. (1983). Validation of a multimethod assessment of post-traumatic stress disorders in Vietnam veterans. *Journal of Consulting and Clinical Psychology, 51,* 488–494.

Mischel, W. (1973). Toward a cognitive social learning reconceptualization of personality. *Psychological Review, 80,* 252–283.

Nelson, R. O., & Barlow, D. H. (1981). Behavioral assessment: Basic strategies and initial procedures. In D. H. Barlow (Ed.), *Behavioral assessment of adult disorders* (pp. 13–43). New York: Guilford Press.

Nezu, A., & Carnevale, G. (1987). Interpersonal problem solving and coping reactions of Vietnam veterans with posttraumatic stress disorder. *Journal of Abnormal Psychology, 96,* 155–157.

Pallmeyer, T. P., Blanchard, E. B. & Kolb, L. C. (1986). The psychophysiology of combat-induced post-traumatic stress disorder in Vietnam veterans. *Behavioral Research and Therapy, 24,* 645–652.

Penk, W. E., Keane, T. M., Robinowitz, R., Fowler, D. R., Bell, W., & Finkelstein, A. (1988). Post-traumatic stress disorder. In R. C. Greene (Ed.), *The MMPI: Use with specific populations* (pp. 198–213). Philadelphia, PA: Grune & Stratton.

Penk, W. E., Peck, R. F., Robinowitz, R., Bell, W., & Little, D. (1988). Coping and defending styles among Vietnam combat veterans seeking treatment for post-traumatic stress disorder and substance use disorder. In M. Galanter (Ed.), *Recent developments in alcoholism,* vol. 6 (pp. 69–88). New York: Plenum Publishing.

Penk, W. E., Robinowitz, R., Roberts, W. R., Patterson, E. T., et al. (1981). Adjustment differences among male substance abusers varying in degree of combat experience in Vietnam. *Journal of Consulting and Clinical Psychology, 49,* 426–437.

Pitman, R. K., Orr, S. P., Forgul, D. F., de Jong, J. B., & Claiborn, J. M. (1987). Psychophysiologic assessment of post-traumatic stress disorder imagery in Vietnam combat veterans. *Archives of General Psychiatry, 44,* 970–975.

Resick, P., Calhoun, K., Atkeson, B., & Ellis, E. (1981). Social adjustment in victims of sexual assault. *Journal of Consulting and Clinical Psychology, 49,* 705–712.

Resick, P. A., Veronen, L. J., Kilpatrick, D. G., Calhoun, K. S., & Atkeson, B. M. (1986). Assessment of fear reactions in sexual assault victims: A factor analytic study of the Veronen-Kilpatrick Modified Fear Survey. *Behavioral Assessment, 8,* 271–283.

Roberts, W. R., Penk, W. E., Gearing, M. L. Robinowitz, R., Dolan, M.P., & Patterson, E. T. (1982). Interpersonal problems of Vietnam combat veterans with symptoms of posttraumatic stress disorder. *Journal of Abnormal Psychology, 91,* 444–450.

Robins, L. N., Helzer, J. E., Croughan, J., & Ratcliff, K. (1981). National Institute of Mental Health Diagnostic Interview Schedule. *Archives of General Psychiatry, 38,* 381–389.

Rychtarik, R. G., Silverman, W. K., Van Landingham, W. P., & Prue, D. M. (1984). Treatment of an incest victim with implosive therapy: A case study. *Behavior Therapy, 15,* 410–420.

Saigh, P. A. (1986). In vitro flooding in the treatment of a 6-year-old boy's posttraumatic stress disorder. *Behavior Research and Therapy, 24,* 685–688.

Saigh, P. A. (1989b). On the development and validation of the Children's Post-traumatic Stress Disorder Inventory. *International Journal of Special Education, 4,* 75–84.

Saigh, P. A. (1989a). *Adult trauma inventory.* Unpublished manuscript.

Schlenger, W., & Kulka, R. A. (1989). PTSD scale development for the MMPI-2. Research Triangle Park, NC: Research Triangle Institute.

Schwarzwald, J., Solomon, Z., Weisenberg, M., & Mikulincer, M. (1987). Validation of the impact of event scale for psychological sequelae of combat. *Journal of Consulting and Clinical Psychology, 55,* 251–256.

Sierles, F. S., Chen, J., McFarland, R. E., & Taylor, M. A. (1983). Post-traumatic stress disorder and concurrent psychiatric illness. *American Journal of Psychiatry, 140,* 1177–1179.

Sierles, F. S., Chen, J., Messing, M. L., Besyner, J. K., & Taylor, M. A. (1986). Concurrent psychiatric illness in non-Hispanic outpatients diagnosed as having posttraumatic stress disorder. *Journal of Nervous and Mental Disease, 174,* 171–173.

Solomon, Z., & Mikulincer, M. (1987). Combat stress reactions, post-traumatic stress disorder, and social adjustment: A study of Israeli veterans. *Journal of Nervous and Mental Disease, 175,* 277–285.

Solomon, Z., Mikulincer, M., & Avitzur, E. (1988). Coping, locus of control, social support, and combat-related posttraumatic stress disorder: A prospective study. *Journal of Personality and Social Psychology, 55,* 279–285.

Sparr, L., & Pankratz, L. D. (1983). Factitious PTSD. *American Journal of Psychiatry, 140,* 1016–1019.

Spitzer, R. L., & Williams, J. B. (1985). Structured clinical interview for DSM-III. New York: Unpublished manuscript, Biometrics Research Department, New York State Psychiatric Institute, New York.

Steketee, G., & Foa, E. B. (1987). Rape victims: Post-traumatic stress responses and their treatment: A review of the literature. *Journal of Anxiety Disorders, 1,* 69–86.

Stretch, R. (1985). Post-traumatic stress disorder among US Army Reserve Vietnam and Vietnam-era veterans. *Journal of Consulting and Clinical Psychology, 53,* 935–936.

Swets, J. A. (1988). Measuring the accuracy of diagnostic systems. *Science, 240,* 1285–1293.

Veronen, L. J., & Kilpatrick, D. G. (1983). Stress management for rape victims. In D. Meichenbaum & M. E. Jaremko (Eds.), *Stress reduction and prevention* (pp. 341–374). New York: Plenum Publishing.

Watson, C. G., Juba, M. P., & Anderson, P. E. D. (1989). Validities of five combat scales. *Psychological Assessment: A Journal of Consulting and Clinical Psychology, 1,* 98–102.

Weisenberg, M., Solomon, Z., Scharzwald, J., & Mikulincer, M. (1987). Assessing the severity of post-traumatic stress disorder: Relation between dichotomous and continuous measures. *Journal of Consulting and Clinical Psychology, 55,* 432–434.

Wilson, J. P., & Krauss, G. E. (1985). Predicting post-traumatic stress disorders among Vietnam veterans. In W. E. Kelly (Ed.), *Post-traumatic stress disorder and the war veteran patient* (pp. 102–147). New York: Brunner/Mazel.

Wilson, J. P., Smith, W. K., & Johnson, S. K. (1985). A comparative analysis of PTSD among various survivor groups. In C. R. Figley (Ed.), *Trauma and its wake: The study and treatment of postraumatic stress disorder* (pp. 142–172). New York: Brunner/Mazel.

Wirtz, P., & Harrell, A. (1987). Effects of post-assault exposure to attack-similar stimuli on long-term recovery of victims. *Journal of Consulting and Clinical Psychology, 55,* 10–16.

Chapter 4

Cognitive-Behavioral Treatment of Posttraumatic Stress Disorder

Barbara Olasov Rothbaum
Edna B. Foa

Since posttraumatic stress disorder (PTSD) was first identified, a variety of treatments have been proposed (e.g., sodium amitol or hypnosis). More recently, there has been an increased interest in the cognitive-behavioral treatments. The literature on the cognitive-behavioral treatments for PTSD is the topic of this chapter. To evaluate the existing body of knowledge about the efficacy of treatments for trauma victims, general methodological issues in the investigation of treatment outcome should be considered. Irrespective of the treatment, a design that allows strong inferences should include the following.

First, clear criteria for inclusion and exclusion of subjects must be provided. The impairment, problems, or symptoms should be defined. If therapy is designed to modify undesired behavior or emotions, the target for such change must be delineated. It is important to remember that having been a trauma victim is not, by itself, an impairment or disorder. "Combat veteran," "rape victim," and "fire survivor" are not psychopathological entities. It is not the trauma victim, but rather the specific impairment caused by the trauma, that is the target of treatment. Traumatic events may

Preparation of this manuscript was supported by NIMH Grant No. 5 R01 MH 42178-02.

cause a variety of problems calling for differential treatment procedures designed for the specific presenting problem. Thus, as with any other treatment outcome study, the investigation of treatment for trauma victims must employ a diagnostically homogeneous sample.

Second, subjects should be randomly assigned to control or comparison groups. Minimally, the treatment condition should be compared to a wait-list no treatment condition. A placebo-control group is preferable because it controls for nonspecific treatment effects. Third, the treatment (or treatments) should be described in detail to enable replication. To facilitate this goal, treatment manuals should be prepared and made available to other investigators. Fourth, reliable and valid measures of the target problems must be included as dependent variables. Assessments should be conducted at pretreatment, posttreatment, and follow-up. Fifth, a logical relationship should exist between the disorder, its conceptualization, its treatment, and the measurement of treatment efficacy.

As PTSD is a fairly new diagnostic category (APA, 1980), the literature on its treatment is sparse, with only a few well-controlled investigations, although the methodologically sound studies are almost exclusively limited to behavioral techniques. Most of the treatment literature on PTSD with combat veterans relies on case studies and is of limited generalizability. Even more problematic is the available literature on rape victims, because most of the subjects did not receive a clinical diagnosis. Few reports exist on the treatment of PTSD resulting from other traumas (e.g., accidents or disasters). The literature on treatments for PTSD will be considered in light of the preceding criteria. In this review we will consider only group studies or case reports that included at least some semistructured procedure to evaluate treatment outcome.

TRADITIONAL INTERVENTIONS

A variety of psychodynamically oriented psychotherapies have been applied with PTSD patients, including individual and group therapy in different institutional settings. No obvious thread ties together the different interventions, and no systematic rationale connects the type of therapy to PTSD, with perhaps the one exception of the use of Horowitz's (1976) theory of trauma. Below we will describe some representative reports.

War Veterans

Psychodynamic psychotherapy was not found effective in the treatment of a traumatized Vietnam veteran (Grigsby, 1987). After 19 months of no progress with psychodynamic psychotherapy, imagery techniques were introduced. This imagery procedure was described by the author as follows: (1) No relaxation was used; (2) little guidance was provided by the therapist in the initial phases; (3) the trauma-related scene was presented and allowed to develop spontaneously through associations rather than by plan; (4) the use of the imagery technique was not planned in advance, but was introduced at appropriate times in the context of a session; (5) generalization to other traumas was not structured, but rather the patient moved on to other traumas on his own; and (6) avoidance was addressed through psychodynamic techniques of dealing with transference and resistance. Ten sessions of this imagery resulted in the amelioration of the patient's PTSD as observed by the therapist and reported by the patient. Although constrained by the limitations of a single case study and devoid of systematic measurement, this report suggests that traditional "talking" therapies do not reduce PTSD, whereas behaviorally oriented techniques appear to be effective.

Rape Victims

Crisis intervention and psychotherapy groups for trauma victims are the most common procedures used in rape crisis centers (see Koss & Harvey, 1987). Based on crisis theory (Burgess & Holmstrom, 1976), these interventions incorporate dissemination of information, active listening, and emotional support (e.g., Forman, 1980). Treatment by dynamic psychotherapy has often been advocated as a final component of crisis intervention (Burgess & Holmstrom, 1974b; Evans, 1978; Fox & Scherl, 1972). However, empirical investigations of their efficacy are scarce.

With psychoanalytic therapy, Bart (cited by Turner and Frank, 1981) reported that trauma victims showed increased symptomatology following treatment. The impact of short-term dynamic group therapy for nine rape victims has been reported by Cryer and Beutler (1980). Measures included the Hopkins Symptom Check List, (SCL-90-R; Derogatis, 1977), and the Fundamental Interpersonal Relations Orientation—Behavior scales (FIRO-B; Schutz, 1978) (assessing interpersonal relationships). Fear and hostility showed significant reduction, but three of the seven victims who completed the study reported only a slight change in their overall level of distress. Unfortunately, no control group was included and the content of the therapy sessions was not specified.

Roth, Dye, and Lebowitz (1988) conducted a study comparing a control group to a group that received 47 2 ½-hour sessions of group psychotherapy ($n = 6$). Treatment was based on Horowitz's (1976) theory of trauma, according to which "the goal of psychotherapy is to help the patient work through the trauma experience through gradually 'dosing' her/himself with the reexperiencing of the trauma event and its implications at manageable levels" (p. 4). Treatment began with a discussion of Horowitz's model and consisted primarily of members sharing experiences and offering support to each other. After eight sessions, the control group fared better than the psychotherapy group on all measures. After session 20, the therapy group showed improvement on fear, functioning, and intrusion measures; however, no control group data were collected. Improvements were maintained through a 6-month follow-up. The results are uninterpretable on several accounts: First, control and treatment groups differed with respect to the initial severity of symptoms, the former being less impaired than the latter; second, group members were not selected randomly; third, no control data were available after eight sessions; and fourth, all subjects in the treatment group also received individual therapy. As such, the observed gains cannot be independently attributed to group therapy.

The effect of time-limited group therapy with female and male cotherapists was reported by Perl, Westin, and Peterson (1985). Treatment consisted of eight weekly 90-minute sessions. A total of 17 subjects were treated in groups of three or four. The treatment focused on helping clients reach realistic solutions for specific problems emphasizing "here and now" issues rather than psychodynamic processes. Only rape-related problems were discussed. The effects of therapy were based on subjective evaluations of the therapists as derived from patients' self-reports. The authors reported striking improvements following therapy for participants on all symptoms (including fear and sexual problems). Unfortunately, this report is difficult to interpret because of the absence of objective measurement and absence of a control group.

Disaster Victims

Twenty-eight victims of the Beverly Hills Supper Club fire were treated with individual short-term (6 to 12 sessions) psychodynamic psychotherapy (Lindy, Green, Grace, & Titchener, 1983). Diagnoses included PTSD, complicated bereavement, major depressive disorder, and adjustment disorder. Therapy was conducted along the following guidelines:

1. The work is best started by asking the victim to relate in detail the thoughts and feelings experienced before, during, and after the fire.
2. When the manifest content of affect-laden associations deviates from the fire and its surrounding circumstances, the therapist should link affects where appropriate back to the fire experience.
3. Where grief is present or is being resisted, the therapist should encourage memories (positive and negative) of the deceased person by identifying and explaining barriers.
4. Where unconscious anticipation of something terrible happening

dominates the present, the therapist should contrast feelings of antici-pation with the actual probabilities.

5. Where guilt and shame about the way one acted at the scene are evident, the therapist should help the patient distinguish rational from irrational affect.

6. Where reactive rage dominates, the therapist should interpret the un-derlying feelings of helplessness and loss of control (p. 609).

Measures included the SCL-90 (Derogatis, Rickels, & Rocks, 1976); three target symptoms noted by the therapist; and the Psychiatric Evalua-tion Form (Endicott & Spitzer, 1972) completed by an independent re-search interviewer. Patients who completed treatment showed more im-provement than did patients with interrupted treatment. Lindy et al. (1983) subsequently observed that all treated patients "improved to a subclinical level two years after the fire" (p. 602). It should be noted, however, that the mechanisms by which such improvement was achieved were not adequately discussed by the authors.

Comments

It is apparent from the preceding review that information about the efficacy of traditional interventions with PTSD is quite limited and open to various lines of interpretation. The most informative study is that of Lindy et al. (1983), because it provides clear treatment guidelines for con-ducting the therapy and evaluates its outcome with standardized measures.

BEHAVIORAL TREATMENTS

Two sets of behavioral procedures have been commonly employed in the treatment of anxiety disorders: exposure-based procedures and anxiety management techniques (AMT). In the following review, we will discuss the application of exposure techniques and will follow with a presentation of the use of AMT for this disorder.

EXPOSURE TECHNIQUES

Exposure treatment is a set of techniques with a common denominator involving the confrontation of feared situations. These techniques can be classified according to the medium of exposure (imaginal vs. in vivo), the length of exposure (short vs. long), and the level of arousal during expo-sure (low vs. high). When the various exposure procedures are ordered along these dimensions, systematic desensitization (Wolpe, 1958), where exposure is imaginal, brief, and minimally arousing, occupies one extreme position. In direct contrast is in vivo flooding (Marks, 1972), where exposure to actual life events is prolonged and designed to elicit high levels of anxiety.

Systematic desensitization was the first contempory exposure technique for reducing arousal to phobic stimuli. As described originally, it consists of an imaginal exposure to the feared situations or objects. The therapist describes short scenarios that focus on the feared stimulus (e.g., "You are five feet away from the *snake*"). Patients are instructed to imagine the scenarios as vividly as possible for a short period of time. Although some fear is said to be necessary, attempts are made to minimize fear during imagery, usually through relaxation. The scenes are arranged hierarchically, with the least fearful one presented first. If the patient indicates anxiety, the presentation of the scene is discontinued, relaxation is reintroduced, and the scene is presented again. Each scene is repeated until it ceases to elicit anxiety. Variants of systematic desensitization include in vivo and imaginal graded exposure without relaxation. When exposure begins with highly feared stimuli, is prolonged, and elicits high levels of anxiety, the treatment technique is called flooding. As in systematic desensitization, flooding can be implemented either imaginally or in vivo until anxiety reduction occurs.

Exposure techniques are used when the disorder involves excessive avoidance and treatments are intended to activate and modify the fear structure. AMT, on the other hand, is used when anxiety pervades daily functioning. In this case, there is no need to activate the fear as much as manage it. In PTSD, both specific fears and general chronic arousal are among the defining characteristics. Chronic arousal among traumatized combat veterans was evident via high levels of autonomic responses during baseline testing (Blanchard, Kolb, Gerardi, Ryan, & Pallmeyer, 1986). Moreover, specific fear activation has been found when PTSD cases were exposed to trauma-related material (Keane & Kaloupek, 1982; Kozak, Foa, & Olasov 1987; Pitman, Orr, Forgue, deJong, & Clairborn, 1987). Therefore, both exposure techniques and AMT may be applicable in the treatment of the disorder.

War Veterans

The behavioral treatment for PTSD was initially employed with war veterans. Several single case studies have been published to date (Fairbank, Gross, & Keane, 1983; Fairbank & Keane, 1982; Johnson, Gilmore, & Shenoy, 1982; Keane & Kaloupek, 1982; Schindler, 1980). They demonstrate the effectiveness of a variety of techniques in which patients were exposed to material related to the original traumatic event. Flooding in imagination (e.g., Fairbank & Keane, 1982; Keane, Fairbank, Caddell, &

Zimering, 1989), as well as flooding in vivo to trauma-related events (Johnson et al., 1982) appeared to be equally therapeutic (cf. Fairbank, Chapter 3). Most of these treatments, however, included additional techniques, such as anger control or relaxation training. In view of this, the contribution of exposure to the overall improvement is unclear.

Based on Celluci and Lawrence's (1978) finding that systematic desensitization was successful in reducing nightmares, Schindler (1980) used it in the treatment of a recurring nightmare of a 29-year-old male Vietnam veteran. The patient reported a nightmare that involved an actual incident in which a soldier was wounded by a land mine. The dream had been recurring at least once a month for 9 years and had induced a chronic level of fear that was associated with sleeping and dreaming. Treatment consisted of five biweekly 30-minute sessions. The exposure hierarchy was based on the temporal occurrence of events in the dream. At a 2-week booster session, the patient reported no nightmares and decreased anxiety about sleeping and dreaming. Treatment gains were maintained at a 7-month follow-up.

Using 16 Vietnam combat veterans with PTSD, Peniston (1986) compared the effect of EMG biofeedback-assisted desensitization with a no-treatment condition. EMG levels were monitored at pre- and posttreatment sessions. The treatment included 48 30-minute sessions conducted three times per week over a 4-month interval. During the first three sessions, patients were trained in visualization-imagery and progressive relaxation and a 10-item hierarchy was constructed. During desensitization, three to five sessions were spent on each item, repeating the presentation until it elicited no anxiety. Results indicated the superiority of the EMG desensitization over no treatment in reducing muscle tension, nightmares, and flashbacks. Additionally, none of the treated patients had been rehospitalized at a 2-year follow-up, whereas five of the eight controls were hospitalized during that time.

Bowen and Lambert (1986) studied the effects of systematic desensitization on muscle tension (EMG) and heart rate (HR) with 10 outpatients at a Veterans Administration hospital. Of these, eight were Vietnam veterans, one was a World War II veteran, and one was a post-Vietnam–era veteran who witnessed an airplane crash. Although all of the patients had been exposed to trauma, all of them did not meet DSM-III criteria for a PTSD diagnosis. The EMG and HR levels of the patients were assessed before and after treatment as verbalized descriptions of combat traumas and noncombat stressors (e.g., marital conflicts) were presented. They were subsequently treated with standard systematic desensitization wherein the combat scenes were presented. Length of treatment varied across patients, with an average of 5.8 months of biweekly sessions. Bowen and Lambert subsequently indicated that the EMG and HR levels of the outpatients to both types of stress scenes decreased significantly. Bowen and Lambert also noted that combat scenes were associated with lower levels of arousal than were the noncombat scenes. The authors (1986) concluded that their results underscored the utility of desensitization in reducing physiological arousal (at least autonomic arousal) that is associated with intrusive trauma-related thoughts.

In a clinical trial, 24 PTSD Vietnam veterans were randomly assigned to 90-minute treatment sessions of relaxation and imaginal flooding or to a waiting-list control group (Keane, Fairbank, Caddell, & Zimering, 1989). During each session, subjects were initially instructed to relax. The subjects subsequently received 45 minutes of imaginal flooding, followed by relaxation. Several measures were administered pre- and posttreatment and at a 6-month follow-up. These measures included the Beck Depression Inventory (BDI; Beck et al., 1961); the Zung Depression Scale (Zung, 1965); the Minnesota Multiphasic Personality Inventory (MMPI; Hathaway & McKinley, 1967); the PTSD subscale of the MMPI (Keane, Malloy, & Fairbank, 1984); the Spielberger State and Trait Anxiety Inventory (STAI; Spielberger, Gorsuch, & Lushene, 1970); the Fear Survey Schedule (FSS; Geer, 1964); and therapist ratings of PTSD symptomatology. The treated group reported significantly less depression (BDI and MMPI), state anxiety (STAI-State), fear (FSS), hypochondriasis (MMPI), and hysteria (MMPI) at posttreatment and at follow-up. Therapist-rated reexperiencing of the trauma, startle reactions, memory and concentration problems, impulsivity, irritability, and legal problems were all significantly lower than in the control group. Differences were not noted on several measures, including the PTSD subscale of the MMPI, other symptoms of PTSD, and social adjustment.

Rape Victims

Systematic desensitization was employed effectively by Wolff (1977) to treat the fear of a 20-year-old female who had been raped at the age of 13. The client had been unable to spend a single night alone since the assault, as she feared the assailant's return. Seven sessions of systematic desensitization resulted in her ability to sleep alone at night. In a series of nine cases, Turner (1979) found that systematic desensitization was associated with improvement in measures of fear, anxiety, depression, and social adjustment.

Frank and Stewart (1983a, 1984) corroborated these findings with a sample of 17 assault victims. Frank and Stewart's procedure deviated from the standard use of systematic desensitization in several ways. First, the scenes were composed of long narratives rather than the customary short scenes. Second, the scenes included pleasant descriptions (e.g., "It's a bright spring day, the trees are budding and the sun is warm," p. 255).

Third, the therapists, contrary to the general custom, moved from one hierarchy to another in the same session. Fourth, the therapists presented each scene a set number of times, whereas usually each item is presented repeatedly until it fails to evoke anxiety.

Fourteen sessions of systematic desensitization resulted in a decrease in the targeted fears, as well as an increase in social adjustment. The authors noted that 75 percent of their subjects voluntarily exposed themselves in vivo to situations previously desensitized in imagination. These results are quite impressive. However, in the absence of a control group, these positive effects are difficult to interpret. Since the criteria for inclusion in the study allowed the clients to receive treatment immediately following the rape, some of the observed improvement may have been due to the natural reduction of symptoms over the first several months following assault (see Kilpatrick and Calhoun, 1988, for a critique discussing these issues).

Accident Victims

PTSD resulting from accidents has also been successfully treated with behavioral techniques. McCaffrey and Fairbank (1985) reported on two cases: one after a helicopter crash and the other after a series of automobile accidents. Treatment included relaxation training, imaginal exposure, and self exposure in vivo. Although modest changes in self-reported anxiety were noted, improvement in specific PTSD symptoms (e.g., nightmares) was substantial.

Fairbank, DeGood, and Jenkins (1981) treated a 32-year-old woman for a persistent posttraumatic motoric startle response (i.e., jerking the steering wheel when a car approached) following a head-on collision in which she and her children were injured. Treatment consisted of three weekly sessions of relaxation training and daily exposure to highway driving. Self-reported anxiety decreased during the relaxation training phase, remained at a reduced level during the driving exposure phase, and decreased further at a 6-month follow-up assessment. Self-monitored motoric startle responses fluctuated during the relaxation phase, totally remitted during the driving exposure phase, and remained in remission at follow-up.

Muse (1986) described the use of systematic desensitization with three automobile accident victims who presented with chronic pain syndromes and PTSD. One month to 2 years following the accident, the clients received 2 to 4 months of traditional pain clinic treatments, including exercise therapy, biofeedback training, supportive group counseling, and medication. At the end of these chronic pain treatments, the patients received traditional systematic desensitization (13 to 18 sessions), with the last two sessions spent in in vivo exposure. All of the patients improved greatly following systematic desensitization, with a reduction in therapist-observed and patient-reported fear and anxiety, PTSD symptoms, depression, and pain, and with a resumption of normal activities. Although limited by the case study approach and absence of hard data, this report offers support for the generalizability of treatment techniques for PTSD across different traumas.

ANXIETY MANAGEMENT TECHNIQUES (AMT)

Whereas exposure techniques are designed to activate fear and promote habituation, AMT aims at anxiety reduction by providing patients with skills to control fear. Among such techniques are relaxation training (e.g., Bernstein & Borkovec, 1973; Jacobson, 1938), stress inoculation training (Meichenbaum, 1974), cognitive restructuring (Beck, 1972; Ellis, 1977), breathing retraining (Clark, Salkovskis, & Chaukley, 1985), social skills training (Becker, Heimberg, & Bellack, 1987), and distraction techniques (e.g., thought stopping, Wolpe, 1973). The most widely used of these techniques is deep muscle relaxation training described by Wolpe (1985) as the "activity of the undoing of the tonic contraction of muscle fibers" (p. 101). It affects the autonomic nervous system such that sympathetic responses are attenuated (i.e., heart rate and breathing slows and blood pressure falls).

War Veterans

The efficacy of EMG biofeedback training and progressive muscle relaxation training was investigated by Hickling, Sison, and Vanderploeg (1986). Six veterans with PTSD received 7 to 14 treatment sessions over an interval of 8 to 16 weeks. Incorporated into these techniques were autogenic phrases (e.g., suggesting increased warmth or a calm, regular heartbeat) (Schultz & Luthe, 1969) and cue-controlled relaxation. Pre- and posttreatment measures included the MMPI, STAI, BDI, Multidimensional Health Locus of Control Scale (Wallston, Wallston, Kaplan, & Maides, 1976), EMG, subjective tension ratings, and assessor ratings of overall improvement. Improvement was evidenced on almost all measures. Although promising, the generalizability of the results are limited because physicians referred only patients they believed would profit from this form of treatment.

Rape Victims

A case report utilizing biofeedback with a rape victim was described by Blanchard and Abel (1976). The target symptoms were cardiovascular:

episodic sinus tachycardia and syncope. Systematic biofeedback training helped her to control her tachycardia both in the laboratory and in her natural environment.

The effects of cognitive therapy targeted at depression and anxiety were studied in 25 rape victims who entered treatment approximately 2 weeks after their assault (Frank & Stewart, 1984). This treatment, modeled on Beck's (1972) procedure, included self-monitoring of activities with mastery and pleasure responses, graded task assignments (e.g., going out alone), and the identification and modification of maladaptive cognitions. The basic tenet underlying this treatment is that individual cognitions are filtered through preexisting assumptions about the world. For example, a rape victim may focus on distorted perceptions of inadequacy, incompetence, and helplessness, as well as on thoughts of feeling responsible for the rape and of being worthless for having been raped. Cognitive techniques are thought to help the client identify such distorted beliefs and test their reality.

The application of this treatment by Frank and Stewart consisted of three phases. The first phase focused on challenging maladaptive thinking and encouraging novel thinking. During the second phase, cognitive distortions were identified, and rational, adaptive responses were constructed. During the third phase, basic assumptions about the world were explored. The outcome of cognitive therapy was similar to that of systematic desensitization. More specifically, ratings of fear, anxiety, depression, and social adjustment as measured by the BDI, STAI, FSS, Janis-Field Feelings of Inadequacy Scale (Janis & Field, 1959); and Social Adjustment Scale-II (Schooler, Levine, Severe, Brauzer, DiMascio, Klermen, & Tuason, 1980) showed significant gains. Although no direct comparison between systematic desensitization (SD) and cognitive therapy was reported by the authors, examination of the mean change scores of the two groups suggested that the treatments produced equivalent outcomes (Turner & Frank, 1981).

In a later study (Frank, Anderson, Stewart, Dancu, Hughes, & West, 1988), data from 84 subjects, some of whom participated in previous studies, was reported. Subjects received either cognitive behavior therapy or systematic desensitization. In each treatment modality, some subjects entered treatment soon after the rape (mean of 20 days), and others were seen several months after their assault (mean of 129 days). Measures included the BDI; STAI; modified version of the Veronen-Kilpatrick Fear Survey Schedule (Veronen & Kilpatrick, 1980); Janis-Field Feeling Inadequacy Scale (Janis & Field, 1959); Social Adjustment Scale-II; Target Complaints Assessment (Battle, Imber, Hoehn-Saric, Stone, Nash, & Frank, 1966); and the Demographic, Assault, and Psychiatric History Interview Schedule which the authors designed for their study. Although the delayed treatment seekers were more symptomatic from the onset of the study, posttreatment results revealed that both groups improved equally well pursuant to systematic desensitization or cognitive behavior therapy. On the other hand, the absence of a control group and the failure to exclude cases who were recently raped limits the conclusions that can be drawn about the efficacy of cognitive therapy with rape victims (Kilpatrick & Calhoun, 1988).

In their review of treatments for rape victims, Holmes and St. Lawrence (1983) concluded that "the most promising treatment strategies appear to be those which provide victims with specific coping mechanisms and alternative responses to anxiety" (p. 430). Two treatment packages that aim at providing such coping strategies (i.e., stress inoculation training and a brief behavioral intervention program) for rape victims were developed by Kilpatrick, Veronen, and their colleagues. These two packages as applied to rape victims are described below.

Stress inoculation training (SIT) was developed for victims who remained highly fearful 3 months after being raped (Kilpatrick, Veronen, & Resick, 1982). The original program, which included 20 therapy hours and homework assignments, consisted of two phases (i.e., an educational phase and a coping skills phase). Treatment began with a 2-hour educational phase in which the treatment program rationale and theoretical basis for the treatment were explained. The program was described as a cognitive-behavioral approach to the management of rape-related fear and anxiety that utilizes coping skills to reduce the anxiety. Rape-related fear was explained as a classically conditioned phenomenon. Anxiety was described according to Lang's (1968) multichannel systems, which included motoric, cognitive, and physiological responses. In addition, anxiety was presented as occurring in stages as opposed to being an all-or-none phenomenon. Accordingly, "if one can identify the early indicators of the fear response, one can better control [the] reaction to it" (Veronen & Kilpatrick, 1983, p. 359).

The second phase of SIT focused on the acquisition and application of coping skills and began with deep muscle relaxation training and breathing control. Muscle relaxation training utilized the Jacobson (1938) method of tensing and relaxing muscles. The relaxation sessions were taped to permit home practice, and the sessions were continued until each patient was capable of relaxing herself within a short period of time across a variety of situations. The breathing control exercises emphasized slowed diaphragmatic breathing similar to the exercises taught in yoga or Lamaze natural childbirth classes. Following this, subjects were taught communication skills through role playing. Covert modeling was also taught. This technique was similar to role playing but used imagery rather than in vivo practice. To control for the intrusive effects of obsessive thinking, thought stopping (Wolpe, 1958) instructions were also provided.

Kilpatrick et al. (1982) considered the last technique, guided self-dialogue, to be the most important. The therapist taught each person to focus on internal dialogue and to identify irrational, faulty, or negative self-statements. Rational and positive statements were generated and substituted for negative ones following Meichenbaum's (1974) stress inoculation training and cognitive restructuring procedure. In investigating the efficacy of this program, Veronen and Kilpatrick (1982b) selected 15 female rape victims who showed elevated fear and avoidance to specific phobic stimuli 3 months postrape. A clear treatment effect emerged on rape-related fear, anxiety, phobic anxiety, tension, and depression as measured by the SCL-90, IES, Veronen-Kilpatrick MFS, and the STAI. Although these data are promising, it should be noted that Veronen and Kilpatrick's study did not include a control group. This omission is significant in that interpretation of the data is limited.

In a later study, Veronen and Kilpatrick (1983) offered a sample of rape victims ($n = 50$) their choice of three forms of therapy (stress inoculation training, peer counseling, or systematic desensitization). More than 50% of the potential subject pool rejected therapy. Of the 15 who opted for treatment, 11 selected SIT, three chose peer counseling, and none opted for systematic desensitization. Although no formal statistical analyses were conducted on the six who had completed SIT, the authors reported noticeable improvement from pre- to posttreatment on most measures. In a similar vein, Pearson, Poquette, and Wasden (1983) described the successful use of a method similar to SIT (with the inclusion of systematic desensitization) with a woman who experienced longstanding fears of rape-related situations. The 1-week, 3-month, and 6-month follow-up report of this study were encouraging in that the patient reported that she was successfully applying the skills that she had developed in therapy to cope with or escape the situation if it actually became dangerous. The patient also reported that she had used the skills learned to cope with situations that she had previously been unable to manage.

The SIT program has consequently been modified. In particular, its duration was reduced from 20 to 8 therapy hours, and the provision of the coping skills was expanded to include rape-related problems other than fear and avoidance. Kilpatrick and Amick (1985) reported the successful application of this treatment package with a 21-year-old woman. Their report is exemplary because of the thoroughness of the assessment procedures, which included physiological, cognitive, and behavioral measures. Measures of psychophysiological reactivity (i.e., heart rate, resting skin conductance, electrodermal responses, and frontalis electromyographic activity) were obtained as well as self-monitored estimates of anxiety-related physical symptoms (e.g., headaches, itchy scalp, nausea, sleep disturbances, and tightness in chest). Cognitive responses were assessed through

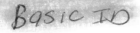

self-report measures, including the SCL-90-R, Veronen-Kilpatrick MFS, Profile of Mood States Scale (McNair, Lorr, & Droppleman, 1971), and the IES, as well as through therapist interviews regarding irrational beliefs about the assault (e.g., self-blame) and dreams. Behavioral responses were measured with self-monitoring of social withdrawal, fear of driving, interpersonal difficulty, and substance abuse of meprobamate and alcohol. The final data analysis determined that the SIT package was highly successful in that most of the therapeutic goals were achieved by the end of the treatment and maintained at follow-up. In addition to helping the patient reduce rape-related intrusive thoughts and symptomatology, the treatment also helped the patient to resume realistic planning regarding the future and to give up the obsession of achieving revenge by having her assailants murdered.

Thirty-seven rape victims participated in a study by Resick, Jordan, Girelli, Hutter, and Marhoefer-Dvorak (1988). Resick et al. compared six 2-hour sessions of three types of group therapy (i.e., stress inoculation training, assertion training, and supportive psychotherapy plus information). The three treatment groups were compared to a naturally occurring waiting-list control group. The SIT procedure was similar to the package described by Kilpatrick, Veronen, and Resick (1982), with two exceptions: (1) cognitive restructuring, assertiveness training, and role play were excluded, because they were used in the comparative treatment, and (2) exposure in vivo was added to the application phase. Assertion training treatment began with an educational phase that included an explanation of how assertion can be used to counter fear and avoidance. Issues concerning social support were discussed within the context of assertiveness. The specific techniques were adopted from Lange and Jakubowski (1976) and from Rational Emotive Therapy (RET; Ellis, 1977). Training included behavioral rehearsal through role play with feedback regarding performance. Supportive psychotherapy plus information consisted of an educational phase after which participants selected topics for discussion. These topics included the reactions of others to their assault and the degree of support they encountered as well as assault-induced anxiety.

Assessment instruments included the Derogatis SCL-90-R; Veronen-Kilpatrick MFSS (Veronen & Kilpatrick, 1980); Tennessee Self-Concept Scale (Fitts, 1965); Adult Self-Expression Scale (Gay, Hollandsworth, & Galassi, 1975); Emotion Thermometer (Obanion & Veronen, 1978); Impact of Event Scale (Horowitz, Wilner, & Alvarez, 1979); and a 221-item structured interview developed for their study. Results indicated that each of the treatments was highly effective in reducing symptoms. Moreover, no significant differences were apparent among the treatment groups. Each treatment group evidenced significantly lower outcome scores than the controls. Improvement was maintained at 6-month follow-up on rape-related fear measures. On the other hand, improvements on depression, self-esteem, and social fears were not maintained. No improvements were found in the waiting-list control group.

A study comparing SIT, exposure treatment, supportive counseling, and a no-treatment control was conducted by Foa, Rothbaum, Riggs, and Murdock (1990). All of the persons were assaulted at least 3 months prior to the receipt of treatment. In addition, all of the persons met criteria for a DSM-III-R Axis I PTSD diagnosis. The SIT treatment that is being presented consists of nine 90-minute sessions that are delivered twice per week. The treatment program involves information gathering, education, and treatment planning, brief breathing retraining, deep muscle relaxation, thought stopping, cognitive restructuring modeled after Beck and Ellis, Meichenbaum's (1974) guided self-dialogue, covert modeling, and role play. This program deviates from the manner in which it is currently being conducted by Kilpatrick and his colleagues in that instructions for in vivo exposure to feared situations are not included.

Each of the coping skills sessions in the Foa et al study is conducted in a similar manner. The sessions begin with a review of the previous session's activity and an update on use of coping skills in the victim's natural environment and review of the victim's homework assignments. The format for teaching coping skills and detailed instructions for each skill follow:

1. *Definition of the coping skill.* Define the skill. What channel (e.g., cognitive, autonomic) will this coping skill fit? Why is it important to the patient?

2. *Rationale and mechanism.* Explain to the patient the behavior, reactions, or symptoms that will be relieved or aided by the new coping skill. Point out similarities and differences between this skill and other skills.

3. *Demonstration.* Demonstrate the skill for the patient or provide a verbal explanation regarding its actual implementation.

4. *Application 1.* The patient first practices the skill with a problem that is not unrelated to the assault (e.g., job-related activities).

5. *Review.* Check to see whether the patient can explain what she did and how it worked.

6. *Application 2.* The patient practices with an example from a rape-related problem.

Some flexibility is needed in the session-by-session format provided here, because skills are acquired at different rates by different individuals. It should be noted in this context that progress may vary on an individual basis (i.e., some cases require only a few minutes to acquire a skill, whereas others require several hours).

Breathing Relaxation

The victim is instructed about the use of breathing relaxation before leaving the information-gathering session as an attempt to countercondition anxiety that may have become conditioned to the therapist as a result of discussing the assault. Rationale includes the following explanation:

Most people realize that our breathing affects the way we feel. For example, when we are upset, people may tell us to "take a deep breath and calm down." However, we don't need to take a *deep* breath, but rather a normal breath and exhale slowly. For example, when our ancestors, thousands of years ago, were walking through the forest and spotted a lion, they probably gasped and held their breath. When the lion walked away, they sighed in relief (exhaled). Therefore, it is *exhalation* that is associated with relaxation, not inhalation.

While concentrating on the exhalation and dragging it out, we will also have you say the word *CALM* to yourself while you are exhaling, and I will say it aloud. *CALM* is a good word to use, because, in our culture it is already associated with nice things. If we are upset and someone tells us to "calm down," usually it is associated with comfort and support. It also sounds nice and can be dragged out to match the long, slow exhalation: c-a-a-a-a-a-a-l-m.

In addition to concentrating on slow exhalation while saying *CALM* to yourself, we want to slow your breathing down. Very often, when people become frightened or upset, they feel like they need more air and they may hyperventilate. However, usually just the opposite is true. Unless we are preparing for one of the three *f*s (i.e., fight, freeze, flee) in the face of a real danger, we often don't need as much air as we are taking in. When we hyperventilate and take in more air, it signals our bodies to prepare for one of the three *f*s and to keep it fueled with oxygen. It is just like a runner before a race who takes deep breaths to fuel her body with oxygen and continues to breathe deeply and quickly throughout the race. Usually when we hyperventilate, though, we are tricking our bodies, and what we really need to do is slow down our breathing and take in *less* air. We do this by pausing between breaths to space them out more. After your slowed exhalation, literally hold your breath for a count of four [may be adjusted if necessary] before you inhale the next breath.

The victim is then instructed to take a normal breath and exhale very, very slowly while saying the word *CALM* as she exhales. Victims are subsequently instructed to pause briefly and to count to four before taking another breath. This entire sequence is repeated 10 to 15 times during the initial session. After this, the victim is instructed to practice these exercises twice a day before the next session.

Deep Muscle Relaxation

The Jacobsonian (1938) tension-relaxation contrast training is used to teach muscle relaxation beginning in session 3. Relaxation training includes a total relaxation of all major muscle groups. An assignment is made for the client to practice relaxation twice daily between sessions. During the fourth session, relaxation training using the "focusing" and "letting go" procedures, is used in conjunction with *breathing control* as previously described. Again, this skill is practiced both in therapy and at home.

Thought Stopping

Thought stopping is taught by having the victim deliberately concentrate on her troublesome thoughts. After doing so for 35 to 45 seconds, the therapist says "STOP!" in a loud, commanding voice (while clapping his or her hands or by hitting the desk). Following this, the therapist asks the victim what happened. Typically, patients report that the thought stopped. This process is repeated several times. The next step involves having the victim stop her thinking with silent verbalizations of the word *STOP.* The victim is instructed to apply this procedure at first to moderately disturbing thoughts and then to quite upsetting ones. If necessary, the victim may wear a rubber band around her wrist, snap it, and say "STOP!" when intrusive thoughts occur.

Cognitive Restructuring

The therapist first presents the A-B-C (A = antecedent, B = belief, C = consequences) paradigm for automatic, irrational thoughts (Beck, Rush, Shaw, & Emery, 1979), focusing on how subjective thoughts affect reactions. An example is given demonstrating how the same event (e.g., hearing a loud noise from the next room) can lead to totally different responses (e.g., intense fear and leaving the house vs. mild annoyance and entering a room) depending on the interpretation (e.g., "There's a burglar in there. I'm in danger." vs. "What did the darned cat get into now?"). The therapist asks the victim to generate a situation unrelated to the assault in which she became upset (e.g., not receiving a raise at work) and proceeds to fill in the A, B, and C. The therapist first completes the A (the antecedent or event) and the C (the consequences, or how the victim felt), and finally asks the victim to assist in generating the B (beliefs/statements she was telling herself that were inducing increased arousal).

The steps for cognitive restructuring include the following:

1. Complete A and C.
2. Complete B, bringing it down to automatic assumption (e.g., "He rejected me. I need to be loved and accepted to feel worthwhile" or "He is a potential assailant and is getting ready to attack me").
3. Reality testing of the assumption under B: Weigh the evidence, as if for a court of law, for and against the assumption.

4. If the evidence is insufficient, dismiss it. The patient may dismiss the assumption or obtain more information.
5. If sufficient evidence exists, respond rationally and adaptively (e.g., "It would be preferable if he didn't reject me, but it doesn't say anything about my worth as a person"), or seek safety response.

The therapist assists the victim in assessing the rationality of the beliefs and consequently challenges and replaces them with more rational self-statements. This process is subsequently applied to an assault-related experience. If necessary, a third example may be used allowing the victim as much independence as possible in completing the process that has been described.

Guided Self-Dialogue

During guided self-dialogue, the therapist teaches the client to focus on her internal dialogue or on what she is saying to herself. Irrational, faulty, or negative dialogue is labeled, and rational, facilitative, or task-enhancing dialogue is substituted. The client is subsequently instructed to ask and answer a series of questions or to respond covertly to a series of statements. The framework for the guided self-dialogue was adapted from Meichenbaum's (1974) examples. The four dialogue categories include statements for (a) preparation, (b) confrontation and management, (c) coping with feelings of being overwhelmed, and (d) reinforcement. For each category listed above, the client and therapist generate a series of questions or statements that encourage the client to (a) assess the actual probability of the negative event, (b) manage overwhelming anxiety, (c) control self-criticism and self-devaluation, (d) engage in the feared behavior, and (e) reinforce herself for attempting the behavior and for following the protocol.

Each set of self-statements is tailored to fit the victim's target problems, although some general statements are nearly always included in a particular victim's set of self-statements. Self-statements are written on 3 × 5-inch index cards, which are used in practice sessions that occur outside the treatment session. As the victim acquires the coping skills, she is encouraged to use them to handle everyday problems and difficulties. Self-statements for most victims focus on the low probability of something traumatic happening again.

Covert Modeling, Role Play, and Termination

Covert modeling is analogous to role playing in the imagination (i.e., covert). First, the therapist describes a scene concerning a difficult situation for the client in which the therapist confronts and successfully works through the situation (i.e., modeling). Next, the client visualizes the same scene wherein she imagines herself successfully completing it. As with all skills, covert modeling is practiced first with a non-assault-related situation and then with an assault-related scene. Scenes used for covert modeling may mimic those that are subsequently used for role-play practice.

During the role-playing training, the client and therapist actually act out scenes in which the client confronts a disturbing situation. The therapist explains that role playing is the acting out of behaviors, rehearsing lines and actions, pretending to be in a particular situation or in a set of circumstances. Role playing is explained as a way to learn new behaviors and words for old habits that provides an opportunity for practice before the event occurs. Like a dress rehearsal, repeated practice reduces anxiety and increases the probability that a new behavior will be appropriately employed.

During role play, the therapist initially enacts the client's role and demonstrates appropriate social skills. Then roles are reversed, with the client playing herself. After each role play, the client is encouraged to identify the positive aspects of her performance and areas for improvement. The therapist subsequently does the same, always emphasizing the positive aspects over the negative aspects. Role plays are repeated until the patient performs satisfactorily or ceases to make further improvements, rarely more than five times.

At the end of the final session, the therapist and patient review the progress made during treatment with respect to the major problem areas identified and addressed during treatment. The therapist solicits information about the skills the client acquired and successfully used. The prospective use of these skills is also discussed.

Exposure treatment consists of nine biweekly, 90-minute sessions. The first two sessions are devoted to information gathering, explanations of treatment rationale, and treatment planning. A hierarchy of avoided situations is constructed for in vivo exposure homework. In vivo exposure begins with situations that evoke relatively low levels of anxiety and progresses up the hierarchy to more feared situations. The next seven sessions are devoted to reliving the rape scene in imagination. Patients are instructed to try to imagine as vividly as possible the assault scene and to describe it verbally in the present tense. For the first two exposure sessions, patients are allowed to refrain from verbalizing details that are extremely upsetting. During the remaining sessions, they are encouraged to describe the rape in its entirety, repeating it several times for 60 minutes per session to facilitate habituation. The patient's narratives are tape recorded and patients are instructed to listen to the tapes at home at least once per day. During the last session, patients are reminded that avoiding safe situations or rape-related thoughts may increase PTSD symptoms and are asked to practice this approach in their everyday lives. Supportive counseling is delivered according to the same nine-session format. Treatment focuses on assisting patients in solving daily problems that may or may not be rape-related and thus aims at promoting the perception of self-control. Discussion of the assault itself is avoided. Patients are encouraged to discuss current daily problems. The therapist plays an indirect and unconditionally supportive role throughout these sessions. Results, as based upon this regimen, support the superiority of SIT and exposure over counseling and waiting-list control condition.

A second treatment program, Brief Behavioral Intervention Program (BBIP), was designed for use immediately after the rape had occurred (Kilpatrick & Veronen, 1983). This 4- to 6-hour treatment was viewed as a prophylactic treatment to prevent the development of phobic reactions and other PTSD symptoms. First, the victim was encouraged to reexperience the rape events in imagery and to permit herself to express feelings associated with the rape. The victim was subsequently informed about learning models that involve the development and maintenance of fear reactions. Victims were also informed about the three-systems model of fear responses (behavioral, cognitive, and physiological). In the third phase, attempts were made to reduce feelings of guilt and responsibility for the rape through discussion of societal expectations and myths about rape. Finally, coping skills such as self-assertion, relaxation, thought stopping, and methods for resuming normal activities were taught. The outcome of a study in which 15 recent victims were randomly assigned to one of three conditions (i.e., repeated assessment, delayed assessment, or BBIP) resulted in no group differences, indicating that active treatment (i.e., BBIP) and repeated assessment were equally therapeutic (Veronen & Kilpatrick, 1982a).

SUMMARY AND THEORETICAL PERSPECTIVES

The few well-controlled studies are consistent with case reports in indicating that both exposure techniques and anxiety management techniques are moderately effective in reducing PTSD symptoms as well as related symptoms such as depression. They also bring attention to the need to understand the mechanisms underlying these techniques so that more effective techniques can be developed. To this end, theoretical issues in the development and maintenance of PTSD will be considered.

Foa, Steketee, and Rothbaum (1989) have proposed that PTSD occurs due to the inability to adequately process the traumata. Indeed, in his classical paper on emotional processing, Rachman (1980) suggested that the index of inadequate emotional processing is "the persistence or return of intrusive signs of emotional activities such as obsessions, nightmares, phobias, or inappropriate expression of emotions . . ." (p. 51). These manifestations resemble the hallmark symptoms of PTSD. If PTSD symptoms are the result of inadequate emotional processing, then therapy, aiming at the reduction of these symptoms, can be perceived as facilitating such processing.

In an attempt to develop the construct of emotional processing with particular attention to the anxiety disorders, Foa and Kozak (1986) integrated concepts of fear, experimental data, and clinical investigations. Adopting Lang's bioinformational theory (1977, 1979), they viewed fear as a cognitive structure that contains three classes of elements: stimuli, response, and the meaning associated with them. They further suggested that the fear structures of anxiety disorders include pathological elements and that treatment should be construed as modifying those elements.

Foa and Kozak (1986) suggested that two conditions are required for the reduction of fear. First, the fear memory must be activated. Second, new information must be provided that includes elements that are "incompatible with some of those that exist in the fear structure, so that a new memory can be formed. This new information, which is at once cognitive and affective, has to be integrated into the evoked information structure for an emotional change to occur" (p. 22). Indeed, exposure procedures activate the structure (i.e., elicit fear) and constitute an opportunity for corrective information to be integrated, and thus modify the fear structure. The result of such modification is the reduction of symptomatology. Treatment by variants of exposure to the feared situations has been applied successfully to those with simple phobias, obsessive-compulsive disorder, agoraphobia, as well as PTSD (cf. Marks, 1987).

Three types of responses during exposure treatment were found to be associated with improvement: (a) degree of initial response (i.e., activation); (b) habituation within the exposure session; and (c) habituation across exposure sessions. Thus, through exposure, situations that aroused intense fear cease to do so. Repeated exposure to the memory of the trauma is expected to result in habituation so that the victim can remember it without intense fear responses. When the fear elements in the structure attenuate, many stimuli that were associated with fear through generalization no longer elicit fear. The generalization gradient sharpens. For example, rape is still perceived as dangerous and therefore would elicit fear, but other stimuli (e.g., being home alone) cease to be associated with the rape and thereby no longer elicit fear.

On the basis of this theory, we hypothesized that PTSD symptoms will decrease following treatment by exposure to the traumatic memory and associated situations. SIT may directly address the pathological elements of the victim's fear structure. Through relaxation training and practice in a variety of situations, associations between stimuli and fear responses are weakened. The cognitive procedures modify the meaning elements, specifically by removing danger interpretations from realistically safe situations, thereby promoting exposure to the situations. Because SIT, unlike exposure, does not directly address the original trauma, it may effect improvement in PTSD symptoms through mechanisms other than exposure. Specifically, we propose that exposure treatment will reduce reexperiencing and avoidance symptoms, whereas SIT will be especially effective for reducing arousal symptoms.

REFERENCES

American Psychiatric Association (1980). *Diagnostic and statistical manual of mental disorders* (3rd ed.). Washington, DC: Author.

American Psychiatric Association (1987). *Diagnostic and statistical manual of mental disorders (3rd ed.—Rev.)*. Washington, DC: Author.

Battle, C. C., Imber, S. D., Hoehn-Saric, R., Stone, A. R., Nash, E. R., & Frank, J. D. (1966). Target complaints as criteria of improvement. *American Journal of Psychotherapy, 20,* 184–192.

Beck, A. T. (1972). *Depression: Causes and treatment.* Philadelphia: University of Pennsylvania Press.

Beck, A. T., Rush, A. J., Shaw, B. F., & Emery, G. (1979). *Cognitive therapy of depression.* New York: Guilford Press.

Beck, A. T., Ward, C. H. Mendelson, M., Mock, J., & Erbaugh, J. (1961). An inventory for measuring depression. *Archives of General Psychiatry, 4,* 561–571.

Becker, R. E., Heimberg, R. G., & Bellack, A. S. (1987). *Social skills training treatment for depression.* Elmsford, NY: Pergamon Press.

Bernstein, D. A., & Borkovec, T. D. (1973). *Progressive relaxation training.* Champaign, IL: Research Press.

Blanchard, E. B., & Abel, G. G. (1976). An experimental case study of the biofeedback treatment of a rape induced psychophysiological cardiovascular disorder. *Behavior Therapy, 7,* 113–119.

Blanchard, E. B., Kolb, L. C., Gerardi, R. J., Ryan, D., & Pallmeyer, T. P. (1986). Cardiac response to relevant stimuli as an adjunctive tool for diagnosing post-traumatic stress disorder in Vietnam veterans. *Behavior Therapy, 17,* 592–606.

Bowen, G. R., & Lambert, J. A. (1986). Systematic desensitization therapy with post-traumatic stress disorder cases. In C. R. Figley (Ed.), *Trauma and its wake,* Vol. II. Brunner/Mazel: New York.

Burgess, A. W., & Holstrom, L. L. (1974b). *Rape: Victims of crisis.* Bowie, MD: R J Brady.

Burgess, A. W., & Holstrom, L. L. (1976). Coping behavior of the rape victim. *American Journal of Psychiatry, 133,* 413–418.

Celluci, A. J., & Lawrence, P. S. (1978). The efficacy of systematic desensitization in reducing nightmares. *Journal of Behaviour Therapy and Experimental Psychiatry, 9,* 109–114.

Clark, D. M., Salkovskis, P. M., & Chaukley, A. J. (1985). Respiratory control as a treatment for panic attacks. *Journal of Behavior Therapy and Experimental Psychiatry, 16,* 23–30.

Cryer, L., & Beutler, L. (1980). Group therapy: An alternative treatment approach for rape victims. *Journal of Sex and Marital Therapy, 6,* 40–46.

Derogatis, L. R. (1977). *SCL-90-R: Administration, scoring, & procedures manual-II.* Towson, MD: Clinical Psychometric Research.

Derogatis, L. R., Rickels, K., & Rocks, A. F. (1976). The SCL-90 and the MMPI: A step in the validation of the new self-report scale. *British Journal of Psychiatry, 128,* 280–289.

Ellis, A. (1977). The basic clinical theory and rational-emotive therapy. In A. Ellis & R. Grieger (Eds.), *Handbook of rational-emotive therapy.* New York: Springer.

Endicott, J., & Spitzer, R. L. (1972). What? Another rating scale? The Psychiatric Evaluation Form. *Journal of Nervous and Mental Diseases 154,* 88–104.

Evans, H. I. (1978). Psychotherapy for the rape victim: Some treatment models. *Hospital and Community Psychiatry, 29,* 309–312.

Fairbank, J. A., DeGood, D. E., & Jenkins, C. W. (1981). Behavioral treatment of a persistent post-traumatic startle response. *Journal of Behavior Therapy and Experimental Psychiatry, 12,* 321–324.

Fairbank, J. A., Gross, R. T., & Keane, T. M. (1983). Treatment of posttraumatic stress disorder: Evaluation of outcome with a behavioral code. *Behavior Modification, 7,* 557–568.

Fairbank, J. A., & Keane, T. M. (1982). Flooding for combat-related stress disorders: Assessment of anxiety reduction across traumatic memories. *Behavior Therapy, 13,* 499–510.

Fitts, W. H. (1965). *Manual: Tennessee self-concept scale.* Nashville, TN: Counselor Recordings and Tests.

Foa, E. B., & Kozak, M. J. (1986). Emotional processing of fear: Exposure to corrective information. *Psychological Bulletin, 99,* 20–35.

Foa, E. B., Rothbaum, B.O., Riggs, D.S. & Murdock, T. B. (1990). *Treatment of PTSD in rape victims: A comparison between cognitive-behavioral procedures and counseling* (unpublished manuscript).

Foa, E. B., Steketee, G., & Rothbaum, B. O. (1989). Behavioral/cognitive conceptualizations of post-traumatic stress disorder. *Behavior Therapy, 20,* 155–176.

Forman, B. D. (1980). Cognitive modification of obsessive thinking in a rape victim: A preliminary study. *Psychological Reports, 47,* 819–822.

Fox, S. S., & Scherl, D. J. (1972). Crisis intervention with victims of rape. *Social Work, 17,* 37–42.

Frank, E., Anderson, B., Stewart, B. D., Dancu, C., Hughes, C., & West, D. (1988). Efficacy of cognitive behavior therapy and systematic desensitization in the treatment of rape trauma. *Behavior Therapy, 19,* 403–420.

Frank, E., & Stewart, B. D. (1983a). Physical aggression: Treating the victims. In E. A. Bleckman (Ed.), *Behavior modification with women.* New York: Guilford Press.

Frank, E., & Stewart, B. D. (1984). Depressive symptoms in rape victims. *Journal of Affective Disorders, 1,* 269–277.

Gay, M. L., Hollandsworth, J. C., & Galassi, J. P. (1975). An assertiveness inventory for adults. *Journal of Counseling Psychology, 22,* 340–344.

Geer, J. H. (1964). The development of a scale to measure fear. *Behaviour Research and Therapy, 3,* 45–53.

Grigsby, J. P. (1987). The use of imagery in the treatment of posttraumatic stress disorder. *The Journal of Nervous and Mental Disease, 175,* 55–59.

Hathaway, S. R., & McKinnley, J. C. (1967). *Minnesota Multiphasic Personality Inventory: Manual for administration and scoring.* New York: Psychological Corporation.

Hickling, E. J., Sison, G. F. P., & Vanderploeg, R. D. (1986). Treatment of posttraumatic stress disorder with relaxation and biofeedback training. *Behavior Therapy, 16,* 406–416.

Holmes, M. R., & St. Lawrence, J. S. (1983). Treatment of rape-induced trauma: Proposed behavioral conceptualization and review of the literature. *Clinical Psychology Review, 3,* 417–433.

Horowitz, M. D. (1976). *Stress response syndromes.* New York: Aronson.

Horowitz, M. D., Wilner, N., & Alvarez, W. (1979). Impact of Event Scale: A measure of subjective stress. *Psychosomatic Medicine, 41,* 209–218.

Jacobson, E. (1938). *Progressive relaxation.* Chicago: University of Chicago Press.

Janis, I. L., & Field, P. B. (1959). Sex differences in personality factors related to persuasibility. In C. I. Hoveland and I. L. Janis (Eds.), *Personality and persuasibility.* New Haven: Yale University Press.

Johnson, C. H., Gilmore, J. D., & Shenoy, R. Z. (1982). Use of a flooding procedure in the treatment of a stress-related anxiety disorder. *Journal of Behavior Therapy and Experimental Psychiatry, 13,* 235–237.

Keane, T. M., Fairbank, J. A., Caddell, J. M., & Zimering, R. T. (1989). Implosive (flooding) therapy reduces symptoms of PTSD in Vietnam combat veterans. *Behavior Therapy, 20,* 245–260.

Keane, T. M., & Kaloupek, D. G. (1982). Imaginal flooding in the treatment of post-traumatic stress disorder. *Journal of Consulting and Clinical Psychology, 50,* 138–140.

Keane, T. M., Malloy, P. F., & Fairbank, J. A. (1984). Empirical development of an MMPI subscale for the assessment of combat-related posttraumatic stress disorder. *Journal of Consulting and Clinical Psychology, 52,* 888–891.

Kilpatrick, D. G., & Amick, A. E. (1985). Rape trauma. In M. Hersen & C. G. Last (Eds.), *Behavior therapy casebook.* New York: Springer.

Kilpatrick, D. G., & Calhoun, K. S. (1988). Early behavioral treatment for rape trauma: Efficacy or artifact? *Behavior Therapy, 19,* 421–427.

Kilpatrick, D. G., & Veronen, L. J. (1983). Treatment for rape-related problems: Crisis intervention is not enough. In L. H. Cohen, W. L. Claiborn, and C. A. Spector (Eds.), *Crisis intervention.* New York: Human Sciences Press.

Kilpatrick, D. G., Veronen, L. J., & Resick, P. A. (1982). Psychological sequelae to rape: Assessment and treatment strategies. In D. M. Dolays & R. L. Meredith (Eds.), *Behavioral medicine: Assessment and treatment strategies.* New York: Plenum Publishing.

Koss, M. P., & Harvey, M. R. (1987). *The rape victim: Clinical and community approaches to treatment.* Lexington, MA: Stephen Greene Press.

Kozak, M. J., Foa, E. B., & Olasov, B. (1987, October). *Psychophysiological response of rape victims during imagery of rape and neutral scenes.* Paper presented at the annual meeting of the Society for Psychophysiological Research, Amsterdam, the Netherlands.

Lang, P. J. (1968). Fear reduction and fear behavior: Problems in treating a construct. In J. M. Schlien (Ed.), *Research in psychotherapy,* Vol. 3. Washington, DC: American Psychological Press.

Lang, P. J. (1977). Imagery in therapy: An information processing analysis of fear. *Behavior Therapy, 8,* 862–886.

Lang, P. J. (1979). A bio-informational theory of emotional imagery. *Psychophysiology, 6,* 495–511.

Lange, A. J., & Jakubowski, P. (1976). *Responsible assertive behavior.* Champaign, IL: Research Press.

Lindy, J. D., Green, B. L., Grace, M., & Titchener, J. (1983). Psychotherapy with survivors of the Beverly Hills Supper Club fire. *American Journal of Psychotherapy, 4,* 593–610.

Marks, I. (1987). *Fears, phobias, and rituals: Panic, anxiety, and their disorders.* Oxford: Oxford University Press.

Marks, I. M. (1972). Flooding and allied treatments. In W. Agras (Ed.) *Behavior modification: Principles and clinical applications.* Boston: Little Brown.

McCaffrey, R. J., & Fairbank, J. A. (1985). Post-traumatic stress disorder associated with transportation accidents: Two case studies. *Behavior Therapy, 16,* 406–416.

McNair, D. M., Lorr, M., & Droppleman, L. F. (1971). *Profile of mood states.* San Diego, CA: Educational and Industrial Testing Service.

Meichenbaum, D. (1974). *Cognitive behavior modification*. Morristown, NJ: General Learning Press.

Muse, M. (1986). Stress-related, posttraumatic chronic pain syndrome: Behavioral treatment approach. *Pain, 25*, 389–394.

Obanion, D., & Veronen, L.J. (1978). *Fear thermometer: An unpublished instrument*. North Texas State University.

Pearson, M. A., Poquette, B. M., & Wasden, R. E. (1983). Stress inoculation and the treatment of post-rape trauma: A case report. *The Behavior Therapist, 6*, 58–59.

Peniston, E. G. (1986). EMG biofeedback-assisted desensitization treatment for Vietnam combat veterans post-traumatic stress disorder. *Clinical Biofeedback and Health, 9*, 35–41.

Perl, M., Westin, A. B., & Peterson, L. G. (1985). The female rape survivor: Time-limited group therapy with female/male co-therapists. *Journal of Psychosomatic Obstetrics and Gynecology, 4*, 197–205.

Pitman, R. K., Orr, S. P., Forgue, D. F., deJong, J. B., & Claiborn, J. M. (1987). Psychophysiologic assessment of post-traumatic stress disorder imagery in Vietnam combat veterans. *Archives of General Psychiatry, 44*, 970–975.

Rachman, S. (1980). Emotional processing. *Behaviour Research and Therapy, 18*, 51–60.

Resick, P. A., Jordan, C. J., Girelli, S. A., Hutter, C. K., & Marhoefer-Dvorak, S. (1988). A comparative outcome study of behavioral group therapy for sexual assault victims. *Behavior Therapy, 19*, 385–401.

Roth, S., Dye, E., & Lebowitz, V. (1988). *Group therapy for sexual assault victims*. Unpublished manuscript.

Rothbaum, B. O. & Foa, E. B. (1988). *Treatments of post-traumatic stress disorder in rape victims*. Paper presented at the World Congress of Behaviour Therapy Conference, Edinburgh, Scotland, September, 1988.

Schindler, F. E. (1980). Treatment of systematic desensitization of a recurring nightmare of a real life trauma. *Journal of Behavior Therapy and Experimental Psychiatry, 11*, 53–54.

Schooler, N. R., Levine, J., Severe, J. B., Brauzer, B., DiMascio, A., Klermen, G. L., & Tuason, V. B. (1980). Prevention of relapse in schizophrenia: An evaluation of fluphenazine decanoate. *Archives of General Psychiatry, 37*, 16–24.

Schultz, F. H., & Luthe, W. (1969). *Autogenic therapy*. New York: Grune and Stratton.

Schutz, W. F. (1978). *The FIRO-B awareness scale manual*. Palo Alto, CA: Consulting Psychologists Press.

Spielberger, C. D. Gorsuch, R. L., & Lushene, R. E. (1970). *Manual for the State-Trait Anxiety Inventory (self-evaluation questionnaire)*. Palo Alto, CA: Consulting Psychologists Press.

Turner, S. M. (1979). *Systematic desensitization of fears and anxiety in rape victims*. Paper presented at the Association for the Advancement of Behavior Therapy, San Francisco, CA.

Turner, S. M., & Frank, E. (1981). Behavior therapy in the treatment of rape victims. In L. Michelson, M. Hersen, & S. M. Turner (Eds.), *Future perspectives in behavior therapy*. New York: Plenum Publishing.

Veronen, L. J., & Kilpatrick, D. G. (1980). Reported fears of rape victims. A preliminary investigation. *Behavior Modification, 4*, 383–396.

Veronen, L. J., & Kilpatrick, D. G. (1982a). *A brief behavioral intervention procedure for rape victims*. Paper presented at the Annual Convention of the American Psychological Association, Washington, DC.

Veronen, L. J., & Kilpatrick, D. G. (1982b). *Stress inoculation training for victims of rape: Efficacy and differential findings*. Paper presented at the Sixteenth Annual Convention of the Association for the Advancement of Behavior Therapy, Los Angeles, November.

Veronen, L. J., & Kilpatrick, D. G. (1983). Stress management for rape victims. In D. Meichenbaum & M. E. Jaremko (Eds.), *Stress reduction and prevention*. New York: Plenum Publishing.

Wallston, B. S., Wallston, K. A., Kaplan, G. D., & Maides, S. A. (1976). Development and validation of the Multidimensional Health Locus of Control Scale. *Journal of Consulting and Clinical Psychology, 114,* 580–585.

Wolff, R. (1977). Systematic desensitization and negative practice to alter the aftereffects of a rape attempt. *Journal of Behavior Therapy and Experimental Psychiatry, 8,* 423–425.

Wolpe, J. (1958). *Psychotherapy by reciprocal inhibition.* Stanford: Stanford University Press.

Wolpe, J. (1973). *The practice of behavior therapy.* Elmsford, NY: Pergamon Press.

Wolpe, J. (1985). Deep muscle relaxation. In A. S. Bellack & M. Hersen (Eds.), *Dictionary of behavior therapy techniques.* Elmsford, NY: Pergamon Press.

Zung, W. A. (1965). A self-rating depression scale. *Archives of General Psychiatry, 12,* 63–70.

Chapter 5

Behavioral Treatment of Posttraumatic Stress Disorder and Co-occurring Substance Abuse

Francis R. Abueg
John A. Fairbank

As the preceding chapters show, our understanding of the phenomenology, prevalence, etiology, and assessment of posttraumatic stress disorder (PTSD) has increased substantially over the past decade. The research findings and clinical observations discussed in these chapters have repeatedly demonstrated that PTSD is a complex disorder that is multiply determined and expressed.

PTSD is increasingly recognized as co-occurring with other major psychological disorders and psychosocial problems. PTSD has been found to be highly comorbid with alcohol abuse and dependence (Keane & Wolfe, 1990; Kulka, Schlenger, Fairbank, Hough, Jordan, Marmar, & Weiss, 1990); affective disorders such as major depressive disorder (Green, Lindy, Grace, & Gleser, 1989); anxiety disorders such as generalized anxiety disorder (Kulka et al., 1990) and panic disorder (Green et al., 1989); somatization disorder (Toland & Goetz, 1988); and Axis II disorders such as antisocial personality disorder (Kulka et al., 1990; Sierles, Chen, Messing, Besyner, & Taylor, 1986).

Not surprisingly, the combination of PTSD and substance abuse or other major psychological problems is reported to be quite difficult to treat (Boudewyns, 1989; Scurfield, 1991). The development of ecologically valid treatment protocols for multiply disordered PTSD patients is a major challenge facing those who provide clinical services to trauma survivors. Unfortunately, little information exists to guide the clinician in the development of potentially efficacious interventions for multiply disordered PTSD patients. The purpose of this chapter is to attempt to provide some heuristic guidelines for treating PTSD, and one of the most prevalent and challenging comorbidities, substance abuse.

We will begin the present chapter with an overview of recent research findings that highlight what we currently know about the relationship between PTSD and substance abuse. This overview will be followed by our rationale for advocating the development and refinement of comprehensive interventions for PTSD and substance abuse comorbidities.

A major focus of the chapter will be to describe in detail a specific model for treating PTSD and substance abuse that takes into account our current state of knowledge about this complex comorbidity. The treatment strategy that we will describe consists of five sequential phases or stages: (a) precommitment; (b) commitment phase; (c) action phase 1: acquisition and practice; (d) action phase 2: generalization and maintenance; and (e) the relapse phase. A brief description of the rationale and empirical support for each stage of this intervention model will be included in this section of the chapter. Detailed information on specific treatment components that should be considered at each stage of the intervention will follow in separate sections. The chapter will conclude with a discussion of the need for research that describes the process by which treatment of PTSD substance abuse patients takes place, as well as studies that examine the outcome efficacy of such interventions.

PREVALENCE OF PTSD AND CO-OCCURRING SUBSTANCE ABUSE

There is now substantial evidence to suggest that many people with PTSD also suffer alcohol or drug abuse and dependence (Davidson, Kudler, Saunders, & Smith, 1990; Friedman, in press; Green, Lindy, Grace, & Gleser, 1989; Keane, Gerardi, Lyons, & Wolfe, 1988; Keane & Wolfe, in press; Kilpatrick, 1990; Kulka et al., 1990; McFarland, 1985; Sierles, Chen, McFarland, & Taylor, 1983; Sierles, Chen, Messing, Besyner, & Taylor, 1986). For example, among the nationally representative, community-based sample of more than 1,600 Vietnam veterans who participated in the National Vietnam Veterans Readjustment Study (NVVRS), nearly a quarter of the men with current PTSD also met DSM-III-R criteria for current alcohol abuse or dependence (Kulka et al., 1990). In comparison, among male Vietnam veterans without PTSD, fewer than 10% met criteria for current abuse of or dependence on alcohol. Thus, male Vietnam veterans with a current diagnosis of PTSD were found to be more than twice as likely to meet criteria for current alcohol abuse or dependence as their counterparts without PTSD. Among Vietnam veteran women with current PTSD, roughly 10% were found to meet criteria for current alcohol abuse or dependence. In contrast, less than 2% of Vietnam veteran women without PTSD met criteria for alcohol abuse or dependence. Thus, among female Vietnam veterans, having a current diagnosis of PTSD predicts a greater-than-fivefold increase in the likelihood that alcohol abuse or dependence is a current problem.

Regarding current drug abuse or dependence among people with PTSD, several findings from the NVVRS are relevant. For men, more than 1 in 20 veterans with PTSD were found to have a serious current problem with drug abuse or dependence. In comparison, less than 1 in 100 Vietnam veteran males who do not have PTSD have a current diagnosis of drug abuse or dependence.

As one might expect, lifetime rates of alcohol and drug abuse among people with current PTSD are even higher. In the NVVRS, nearly three-quarters of the men with a current diagnosis of PTSD met criteria for a lifetime diagnosis of alcohol abuse or dependence ("lifetime" diagnosis of substance abuse was operationally defined as "ever" having met criteria for substance abuse or dependence at any time during the course of one's life). Among women with current PTSD, nearly 3 in 10 have met criteria for alcohol abuse in their lifetime. Regarding the lifetime prevalence of PTSD and co-occurring drug abuse or dependence, roughly 10% of men and women met diagnostic criteria. Compared to Vietnam veterans without PTSD, veterans with PTSD have lifetime rates of alcohol and drug abuse and dependence that are significantly higher.

In addition to combat-related PTSD, PTSD that results from exposure to other types of extreme events is associated with high rates of co-occurring substance abuse. For example, among 2,009 women who participated in a national epidemiological study of the psychological impact of violent crime, crime victims with PTSD were found to be at increased risk for co-occurring substance abuse problems (Kilpatrick, 1990). Specifically, crime victims with PTSD were 3.2 times more likely than crime victims without PTSD to have had serious problems with alcohol and 3.4 times more likely to have had a serious problem with drugs.

Among treatment-seeking populations, the prevalence of dual PTSD and substance abuse disorders is generally found to be higher than in the community-based samples (Davidson et al., 1990; Keane & Wolfe, 1990; McFarland, 1985; Sierles et al., 1986). For example, Keane and Wolfe (1990) reported that 84% of 50 patients who sought treatment at the

Boston Veterans Administration Medical Center for PTSD had at least one substance abuse problem: 70% met criteria for alcohol abuse or dependence, while 42% met criteria for drug abuse or dependence.

CHALLENGE OF TREATING THE PTSD SUBSTANCE ABUSER

A major challenge in treating the PTSD substance abuser is the development of an individual treatment plan that adequately addresses the array of problems associated with this complex comorbidity. At least three different general treatment goals usually should be considered in addressing the problems of PTSD substance abusers. One treatment goal is to attempt to decrease positive symptoms of PTSD, such as anxiety, arousal, intrusive recollections of extreme events, anger, and hostility. A second goal is to attempt to increase approach behavior to counteract negative symptoms associated with both PTSD and substance abuse, such as interpersonal withdrawal and flattened emotional reactivity. A third general goal is to attempt to decrease the frequency of an appetitive addictive behavior. Clearly, the task of devising interventions to address all three goals concurrently or sequentially represents a major challenge for treatment providers.

Additional reasons why treatment of the PTSD substance abuse patient is challenging include the following: (a) many PTSD substance abuse patients continue active alcohol or drug abuse during treatment; (b) alcohol or drug dependence comorbidities are associated with treatment noncompliance; and (c) therapists often report that they feel overwhelmed by the chronic and recalcitrant problems of the PTSD substance abuser (cf. Lyons & McGovern, 1989).

Conceptual Model for Treating the PTSD Substance Abuser

This section is designed to elaborate upon an integrative model for conceptualization of the interaction between PTSD and substance abuse and dependence, with an emphasis on the most prevalent comorbid addiction, alcoholism. The aim of this model is threefold: (a) to account for the complexity of alcohol-anxiety (and PTSD) interactions, from both an etiological as well as a maintenance perspective; (b) to provide a logical foundation for generating clinical interventions; and (c) to articulate components of a model that can generate testable hypotheses for clinical and field research in comorbid PTSD. We hope to cast a broad conceptual net in reviewing relevant work to provide a logical springboard for a rather novel multidimensional behavioral approach. Although this model was developed largely through work with patients with combat-related PTSD, it should, in general, serve as a useful heuristic for treatment of PTSD resulting from exposure to other types of extreme events.

Rationale for Model Development

Several practical, theoretical, and more speculative treatment considerations have led to the need for an integrative model for understanding the sequelae to trauma and the addictions. PTSD is a relatively new addition to the clinical taxonomy of psychiatric disorders (American Psychiatric Association, 1980), and most empirically based information about the disorder has been collected only in the last few years. It is therefore not surprising that many clinicians who have been treating individuals with PTSD often have had little exposure to this increasingly sophisticated knowledge base and are unaware of the complex nature of the disorder. Of particular concern is that little attention is typically paid in clinical practice to developing treatment plans and interventions that consider how to treat PTSD that is comorbid with other serious problems such as alcohol and drug abuse, major depression, and antisocial or borderline personality disorders. This issue raises important questions about the type and focus of treatment and whether various combinations of PTSD and other disorders provide differential information about matching clients to treatment and prognosis. What is now needed is the development of behavioral approaches to treating PTSD that are commensurate with our current level of understanding regarding the complexity of the disorder.

We will consider four substantive arguments for the careful joint consideration of PTSD and alcoholism. The first argument accounts for the interaction of the disorders. Here, we will discuss studies that have relevance for the influence of one disorder upon the other, in a causal or directional fashion. The second argument involves the respective impairment of individuals with PTSD and substance abuse. This discussion will review symptom constellations that are common to both alcoholism and PTSD and the recalcitrance of the chronic forms of these disorders. The third argument—relapse rates—is based upon extensive addiction literature and growing PTSD literature regarding relapse rates posttreatment. The fourth and final argument is one of cost effectiveness. This rationale is based solely on the logic that combined, better conceived interventions are less costly and more likely to provide a complete continuum of care.

Interaction Argument. Currently we know little about the directionality of the etiological relationship between PTSD and substance abuse and dependence. We have yet to determine whether PTSD is a risk factor for alcohol or drug abuse, or whether substance abuse operates as a risk factor for the development of PTSD. Recently, Davidson et al. (1990) have reported some preliminary data regarding the sequencing and course of alcoholism with PTSD. These investigators administered the Schedule of Affective Disorders (SADS-L; Endicott & Spitzer, 1978) to a sample of 44 World War II and Vietnam veterans with PTSD to establish (a) age at first diagnosis of alcoholism and other psychiatric disorders; (b) age at onset of PTSD; and (c) chronology and number of other diagnoses. Alcoholism was found to precede the onset of PTSD by a mean of 3.1 years among Vietnam veterans but follow PTSD by a mean of 6.9 years in WWII veterans. As noted by the authors, the finding that alcohol abuse or dependence preceded or occurred at the same time as PTSD in most Vietnam veterans does not indicate causality. Alcohol abuse still may have represented an attempt to cope with significant early PTSD symptoms before the emergence of the full disorder.

Khantzian (1985) has proposed a self-medication theory of substance abuse, suggesting that drugs of abuse are selected because of their specific psychotropic effects. Heroin, for example, may be chosen for its powerful muting effect on rage and aggression, while cocaine may be adopted for its antidepressant action. Neff and Husiani's (1982) study of the "stress-buffering" function of alcohol consumption suggested that drinking is a mediating factor in the relationship between certain life events and depressive symptomatology, particularly in response to extreme ("calamitous") events.

A growing body of literature has begun to point toward the insidious manner in which the urge or craving to drink may be precipitated by PTSD symptomatology (Keane et al., 1988; Jellinek & Williams, 1984, 1987). Although the tension-reduction hypothesis has received mixed support in the alcohol and anxiety literature, there is clinical consensus that a proportion of PTSD patients self-medicate their anxiety in the absence of other, more adaptive ways of coping. Brinson and Treanor (1988) have concluded that individuals with PTSD abuse alcohol to dampen adverse emotional reactivity, cope with sleep disturbance, and escape intrusive PTSD reexperiencing phenomena.

Initial associations between extreme stress and drinking can contribute to later vulnerability to multiple diagnosis through changes in expectancies about the effects of alcohol (cf. Brown, Goldman, Inn, & Anderson, 1980; Brown, Goldman, & Christiansen, 1985). One study directly asked dually diagnosed patients what led to their last return to drinking (Abueg, Chun, & Lurie, 1990). These PTSD alcoholics reported many of the relapse precipitants evident in the literature regarding relapsing alcoholics, i.e., negative affect, external stressors, or simple urges. Nearly 25% of the responses in this study, however, needed to be scored in an entirely independent category of precipitants related specifically to symptoms of PTSD (sleep loss, nightmares, being "on guard," and trauma-related ideation). These data suggest that, at the very least, PTSD alcoholics' attributions regarding what precedes a relapse may be intimately bound to the unique symptoms from which they suffer.

Recent work in the alcohol field has centered on biological aspects of extreme stress symptoms and their interaction with the CNS depressant properties and disinhibitory mechanisms of alcohol ingestion (cf., Kosten & Krystal, 1988). Volpicelli (1987), for example, developed a model for understanding drinking in response to uncontrolled stress, emphasizing constructs from the learned helplessness paradigm. Although experimental studies in toto appear to fail to support the tension-reduction hypothesis, reexamination of uncontrollable stress paradigms clearly indicates a temporal link between drinking and stress. Increases in alcohol consumption follow uncontrollable aversive events (Volpicelli, 1987, p. 385). Volpicelli's analysis suggests that "tension relief"—or the termination of the aversive stimulus—reliably precedes drinking. A secondary hypothesis postulated by that author is that alcohol ingestion is reinforced by effects that substitute for decreased endorphin activity after presentation of shock. Examination of historical variables such as alcohol exposure during combat duty and its link to course and current presentation of the disorders appears to be an important area for assessment and further research.

Alcohol use has also been shown to potentiate anxiety in both normal and clinical samples (Stockwell, Small, Hodgson, et al., 1984; Vaillant, 1980). Thus, continued drinking may exacerbate PTSD symptoms, which, in turn, can precipitate episodes of abusive drinking. Classical conditioning may account for this influence. However, higher order conditioning as well as cognitive influences are likely to be as influential. Withdrawal symptoms experienced as anxiety or PTSD symptoms per se have indeed been identified by a number of authors as precipitants to symptom exacerbation (Kosten & Krystal, 1988; Risse, Whitter, Burke, et al., 1990). One hypothesis is that the withdrawal symptoms can directly potentiate preexisting psychopathology of PTSD, such as rage and aggression (Risse et al., 1990). Another hypothesis may occur at an attributional level. For example, "What is happening to me?" "Am I falling apart?" or "Is this my PTSD worsening again?" are questions that may plague comorbid patients. Finally, at least one author has suggested that alcoholism, because of its numerous tragic consequences for the sufferer and his or her family, can be considered a traumatic stressor (Bean-Bayog, 1988).

A recent review by Kushner, Sher, and Beitman (1990) suggests that the interaction for clinical anxiety and alcohol use differs significantly across the anxiety disorders. Although the literature on generalized anxiety disorder (GAD) and panic patients suggests that tension reduction and self-medication may account for some drinking, agoraphobics and simple phobics do not show such trends. Data suggest that agoraphobics, for example, drink in a variety of situations and tend to show greater interaction between their anxiety and alcohol use. Based on these observations, it is not unlikely to expect a unique covariation in the symptoms of the PTSD-alcoholic, again warranting model development, treatment, and research in this specific area.

Impairment Argument. During the 1980s, much progress was made in identifying and clarifying the nature of the relationship between substance abuse and psychological disorders. First, studies conducted in a variety of drug treatment settings demonstrated that many people who seek drug abuse treatment have coexisting psychological impairments. Several groups of independent investigators all found high levels of psychological disorder among people seeking drug or alcohol treatment (Dorus & Senay, 1980; Rounsaville, Weissman, Crits-Cristoph, Wilber, & Kleber, 1982; Rounsaville, Weissman, Rosenberger, Wilber, & Kleber, 1979; Steer & Kotzker, 1980). Similarly, McLellan and his colleagues (McLellan, Childress, Griffith, & Woody, 1984; LaPorte, McLellan, O'Brien, & Marshall, 1981) found different psychiatric diagnoses among those seeking treatment for the abuse of different drugs.

In addition to documenting the prevalence of psychopathology among people seeking treatment at drug or alcohol abuse facilities, recent studies have demonstrated the important role of comorbid diagnoses in predicting response to treatment. For example, Rounsaville and his colleagues (e.g., Kosten, Rounsaville, & Kleber, 1983) found both severity of psychological impairment and the presence of specific psychiatric diagnoses at intake to be predictive of long-term treatment outcome for opiate addicts. Additionally, in a controlled trial of the efficacy of psychotherapy as an adjunct to methadone maintenance treatment for opiate addicts, Woody, McLellan, Luborsky, and O'Brien (1985) found that the presence of specific psychiatric disorders, such as major depression and antisocial personality disorder (ASP), interacted with drug dependence to affect client response to treatment. Opiate addicts with no pretreatment psychological impairment were found to improve significantly with treatment, as did those who met criteria for major depression. Addicts with ASP alone, however, showed little improvement as a function of treatment, whereas addicts with ASP and depression at intake responded almost as well as those with depression alone. Thus, although ASP alone was a negative predictor of opiate addicts' response to treatment, its effects appear to be mollified substantially by the presence of a co-occurring depressive disorder and other psychiatric symptoms (cf. Gerstley, Alterman, McLellan, & Woody, 1990).

Recent drug abuse treatment studies have also demonstrated that psychotherapy can be an important part of a comprehensive treatment plan for at least some substance abusers. In the controlled trial of psychotherapy in the treatment of methadone-maintained opiate addicts described previously, Woody and his colleagues demonstrated that both cognitive-behavioral and supportive-expressive interventions, when added to standard drug abuse counseling, resulted in improved treatment outcome. This study is important because it speaks to client treatment in the study of multiple disorder patterns.

"Patients with PTSD seen at VAMCs (Veterans Affairs Medical Centers) consistently function at a lower adaptive level (e.g., DSM-III Axis 4) than patients with other psychiatric disorders," at least according to the ratings provided by surveyed clinicians (VA Health Systems Research & Development, 1987; Chief Medical Director's Special Committee on PTSD, 1987). The lower level of reported adaptation may be due in part to the chronicity of PTSD in Vietnam combat veterans (Kolb, 1987) as well as the pervasive symptom complex. With chronic PTSD comes a host of other life dysfunctions that parallel problems suffered by alcoholics. Broadly speaking, these include intrapersonal factors (biological and psychological) and interpersonal problems in the life system, such as marital and family difficulties, deficits in occupational functioning, and social and communication skills. To underscore the impairment argument for model development, we will briefly review areas of convergence in PTSD and substance abuse.

In a meta-analysis of the psychological problems of Vietnam veterans, Kaylor and colleagues (1987) found that they were more likely than their civilian counterparts to have difficulties with depression, anger, anxiety, and suicidal tendencies. Furthermore, combat veterans who meet criteria for PTSD are more likely than their non-PTSD counterparts to have such problems (Kulka et al., 1990).

First, the biological sensitivity documented in both PTSD patients and alcoholics to stimuli relevant to their conditions is an area of remarkable convergence. The psychophysiological reactivity of veterans with combat PTSD is well documented (Malloy, Fairbank, & Keane, 1983; Blanchard, Kolb, Pallmeyer, & Gerardi, 1982). In the presence of stimuli reminiscent of the original trauma, measures of autonomic arousal rise precipitously, and to a degree that is difficult to fake (see chapter by Litz et al. for a more detailed review of this work). Moreover, PTSD sufferers appear to exhibit a continual state of hyperarousal (Gerardi, Keane, Cahoon, and Klauminzer, 1989). These hallmark symptoms of PTSD have been conceptually linked directly to the traumatic exposure. Two-factor theory of avoidance conditioning combines classical conditioning principles with operant avoidance and has become a fruitful way of studying PTSD (Fairbank & Brown, 1987; Keane, Fairbank, Caddell, Zimering, & Bender, 1985).

In a manner similar to the PTSD victim's response to traumatogenic stimuli, it can be argued that alcoholics are psychophysiologically reactive to stimuli that remind them of drinking. Indeed, physiological differences have been demonstrated between alcoholics and nonalcoholics when exposed to the sight and smell of alcohol (Pomerleau, Fertig, Baker, & Cooney, 1983; Kaplan, Meyer, & Stroebel, 1983).

Poulos, Hinson, & Siegel (1981) outlined a model of classical conditioning of alcohol cues, both interoceptive and exteroceptive, that increase the likelihood of drinking. This type of conceptual reasoning has led to a number of studies on alcohol cue exposure, with various manipulations relevant to the ecology of relapse (Niaura, Rohsenow, Binkoff et al., 1988). After a priming dose of alcohol, for example, alcoholics report a significantly increased desire to drink in the presence of alcohol cues (Hodgson, Stockwell, & Rankin, 1979; Kaplan, Meyer, & Stroebel, 1983; Laberg & Effertsen, 1987). Negative mood states can also elicit a desire for alcohol in the absence of external cues for drinking (Litt, Cooney, Kadden, & Gaupp, 1990). Cognitive changes have also been documented in response to alcohol cues (Cooney et al., 1987).

As research progresses, more and more links have been found between cue reactivity and treatment progress, outcome and relapse (Niaura et al., 1988). Continued theoretical development is needed in the area of cue reactivity among PTSD substance abusers. Does the presence of traumatogenic conditioned stimuli increase the psychophysiological urge to drink? Is there incremental enhancement of the urge in the added presence of alcohol cues?

Finally, and at an even more complex level, the approach-avoidance conflict observed in patients posttrauma (Roth & Cohen, 1986) is mirrored in the conflict observed in the alcohol reactivity literature. That is, depending upon motivational states, the patient may view exposure to alcohol-related stimuli as highly objectionable and aversive, particularly if a great deal of energy is being expended toward behavioral restraint. Another individual who is not so conflicted may welcome a challenge or may indeed be less invested in absolute abstinence, thus automatically responding to the stimulus as a reinforcer.

Another area of convergence between disorders is in coping strategies and coping skills deficits. Penk, Peck, Robinowitz, Bell, and Little (1988), and Penk et al. (1981) reviewed the literature on coping among substance abusers. They found that a common theme in this work is that the use of a substance indeed indicates a failure to cope adequately. Moreover, substance abusers as a group show a clear bias toward avoidant styles of coping. These data are fully consistent with other psychometric data on the social withdrawal and avoidance coping style of veterans with PTSD (Fairbank, Hansen, & Fitterling, 1991) and some victims of sexual assault (Foa, Steketee, & Olasov Rothbaum, 1989). In addition, there is an increased likelihood that a PTSD patient and an alcoholic patient will struggle concomitantly with depression (Kulka et al., 1990). Taken as a whole, these data suggest that the interaction of such problem categories would only strengthen a defensive avoidance and withdrawal.

Relapse Rates Argument. A substantive body of evidence has been amassed regarding the high relapse rates in the addictions posttreatment. As Saunders and Allsop (1987) succinctly summarize, "If a relapse is any drug use after initiating a period of abstention, then over 90% of clients will, in any 12-month period, exhibit such behavior" (p. 418). They also note that defining relapse as a return to pretreatment levels of substance use typically generates relapse rates in the 45% to 50% range. Although these particular definitions of relapse have been challenged in this literature, the fact remains that addictive behavior is highly resistant to long-term change. In addition to strong behavioral advances (e.g., Marlatt & Gordon, 1985; Brownell, Marlatt, Lichtenstein, & Wilson, 1986) that conceptualize the process of relapse and precipitants or predictors of relapse, significant theorizing has begun to examine the reciprocal influences of the patient's natural environment on relapse and recovery (Moos, 1990). These developments have not only increased explanatory power in behavioral prediction, but have also led to additional entry points for intervention.

When one considers the convergence of PTSD and substance abuse, then certainly it is reasonable to expect an increased likelihood of relapse among dually diagnosed individuals versus a non-PTSD alcoholic, for example. Whether the events leading to the relapse are conditioning based, are rooted in the chronicity of one of the disorders, or in the poor social support of a poorly adapted person with PTSD, risks for relapse seem to be more abundant. These questions have yet to be formally addressed by any research. However, a few studies have begun to attend to the recalcitrance of PTSD alone posttreatment.

Perconte, Griger, and Bellucci (1989) followed 102 Vietnam combat veterans treated in a partial hospitalization program for PTSD. Within a 2-year follow-up period, 26 of 47 patients (55.3%) who were initially rated as improved suffered a subsequent hospitalization for their PTSD. Only 21 of 74 veterans (28.4%) remained improved over that follow-up period. Preliminary outcome data such as these confirm the risk inherent in having PTSD. The question remains: Does the dual diagnosis predict even greater relapse potential?

Cost Effectiveness Argument. Some data suggest that substance abuse treatment in conjunction with PTSD treatment improves outcome for dually diagnosed patients (Kuhne, Nohner, & Baraga, 1986). Unfortunately, this is an isolated piece of evidence. A great deal of concern has been expressed regarding the lack of continuity of care in this area (Lehmann, 1990). One common clinical observation is that patients have received piecemeal interventions, obtaining treatment for substance abuse problems and then PTSD, or vice versa, but rarely an integration of the two (Schnitt & Nocks, 1984). Formal aftercare that addresses the dual diagnosis has not been reported to our knowledge. In response to this reality, a progressive approach has already been adopted in the Department of Veterans Affairs. A number of PTSD substance abuse units have been funded to augment existing outpatient and inpatient care in these areas (Lehmann, 1990). It seems quite logical to conclude that programs conceived with the unique problems of the PTSD substance abuser will be more cost effective than a piecemeal or additive approach to therapy. Progressive administrative moves mirror important advances in the theoretical and clinical literature. Increasing sophistication does not necessarily mean increasing complexity. Rather, efficiency is enhanced by focusing a limited set of resources, in an interactive conceptual framework, upon a unique problem population.

BUILDING AN INTEGRATED MODEL

After reviewing the epidemiology, the descriptive data, and the reasons we need a working model for treating the PTSD substance abuser, it becomes clear what significant questions must at least be addressed, if not answered, in a practical, multidimensional treatment model. Some of these questions are listed below:

- How can therapists increase the PTSD substance abuser's motivation for therapy?
- What should be the first course of action?
- What places a patient at risk for future failure?
- Given the strong technology for change, what do we know about timing of interventions, effects of practice, and beliefs or expectancies about change, which will strengthen what is learned?
- How should we proceed if the patient is not amenable to imaginal techniques?

To provide a coherent framework from which to consider these difficult questions, we will outline a stage model of change and intervention sensitive to drug and alcohol interactions with PTSD symptoms. Social learning theory (Bandura, 1978a; Bandura, 1978b, 1982) has become fertile ground for the development and understanding of the process of change in individuals in therapy. In addition to borrowing constructs from this area of theory development, we will incorporate observations from other approaches to understanding addictive process, abstinence, and relapse. Finally, an important novel component complementing a stage model is a recursive analysis of self-regulatory strategies occurring in response to therapy.

The mainstays of learning theory that have served as reliable guideposts to therapy for so long continue to be relevant here. New behaviors are acquired in the presence of appropriate reinforcement, are emitted and practiced over time, are generalized across settings, and become maintained in those settings. Psychotherapy of all orientations can be conceptualized as an ongoing process of differential reinforcement, counterconditioning, and other types of learning within the interpersonal context, with the aim of producing more adaptive strategies or skills in living.

Arnold Lazarus broadened the scope of behavior therapy to capitalize upon its functional properties (Lazarus, 1971). That is, to examine the context in which a behavior is maintained or reinforced is critical. Thus, the PTSD alcoholic, for example, must be assessed for what conditions appear to lead to heavy drinking, what evokes memories of extreme events, and what precedes isolation and withdrawal. Prior to making these functional assessments, however, we strongly believe that an understanding of the potential patient's stage of change must be acknowledged. Indeed, such an orientation inherently conveys a respect for the patient's stage of adjustment and does not place a value judgment upon those who do not wish to engage in therapy.

Prochaska and colleagues (Prochaska & DiClemente, 1983) significantly influenced the field in their attempt to understand the naturalistic stages of change in which smokers attempt to quit. They classified the strategies smokers were employing into five stages: precommitment, commitment, action, maintenance, and relapse. The precommitment stage involves the contemplation of stopping the addictive behavior and considering the options, risks, and consequences. The commitment stage involves a resolution or formal decision to quit with strong intentions to engage in activities that will reduce the behavior. Some experimentation with actual change techniques was noted in this group. The third stage, the action stage, was marked by strong efforts at behavior change and "deaddiction." This sample of "self-changers" intuitively adopted many traditional behavioral techniques such as stimulus control, thought stopping, delays to use, and relaxation. These individuals reported strengthening their abstinence through stimulus and response generalization. Finally, the relapsers characterized those individuals who were facing difficulties in maintaining their goals at reduction or cessation of tobacco use. Anecdotally they appeared to be in emotional conflict over the inconsistent behavior.

We have chosen to modify this stage model to accommodate observations of these patients in therapy as well as the realistic demands and therapeutic constraints in treating the addicted PTSD patient. Much of the model development can be attributed to direct experience at the National Center for PTSD in Menlo Park, California, where the first clinical demonstration project for the treatment of the combined disorders was founded. The 30-bed program was fully incorporated into the therapeutic community for combat veterans, still the largest inpatient program in the Department of Veterans Affairs (Berman, Price, & Gusman, 1982).

Our model proposes five stages that vary slightly from Prochaska in how each stage is demarcated. These stages include precommitment, commitment, action phase 1 (practice), action phase 2 (generalization and maintenance), and the relapse stage (see Figure 5.1). The second, separate action phase is intended to emphasize an active therapeutic focus on encouraging the patient to implement new skills in broader contexts.

The precommitment stage precedes the formal therapeutic contract to work on the patient's problems. Usually, this stage means stabilization through detoxification or inpatient hospitalization for suicidal or homicidal acts or intentions. In some instances, it may mean stabilizing highly disorganized, psychotic, or aggressive behavior. Although the challenge of therapy cannot be fully appreciated by the PTSD substance abuser at this stage, the respite provided by the therapist from often-dramatic life circumstances can create powerful positive expectancies about psychotherapy. If the crisis was precipitated by war-related stress, acknowledging that pain can build immediate rapport in preparation for subsequent trauma exposure procedures. Also, broaching the use of medication to control substance use—such as disulfiram or naltrexone—is useful at this stage, when the negative consequences of the substance use are still salient.

The commitment stage may be the most important step in helping the

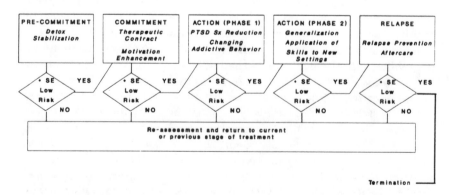

FIGURE 5.1. Stage model for treating the PTSD substance abuser. Note: + SE (self-efficacy) refers to increased confidence to resist the urge to drink or use substances; Low Risk refers to other vunerability factors that may be evident to the clinician (physiological factors, social, occupational, etc.).

individual obtain the most from the therapy available. Two goals are prominent here: to contract with the patient to engage in therapy by explaining what can be gained from therapy (and what is lost by not attempting therapy) and to increase the motivation for this substantive task. William Miller (1985) provides a comprehensive review of how motivation can be influenced, usually through simple behavioral procedures. These can include helping the patient set manageable short-term goals (see Bandura & Schunk, 1981), setting realistic expectations about therapy in general, reinforcing the patient for past successes and cognitions that are consistent with change in therapy ("Maybe I can do things differently and maybe I'm not a bad person after all"). In the commitment stage, brief education about the addiction as well as PTSD is highly recommended. The patient can begin to understand how the disorders have interacted based upon personal experiences highlighted by the therapist.

As learning progresses, the patient moves from commitment to action (phase 1: practice). Here the substance of the interventions is aimed at satisfying the three therapeutic goals in the multiply diagnosed (reducing positive symptoms, negative symptoms, and reversing the addiction). Problem-solving training, direct therapeutic exposure (DTE), and self-control training in the addictions including cue exposure, are all appropriate interventions for this phase of change. Relief from disturbing symptoms typically marks precipitous progress in therapy. These interventions will be described in detail later in this chapter. Close monitoring of expectancies is important to maintain a realistic view of the future for the patient.

The next phase, the action stage (phase 2: generalization), reflects the improvement in the skills of the patient to anticipate opportunities to use previously learned techniques. Here the therapist is invaluable in modulating the degree to which new challenges are undertaken—in intimate relationships, as a parent, in the work setting, in the community. Emphasis is placed upon broadening the social support network and deepening existing ties.

Finally, the relapse stage is ideal for focusing upon the potential for lapse and relapse, particularly in the area of returning to use the substance of choice. Formal intervention through relapse prevention training, with adaptations that incorporate a conceptualization of PTSD themes and symptoms, appears to hold promise for forestalling relapse. Cue exposure in imagination is repeated here through the use of the relapse fantasy. Positive coping imagery followed by role play increase the likelihood of emitting an adaptive response when faced with urges or cravings. Drink- and drug-refusal training is seen as practical and effective by PTSD substance abusers and is the last component of the intervention.

As is evident from the above elaboration of stages, this model is not strictly linear. PTSD has been conceptualized in terms of the person-environment interaction (Keane, 1989), and behavior therapy has been strongly influenced by systems approaches to assessment and treatment (Evans, 1985; Staats, 1978). Rosenbaum (1990) has elaborated upon an elegant model of self-regulation that attempts to integrate findings from a wide range of literature. Acknowledging the importance of some of these conceptual developments in behavior therapy, we will attempt to address the complexity of treatment decision making and the vicissitudes of individual patient development through the inclusion of a recursive analysis of two central variables.

Consideration of two important variables—vulnerability and self-efficacy—may lead the therapist and patient to reconsider what the subsequent steps in the treatment plan will be. We propose that the first construct, *vulnerability* factors, must be consistently monitored to help the patient maintain gains. With the rich fund of information amassed regarding relapse, forewarning the patient early of these risks can avert therapeutic backsliding; the awareness of these risks by both patient and therapist can also help regulate the pace of therapy. One Korean veteran, a PTSD alcoholic who was treated by one of the authors (FRA), showed significant improvement in response to implosive therapy and relapse-prevention training. Although the gains were remarkable, 1 full year after the most intensive part of therapy, other vulnerabilities in the area of anger management and his fear of loss of control arose in the context of an increasingly intimate relationship. As he became closer and more emotionally expressive, these feelings began to emerge. His "vulnerability profile" helped guide therapy well before these issues actually confronted the patient. Moreover, the patient himself experienced a great deal of control in anticipating these feelings prior to their occurrence.

The second construct that bears repeated scrutiny in each developmental stage is self-efficacy, or the confidence the patient has to engage in a particular behavior (Bandura, 1978a). Progress in therapy has been shown to be well predicted by changes in self-efficacy, even prior to enacting the early learned behavior (Bandura, 1982). Incorporating a repeated assessment of self-efficacy is particularly useful for periods of therapy in which changes progress at a slower rate, become stalled, or actually reverse. With the convergence of these disorders, it is common that anxiety will markedly diminish, but the broad goal of abstinence still remains. This may involve constructing an environment that promotes nondrug-related activities and severing or at least restricting old ties to alcohol and drug use. With these new challenges, we often observe a deflated sense of self-efficacy. Immediate interventions may be aimed at directly enhancing these self-perceptions through reminders of past success, setting even smaller goals in therapy, cognitive restructuring or taking a therapeutic "breather" (Goldfried & Robins, 1982).

Many long-term alcohol abusers have had little experience predicting the level of effort that therapy can require. What has commonly been observed as a process of denial can be operationalized as excessively high perceptions of self-efficacy. One recent study found that excessively high ratings of self-efficacy can predict relapse postdischarge in hospitalized alcoholics (Burling, Reilly, Moltzen, & Ziff, 1989). If the patient appears excessively self-assured or appears to be ignoring important details of his or her behavior, then interventions heightening the salience of ignored or minimized information can be therapeutically mobilizing.

SPECIFIC BEHAVIORAL INTERVENTIONS

Direct Therapeutic Exposure

Direct therapeutic exposure (DTE) has been operationally defined as repeated or extended exposure, either in vivo or in imagination, to objectively harmless but feared stimuli for the purpose of reducing anxiety (cf. Boudewyns & Shipley, 1983). Both graded (e.g., systematic desensitization) and nongraded (e.g., flooding and implosive therapy) forms of DTE have been applied to PTSD to reduce anxiety associated with intrusive memories of extreme events and exposure to stimuli or events that resemble aspects of the precipitating traumatic event. A review of the extant literature on the use of DTE for PTSD appears in the preceding chapter by Barbara Olasov Rothbaum and Edna Foa. For a review and discussion of the behavioral conceptual models from which DTE strategies are derived, the reader should refer to the earlier chapter by Foy and colleagues.

Recently, three independent research teams have completed controlled clinical trials of DTE for combat-related PTSD and have reported generally positive findings regarding the efficacy of this strategy for reducing PTSD symptomatology (Boudewyns & Hyer, 1990; Cooper & Clum, 1989; Keane, Fairbank, Caddell, & Zimering, 1989). In particular, DTE appears to be effective in reducing positive PTSD phenomena, including reexperiencing symptoms, sleep disturbance, hypersensitivity to sound, and state anxiety (Cooper & Clum, 1989; Keane et al., 1989).

Unfortunately, the encouraging findings from these controlled, outcome studies are difficult to generalize to the substantial population of patients with concurrent PTSD and substance abuse problems. In these studies, PTSD-substance abuse patients were either excluded from the study protocol (Boudewyns & Hyer, 1990) or the prevalence of concurrent substance abuse among study participants with a diagnosis of PTSD was not reported (Cooper & Clum, 1989; Keane et al., 1989). Thus, an important question that is largely unanswered involves the extent to which DTE is effective in the treatment of patients with comorbid PTSD and substance abuse.

Indeed, despite promising preliminary research findings on the utility of DTE for PTSD, some clinicians express reluctance to use this intervention with PTSD substance abusers. Recently, Litz, Blake, Gerardi, and Keane (1990) surveyed clinicians experienced in the use of DTE for PTSD and found that 27% consider "concurrent character or substance abuse disorder" as contraindicating the use of DTE with PTSD patients. One concern, for example, is that PTSD patients with longstanding problems with alcohol or drug dependence may experience cognitive deficits that impair their ability to image. Cognitive impairment could render ineffective DTE techniques based upon imaginal flooding. Another concern is that patients who rely on alcohol or illicit drugs as a primary coping strategy for PTSD symptoms may tolerate poorly the increased arousal elicited by exposure techniques. The concern expressed here is that DTE may increase the potential risk of relapse to alcohol or drug abuse among poorly stabilized PTSD substance abusers.

Although hypotheses about the utility of DTE for PTSD-substance abusers have yet to be tested empirically in randomized clinical trials, several studies using single case designs have reported that treating PTSD symptoms with DTE was associated with reductions in concurrent substance use. For example, Black and Keane (1982) treated a 55-year-old male naval veteran of World War II with severe anxiety associated with combat memories and a 10-year history of alcohol abuse. Treatment consisted of repeated imaginal exposure to two scenes involving traumatic combat experiences. Improved functioning, including decreased anxiety and alcohol abuse, occurred over 24 months of posttreatment follow-up. One episode of alcohol abuse occurred during the 24-month follow-up period.

Keane and Kaloupek (1982) reported reductions in PTSD symptoms and alcohol abuse in a Vietnam veteran following treatment for PTSD that included DTE as a major component of the intervention. The patient was a 36-year-old divorced male whose presenting problem was alcohol abuse (1 quart of gin per day for nearly 5 years) for which he was treated in a 4-week inpatient alcohol program. He returned intoxicated to two consecutive follow-up appointments, where it was learned that he was experiencing severe symptoms of combat-related PTSD. In this study, three extreme events that comprised the content of the veteran's intrusive memories of combat were presented repeatedly until they evoked low levels of anxiety relative to pretreatment levels. One-year follow-up indicated improvement across multiple domains of functioning, including no abusive drinking.

We often include DTE in action phase 1 because, as stated earlier, a major goal of treatment of the PTSD substance abuser is to reduce the distressing positive symptoms of PTSD: the various symptoms of reexperiencing and hyperarousal. We view the reduction of positive PTSD symptoms as essential to the treatment of most PTSD substance abusers, since positive PTSD symptoms per se are viewed by patients as major precipitants of alcohol and drug abuse relapse (Abueg et al., 1990).

Implementing DTE. Since imaginal flooding and implosive therapy are among the more frequently used DTE techniques for PTSD, we will focus our comments on these procedures (Fairbank & Brown, 1987; Brown, Abueg, & Fairbank, 1991). However, the reader should keep in mind that other forms of DTE may be appropriate, such as, for example, in vivo systematic desensitization.

Unfortunately, the utility of systematic desensitization for PTSD would appear to be diminished by the fact that it is frequently difficult to implement. For example, given the high levels of tonic and phasic arousal associated with PTSD (Malloy et al., 1983), we have found that PTSD patients have difficulty identifying meaningful low-level conditioned stimuli (CS) that they can tolerate while maintaining a relaxed state. Perhaps as a function of the relatively broad stimulus generalization gradient associated with PTSD, we have also found that the presentation of relevant "low-stress" stimuli often quickly elicits intrusive thoughts about "high-stress" traumatic stimuli in veterans with PTSD. As a result, progression through the stimulus hierarchy often occurs at an extremely slow pace. From the perspective of implosive theory, systematic desensitization is contraindicated because of the insufficient presentation of the CS complex. The potential for anxiety enhancement during partial CS presentation has been established in the laboratory but not in any human clinical studies (cf. Brown et al., 1991).

In implementing imaginal flooding or implosive therapy for PTSD, the therapist is confronted with three major tasks. The first of these involves setting the scene in which the extreme event occurred and presenting the details of the event in a meaningful way. Setting the scene is accomplished by describing the situation in which the specific event occurred—usually based on prior information obtained from the patient. In presenting the details of the extreme event, it is important to carefully describe both characteristics of the event itself and aspects of the patient's response at the time that the event occurred. Our experience has been that the more elaborate and complete the details of the extreme event, the better the responsivity of the patient. Accordingly, a full depiction of the extreme event should include details registered in all sensory modalities—sight, sound, smell, and touch. In general, we have found that it is most effective to elicit this information for the time periods immediately prior to, during, and following the traumatic event. Additionally, exposure should include the presentation of cues associated with the patient's response at the time of the event. Response cues should also be as rich in detail as possible, focusing on thoughts, emotions, somatic reactions, and feelings that the client experienced at the time of the event. Examples of clinical dialogues that demonstrate how to implement this component of imaginal flooding and implosive therapy with adult PTSD patients can be found in articles by Keane, Fairbank, Caddell, Zimering, and Bender (1985) and Lyons and Keane (1989). Examples from the child clinical area can also be found in articles by Saigh (1987a, 1987b). In a similar vein, Rychtarik, Silverman, Van Landingham, and Prue (1984) provide a description of imaginal flooding in the treatment of a 22-year-old incest victim.

A second key aspect of implementing imaginal flooding or implosive therapy is to monitor carefully the patient's reactions to the traumatic scene and to watch carefully for obvious and subtle signs of arousal to specific aspects of the scene. In working with combat veterans with PTSD, we have found that individuals vary greatly in their modes of expressed arousal and in the intensity of their arousal responses. Indicators of arousal during DTE may range from clearly observable changes in motoric activity (e.g., increased fidgeting and hand wringing) to subtle (yet detectable) changes in respiration (Fairbank et al., 1983).

A third critical component of implementing DTE is to encourage the patient to maintain exposure to the most salient aspects of the traumatic memory. In technical terms, this component of DTE is referred to as response prevention, which is the prevention of avoidance responses that are assumed to play a critical role in the maintenance of adverse arousal to reminders and memories of combat events. Operationally, response prevention is often accomplished by exposing the patient to the most meaningful aspects of the traumatic event repeatedly within a single session or over the course of sequential sessions. The reader is again referred to Keane et al. (1985), Saigh (1987a, 1987b), Rychtarik et al. (1984), and Lyons and Keane (1989) for practical guidelines on how to implement this component of DTE.

A legitimate question for treatment providers to ask is, How will my patient and I know when DTE is complete? The answer is criterion based. You will know that the goal of DTE for PTSD has been accomplished when memories and reminders of traumatic events cease to elicit dysfunctional levels of anxiety and arousal.

Problem-Solving Skills Training

Treatment providers have long observed that individuals with PTSD who abuse drugs and alcohol often have histories of poor problem solving. The daily lives of PTSD substance abusers often are chaotic and appear to evolve from one crisis to another. Alcohol- or drug-dependent individuals often act impulsively when confronted with a problem and fail to consider either the consequences of their actions or the possible range of alternative solutions (O'Farrell & Langenbucher, 1985). Deficits in effective problem solving often lead to unsatisfactory solutions, especially when drug or alcohol use is the solution for coping with problems. Clearly, patients who rely on drugs or alcohol as a strategy for coping with situational and emotional problems are at increased risk for continued substance abuse and relapse following treatment. Relapse among PTSD substance abusers is especially likely when they do not have the problem-solving skills necessary to cope with the stress of low-status employment, specific situations of the nonabusing world such as recreational alcohol use of co-workers, and the effort of maintaining gains made in treatment (cf. Platt & Metzger, 1987).

One promising intervention strategy is to teach PTSD substance abusers flexible, practical, and relevant skills for resolving problems associated with both PTSD and substance abuse. The purpose of problem-solving therapy is to teach an adaptive approach to resolving problems that will enhance the patient's self-efficacy and reduce the likelihood of alcohol or drug use. The general approach adopted by most problem-solving-oriented therapies is to teach individuals to adopt a multistep approach toward resolving problematic life situations (D'Zurilla, 1986; Goldfried & Davidson, 1976; Nezu, Nezu, & Perri, 1989; Platt, Taube, Metzger, & Duome, 1988; and Spivak, Platt, and Shure, 1976). The basic components of most problem-solving interventions include several interdependent processes, including (a) adopting a problem-solving orientation, (b) defining problems accurately, (c) generation of alternative solutions, (d) decision making, and (e) implementation and monitoring.

We recommend that at least one treatment session during action phase 1 be dedicated to each of the major component processes of problem solving (problem orientation, problem definition, generation of alternative solutions, decision making, and implementation). Our expectation is that earlier treatment sessions will require considerable instruction and training and may often be entirely dedicated to teaching basic problem-solving skills. For some patients, effective learning will occur relatively rapidly, such that later sessions will focus primarily on the maintenance and generalization of problem-solving skills. For these patients, the portion of a session dedicated to problem-solving skills maintenance may be comparatively small (e.g., 10 to 15 min.). In terms of implementing problem-solving therapy, we advocate the use of procedures that have been found to be effective in skills training in general, such as instruction, prompting, modeling, behavioral rehearsal or practice, homework assignments, shaping, reinforcement, and feedback.

The initial session of problem-solving skills training should focus on providing the patient with information on the rationale and relevance to PTSD, substance abuse, and other specific problem areas of each of the five major problem-solving operations. A clear presentation of the purpose and goals for problem-solving skills training should occur before actual training begins to increase the likelihood that the patient and treatment provider will operate from a common treatment framework.

The following is an example of a rationale for PTSD substance abusers adapted from Nezu et al. (1989).

> Another approach to treatment that I am recommending is problem-solving skills training. In addition to having to deal with the debilitating symptoms of PTSD, such as distressing and unwanted thoughts about extreme events, people who have PTSD usually have to cope with lots of other problems. These often include severe problems with family and friends; serious problems with employment and financial support; legal difficulties; and problems with alcohol, drugs, and other forms of psychological distress, such as depression. According to this approach, some people are especially prone to abusing alcohol when they think that they are unable to cope with symptoms of PTSD and other associated problems. Of course there are lots of reasons why people have difficulty coping. At times people are overwhelmed by the severity of their PTSD symptoms and other problems, and think that they can't do anything to change these problems. At other times people are unable to cope because they don't know how to deal with a particular problem because they never learned the skills necessary to effectively resolve problems. Clearly, the kinds of things that we think and do when confronted with a problem will have a big influence on how effectively we cope with and resolve it. Effective problem solving is a skill that has many components that are likely to be helpful in learning to resolve problems associated with having PTSD. We will be focusing on five major components of problem solving: how we think about problems associated with PTSD; how we define these problems; how we arrive at solutions; how we make decisions about what to do to solve a problem; and how we go about implementing the solution and determining how well it worked.

Training in Adopting a Problem-Solving Orientation. In this initial stage the clinician focuses on teaching the patient how to adopt a problem-solving coping style when confronted with problems. It is important to explain this step carefully to patients, as PTSD substance abusers commonly react impulsively when confronted with a problem. Nezu et al. (1989) have suggested that training in this stage be geared toward providing patients with a rational orientation to problems in living and problem solving as a means of coping effectively. They recommend that goals include encouraging the patient to adopt the following aspects of a positive and realistic orientation: (a) acceptance of problems as a normal part of living; (b) belief in one's ability to solve problems effectively; (c) labeling of one's experience of distress as a cue that a problem exists; (d) inhibiting the tendency to respond automatically or impulsively and developing the ability to think things through carefully; and (e) recognizing that problem resolution often entails considerable time and effort.

Many PTSD substance abusers, whose reflexive reactions to problems are elicited by high levels of anxiety, may benefit from training in the use of self-control calming strategies. In our experience, an intervention that appears to be helpful to PTSD substance abusers who are unable to "stop and think" because of overwhelming anxiety is relaxation training using progressive muscle tense-and-release procedures and cue-controlled relaxation strategies (e.g., Bernstein & Borkovec, 1973; Fairbank, Gross, & Keane, 1983). The thesis here is that once the patient is able to calm down and arrest "out-of-control" thoughts, anxiety, and arousal, she or he can begin the process of thinking things through logically and carefully. An example of a script for relaxation training is contained in the preceding chapter by Olasov Rothbaum and Foa.

Training in Defining Problems and Setting Goals. In this stage, you should help the patient to develop skills that will enable him or her to understand the problems at hand. Not uncommonly, PTSD substance abusers have unspecified, vague, or very general presenting complaints (e.g., "My nerves are shot and I need some help," "My old lady is driving me nuts"). The overall goal of this stage of problem-solving training is to teach patients to be able to define and formulate problems on their own and in a manner that permits the implementation of subsequent steps. As noted by Nezu et al. (1989), this may be accomplished by teaching the patient to (a) seek all available facts and information about the situation; (b) describe the facts in clear and unambiguous terms; (c) identify those factors that actually make the situation a problem; (d) differentiate relevant from irrelevant information and objective facts from unverified assumptions and interpretations; and (e) set realistic problem-solving goals.

As recommended by D'Zurilla (1986), this task can be facilitated by asking *who, what, when, where,* and *why* questions about each problem. Who is involved? What happens (or does not happen) that bothers you? Where does it happen? Why does it happen (i.e., known causes or reasons for the problem)? What is your response to the situation (i.e., actions, thoughts, and feelings)?

Below is an abbreviated excerpt from a session that focuses on the issue of problem definition and formulation.

Therapist: Tell me again what happened when the nurse gave you your medication today?

Patient: She insulted me. She threw the meds at me. I tell you, the woman hates me.

Therapist: You are telling me that the nurse told you that she hates you.

Patient: No, she didn't say that. She didn't have to. The way that she threw the cup at me was clear enough. It makes me mad. She wouldn't treat a dog that way. It's insulting.

Therapist: Describe the circumstances at the nurses' station this morning.

Patient: Well, as usual, it was busy. There were more folks in line than usual, though. Only that nasty nurse was on duty.

Therapist: Describe exactly what happened when you received your medication. As we've discussed before, give me a brief, clear, and accurate description of the event itself, with no interpretive language.

Patient: After waiting about 20 minutes I finally got to the front of the line. She gave me my meds and ordered me to take them fast.

Therapist: She ordered you? What did she say exactly?

Patient: Dave, quick, down the hatch, we're busy today (client laughs).

One of the things that occurred in this example of a dialogue was the evolution of the patient's emotional, exaggerated, and overstated description of a problematic interpersonal interaction to a brief description of the event itself with no speculation as to hidden meanings. Frequently, therapists choose to begin the process of problem-definition training by focusing on examples of recent problems of relatively minor significance to the patient. Once the patient has demonstrated the ability to define minor problems accurately, then he or she is ready to advance to the more difficult task of objectively defining problems of a more severe nature.

Training in Generation of Alternative Solutions. In this process, the therapist teaches the patient to generate a range of possible solutions to problems using brainstorming techniques. In the following passage, Nezu et al. (1989) provide an excellent rationale for the importance of this process to effective problem solving.

> Training patients to develop a range of coping options is based on the premise that the availability of a large number of alternative actions will increase the chances of eventually identifying an effective solution. Often patients expect that there is one right answer for each problem and that therapy, or the therapist, will provide it for them. Moreover, in trying to find the right solution to a problem, patients sometimes believe that the first idea that comes to mind is the best one. Therefore, in order to maximize problem-solving effectiveness, the therapist needs to convey to patients the necessity of generating as many different options as possible (p. 180).

The two key aspects of brainstorming—quantity and deferment of judgment—suggest the following rules. First, generate as many ideas as possible. Second, don't criticize the ideas at this stage of problem solving. It is important to note within this context that PTSD substance abusers often complain that they are unable to brainstorm because they can't imagine that there are other solutions to their problems. Therapists are advised to be persistent, tenacious, and patient with attempts to avoid this essential aspect of problem solving. Therapists are also advised against passively accepting standard complaints such as "I can't think of any other solution to this problem. Besides, if I could, I wouldn't need to come see you." Indeed, therapists should strongly resist the temptation to accept a patient's insistence on helplessness regarding the generation of solutions.

PTSD substance abusers also often have difficulty generating alternatives without immediately evaluating and rejecting them. Through repeated practice and reinforcement, the therapist teaches the patient to generate as complete a list as possible of alternative solutions prior to proceeding to the next stage of problem solving (i.e., decision making).

Training in Decision Making. At this stage, the therapist teaches the patient to predict which alternative solutions are worth pursuing and then to take action. Therapists discuss each potential solution with the patient and encourage him or her to anticipate the likely long-term and short-term consequences of each alternative. In addition, patients should be urged to evaluate the usefulness of each of these consequences for resolving the problem situation.

Resick and Jordan (1988) have noted that when patients have difficulty choosing among the alternatives, it is often helpful to have them assign weights (i.e., scores) to the positive and negative consequences to estimate their relative importance. For example, positive consequences could receive scores from 1 to 100, while negative consequences could be assigned scores from -1 to -100. Although one alternative may have a longer list of positive consequences, it may also have more important drawbacks, while another alternative has fewer important drawbacks and more important gains. While the patient is unlikely to base his or her final decision only upon the total score obtained from the weightings, the process may help the patient in determining what factors are most important in deciding upon a course of action.

Training in Implementing Solutions and Monitoring Effectiveness. At this stage, the patient is encouraged to carry out the selected course of action. Some patients are likely to need considerable encouragement at this stage of problem-solving counseling, given that many of the men and women in treatment for PTSD substance abuse use avoidance as a major coping strategy. Toward this end, the therapist urges the patient to observe the consequences of his or her actions and the actions of the therapist or others who serve as problem-solving role models. It is also important to train the patient to match real outcomes of the solution against the expected or predicted outcomes. If the match is satisfactory, the problem-solving process is complete. If the match is unsatisfactory, the patient should return to step 2—problem definition.

This approach is based on the thesis that problem solving is a skill that PTSD substance abuse patients can learn to use effectively to cope with a variety of problem situations. Whether it is learning how to resolve a conflict with one's employer, control explosive anger episodes with one's family, or avoid the places and people associated with drug abuse, the goal is to teach the patient practical and flexible problem-solving skills. As an intervention for PTSD substance abuse, problem-solving skills training shapes new, more adaptive behaviors for coping with PTSD symptoms that may trigger episodes of alcohol or drug use and relapse.

Relapse-Prevention Training (RPT)

G. Alan Marlatt and his colleagues (Marlatt & Gordon, 1985) have developed one of the most comprehensive addiction treatment models based upon constructs of social learning, particularly Bandura's self-efficacy theory (Bandura, 1978a). Marlatt's model holds that addiction is a habit that can be altered through active behavioral and cognitive methods. Most central to his theorizing, however, is that without a growing sense of self-control over the habit, the individual is highly prone to return to using the substance. This fact has been borne out by the high relapse rates in the addictions regardless of treatment strategy.

Marlatt and Gordon (1980) addressed the lack of attention to the maintenance of abstinence by analyzing in depth the relapse process. First, the ex-addict's expectation of the immediate positive effects of using the substance combines with both the actual initial reinforcing sensations of consumption and social/situational pressures that encourage a "slip" (high-risk situations). Second, the individual experiences what Marlatt called the abstinence violation effect (AVE), a cognitive process that further increases the probability of a complete relapse. Guilt is central to the AVE ("I've engaged in a proscribed behavior.") as well as negative global self-attributions to reduce cognitive dissonance ("If I take a drink then I must be weak. Yeah, I'm a drunk".) (Curry, Marlatt, & Gordon, 1987). Marlatt uses the construct of self-efficacy—confidence in one's ability to engage in a particular behavior—in this case resisting the urge—as a predictor of abstinence and resistance to relapse in high-risk situations.

The relapse prevention model provides a strong conceptual framework for coping, or failures to cope, among individuals with PTSD and alcohol problems. Three areas are especially relevant to this population, as observed consistently in our clinical work:

1.   The PTSD victim's high-risk situations are numerous. Beyond emotional states similar to original traumatic situations (e.g., loss, guilt, disappointment, confusion), the actual symptoms of PTSD (e.g., cognitive intrusions, sleep loss, social avoidance) are extremely high-risk cues.

2.   Global attributions of low self-efficacy are prevalent, and resistance to high-risk situations such as those cited above is consequently quite low.

3.   The PTSD patient has rather severe self-attributions regarding failure. For example, combat training compels the soldier to acquire the notion

that mistakes can be lethal; actual loss of life due to errors only strengthens that belief or expectancy. The AVE appears to be especially severe for the traumatized patient.

Abueg et al. (1989) conducted a two-group outcome study of relapse-prevention training as an adjunct to a full-spectrum inpatient hospitalization for PTSD. Forty-two well-diagnosed PTSD alcoholics received RPT, a 12-session treatment adapted to attend to the special needs of these patients; 42 patients did not receive the additional intervention. At a 6-month follow-up, 63% of the experimental RPT group had not returned to drinking, as compared to 41% of the controls who were abstinent. Modified RPT successfully forestalled a return to drinking. Relapse rates converged at 9-month follow-ups (44% of experimental groups versus 38% of controls abstinent), but the treated group showed a significantly lower degree of relapse, as measured by self-reported number of drinks consumed.

Modified Relapse-Prevention Training for PTSD Substance Abusers. Given the comorbidity of PTSD and alcoholism and the fact that the high-risk situations or stimuli for drinking behaviors are generalizations or representations of traumatic experiences, successful intervention must necessarily include identification and recognition of these high-risk profiles by the patient. The identification and exploration of these high-risk or trauma experiences is often best accomplished in a group designed for this purpose (i.e., a "trauma focus group"). In the program described here, the formal relapse-prevention groups are conducted concurrent with or after the patients have completed their focus group or DTE; such timing provides the foundation for identifying unique high-risk areas. This focus work is built on and extended in the relapse-prevention groups as each member's "road to relapse" is explored in depth. The self-knowledge gained in working on trauma experiences from their past is an important first step in the prevention of relapse in this population.

The modified relapse-prevention training takes place in 8-12 sessions. In keeping with the social learning model, these sessions include didactic and experiential components of role play and imagery as the primary methods of teaching. Ongoing assessment in the form of both process and outcome measures is also conducted throughout the period of intervention and as follow-up after its completion. One relapse prevention treatment manual is available specifically for Vietnam veterans with the dual diagnosis (Abueg & Kriegler, 1988).

After the provision of a statement of the purpose, goals, and method of the group, the initial session continues with an exploration of the members' expectations, both of drinking and of failure (i.e., their attributions and personal definitions of relapse). A didactic segment is repeated on the long- vs. the short-term consequences of alcohol consumption. In sessions 2 and 3 this is followed by an initial assessment of each member's potential high-risk situations based on history and their own expectations. This is accomplished through group discussion of trauma-related issues and experiences from the past through imagery of their first "failure" experience, a discussion of those experiences and their emotional responses to these experiences, and written assignments. The Annis Situational Confidence Questionnaire (SCQ-39) is especially useful as a springboard for identifying particular areas of low self-efficacy to resist the urge to drink (Annis, 1985).

Based on the information gathered in these sessions, each member's "high-risk profile" and their potential "roads to relapse" are mapped out or defined. The following session is focused on the development of stimulus-control strategies—that is, skills that will help to reduce the patient's opportunity to drink. Such opportunities include the development of new or alternative social support networks or cognitive techniques to manage negative or high-risk emotions identified for each patient. Extensive role play and the use of relaxation and imagery (visualization) techniques are employed during this session. Continued problem solving of daily high-risk situations is discussed in sessions 5 and 6.

In these sessions, stimulus-control and cognitive techniques including problem solving and thought stopping are emphasized. Two sessions are devoted to an additional technique based upon the cue reactivity literature, alluded to earlier in this chapter. If alcohol- or drug-related cues evoke less psychophysiological and cognitive urges, then relapse risk would be presumably lowered. Subjective reports suggest that this may be the most memorable aspect of modified relapse-prevention training for PTSD alcoholics.

Patients are asked to picture the "relapse fantasy" in imagination up to the point of alcohol or drug use without letting the substance use occur. After obtaining two scenes per patient, positive coping imagery is employed to "turn the drinking scene around," thus strengthening alternative coping responses. These scenes are often quite revealing and provide substantive core themes to be used for later drink-refusal role playing or further problem solving.

The two sessions to follow (7 and 8) are devoted to drink-refusal training. This involves using visualization techniques in which the group members imagine themselves in an actual high-risk situation complete with feelings, sensations, and potential urge to drink. Then they are asked what type of response they would provide to an offer of a drink in the context of the situation they had just visualized. The various responses are discussed in terms of their probability for success, and alternatives are generated. Three types of refusals are highlighted: aggressive, assertive, and passive refusals. The potential difficulties encountered when using the first and third types of refusal are highlighted. Once each member has produced an assertive drink-refusal strategy appropriate to his or her situation, the entire sequence (entering a high-risk situation, being offered a drink, and using an assertive drink refusal strategy) is enacted through role play. In the following session, drink-refusal training continues. However, at this point the learning involves in vivo exposure to actual drink stimuli. That is, patients are asked to participate in a reenactment of their imagined high-risk situation through role play involving an actual refusal of their drink of choice.

The following session involves preparation for coping with actual relapse through a discussion of the "abstinence violation effect" (AVE), the reaction they will have when they take their first drink after not drinking for some period of time. Coping with the guilt this behavior induces and working on the negative attributions or labeling that may follow is the focus of this work. If patients react by assigning global, internal, stable attributions about this behavior (e.g., "See, I am a drunk. I can't do anything right. I might as well keep on drinking since there really is no hope," etc.), then the AVE will be greater and the potential for a full-blown relapse is also greater. If patients are able to assign specific, external, unstable attributions to this behavior (i.e., to identify the high-risk situational or affective characteristics surrounding their behavior), and to generate coping strategies to alter the course of their behavior, then the relapse becomes a learning experience rather than a failure experience, and feelings of self-efficacy can be restored or maintained. The final two to three sessions involve the establishment of a "buddy system," final evaluation of skills, and arrangements for follow-up with the patient.

SUMMARY AND FUTURE
DIRECTIONS

We have learned much about the complexity of PTSD over the course of the past decade. Our growing base of information includes the knowledge that chronic PTSD frequently co-occurs with substance abuse. Unfortunately, clinical experience has shown that PTSD and substance abuse comorbidities are especially difficult and challenging to treat. In this chapter, we have presented the conceptual basis and operational components of a behavioral multidimensional stage model for treating the PTSD substance abuser.

Research and clinical practice need to answer many basic questions regarding the efficacy and utility of behavioral stage interventions for treating PTSD substance abusers. Among the many important questions that should be addressed are: (a) What is the efficacy of this intervention as measured by changes in PTSD symptomatology, alcohol abuse, and other important psychosocial outcomes? (b) Which components and stages of the model contribute to treatment outcome? (c) What is the relationship between important client characteristics (e.g., level of impairment, self-efficacy, and expectations of treatment) and outcome? (d) To what extent does this intervention generalize to PTSD substance-abusing victims of other types of extreme events (e.g., violent crime, sexual assault, natural or technological disasters) and what modifications should be made to the treatment protocol for various populations of trauma survivors? (e) To what extent is this intervention effective for individuals with PTSD who abuse other substances besides alcohol (e.g., illicit opioids and cocaine)? (f) To what extent can this intervention be implemented in other settings, such as community-based outpatient treatment programs? Future progress in successfully treating individuals with PTSD and substance abuse is linked to our ability to answer these and other questions about the interventions that we design for this complex comorbidity.

REFERENCES

Abueg, F. R., Chun, K., & Lurie, D. (1990, August). Precipitants to alcohol relapse among PTSD-alcoholics. In T. M. Keane (Chair), *Recent advances in the study of combat-related post-traumatic stress disorder.* Symposium conducted at the annual meeting of the American Psychological Association, Boston.

Abueg, F. R., Dondershine, H., & Gusman, F. D. (1989, October). Relapse vulnerability in PTSD-substance abuse: An integrated model for service delivery. In R. Zimering (Chair), *Co-morbidity in combat veterans.* Symposium conducted at the annual meeting of the Society for Traumatic Stress Studies, San Francisco.

Abueg, F. R., & Kriegler, J. A. (1988). *Treatment manual for modified relapse prevention training in PTSD-substance abusers.* Unpublished manuscript. National Center for PTSD, 3801 Miranda Ave (323-A8-MP), Palo Alto, CA 94304.

Abueg, F. R., Kriegler, J., Falcon, H., Dondershine, H., & Gusman, F. (1989, November). Relapse prevention training with PTSD-Alcoholics: A treatment outcome study with one year followup. In F. Abueg (Chair), *Co-morbidity in traumatic stress disorders with special attention to substance abuse and dependence.* Symposium conducted at the annual meeting of the Association for Advancement of Behavior Therapy, Washington, DC.

American Psychiatric Association (1980). *Diagnostic and statistical manual of mental disorders* (3rd ed.). Washington, DC: Author.

Annis, H. (1985). Situational confidence questionnaire-39 (SCQ-39). Alcohol Research Foundation, Toronto.

Bandura, A. (1978a). Self-efficacy: Toward a unifying theory of behavior change. *Psychological Review, 84,* 191–215.

Bandura, A. (1978b). The self-system in reciprocal determinism. *American Psychologist, 33,* 344–358.

Bandura, A. (1982). Self-efficacy mechanism in human agency. *American Psychologist, 37,* 122–147.

Bandura, A., & Schunk, D.H. (1981). Cultivating competence, self-efficacy, and intrinsic interest through proximal self-motivation. *Journal of Personality and Social Psychology, 43,* 5–21.

Bean-Bayog, M. (1988). Alcoholism as a cause of psychopathology. *Hospital and Community Psychiatry, 39,* 352–354.

Berman, S., Price, S., & Gusman, F.D. (1982). An inpatient program for Vietnam combat veterans in a Veterans Administration hospital. *Hospital and Community Psychiatry, 42,* 115–119.

Bernstein, D. A., & Borkovec, T. D. (1973). *Progressive relaxation training.* Champaign, IL: Research Press.

Black, J. L., & Keane, T. M. (1982). Implosive therapy in the treatment of combat related fears in a World War II veteran. *Behavior Therapy, 13*(2), 163–165.

Blanchard, E. B., Kolb, L. C., Pallmeyer, T. P., & Gerardi, R. J. (1982). The development of a psychophysiological assessment procedure for post traumatic stress disorder in Vietnam veterans. *Psychiatric Quarterly, 4,* 220–229.

Boudewyns, P. A. (1989, November). Concurrent psychiatric diagnoses (comorbidity) in Vietnam veterans with PTSD: Treatment implications. In F. Abueg (Chair), *Comorbidity in traumatic stress disorders with special attention to substance abuse and dependence.* Symposium conducted at the annual meeting of the Association for Advancement of Behavior Therapy, Washington, DC.

Boudewyns, P. A., & Hyer, L. (1990). Physiological response to combat memories and preliminary treatment outcome in Vietnam veteran PTSD patients treated with direct therapeutic exposure. *Behavior Therapy, 21,* 63–87.

Boudewyns, P. A., & Shipley, R. H. (1983). *Flooding and implosive therapy.* New York: Plenum Publishing.

Brinson, T., & Treanor, V. (1988). Alcoholism and posttraumatic stress disorder among combat Vietnam veterans. *Alcoholism Treatment Quarterly, 5*(3/4), 65–83.

Brown, T. A., Abueg, F. R., & Fairbank, J. A. (1991). Patterns of adjustment following exposure to extreme events: Psychological aftermath of combat and sexual assault. In M. S. Gibbs, J. R. Lachenmeyer, & J. Sigal (Eds.), *Community Psychology and Mental Health.* New York: Gardner.

Brown, S. A., Goldman, M. S., & Christiansen, B. A. (1985). Do alcohol expectancies mediate drinking patterns of adults? *Journal of Consulting and Clinical Psychology, 53,* 512–519.

Brown, S. A., Goldman, M. S., Inn, A., & Anderson, L. R. (1980). Expectations of reinforcement from alcohol: Their domain and relation to drinking patterns. *Journal of Consulting and Clinical Psychology, 48,* 419–426.

Brownell, K. D., Marlatt, G. A., Lichtenstein, E., & Wilson, G.T. (1986). Understanding and preventing relapse. *American Psychologist, 41*(7), 765–782.

Burling, T. A., Reilly, P. M., Moltzen, J. O., & Ziff, D. C. (1989). Self-efficacy and relapse among inpatient drug and alcohol abusers: A predictor of outcome. *Journal of Studies on Alcohol, 50*(4), 354–360.

Chief Medical Director's Special Committee on PTSD. (1987). *Third Annual Report of the Chief Medical Director's Special Committee on PTSD.* Washington: Veterans Administration Central Office.

Cooney, N. L., Gillespie, R. A., Baker, L. H., & Kaplan, R. F. (1987). Cognitive changes after alcohol cue exposure. *Journal of Consulting and Clinical Psychology, 55,* 150–155.

Cooper, N. A., & Clum, G. A. (1989). Imaginal flooding as a supplementary treatment for PTSD in combat veterans: A controlled study. *Behavior Therapy, 20,* 381–391.

Curry, S., Marlatt, G. A., & Gordon, J. R. (1987). Abstinence violation effect: Validation of an attributional construct with smoking cessation. *Journal of Consulting and Clinical Psychology, 55,* 145–149.

Davidson, J. R. T., Kudler, H. S., Saunders, W. B., & Smith, R. D. (1990). Symptom and comorbidity patterns in World War II and Vietnam veterans with posttraumatic stress disorder. *Comprehensive Psychiatry, 31*(2), 162–170.

Dorus, W., & Senay, E. C. (1980). Depression, demographic dimensions, and drug abuse. *American Journal of Psychiatry, 137,* 699–704.

D'Zurilla, T. J. (1986). *Problem-Solving Therapy: A social competence approach to clinical intervention.* New York: Springer.

Endicott, J., & Spitzer, R. L. (1978). A diagnostic interview: The Schedule for Affective Disorders and Schizophrenia. *Archives of General Psychiatry, 35,* 837–844.

Evans, I. M. (1985). Building systems models as a strategy for target behavior selection in clinical assessment. *Behavioral Assessment, 7,* 21–32.

Fairbank, J. A., & Brown, T. A. (1987). Current behavioral approaches to the treatment of post-traumatic stress disorder. *The Behavior Therapist, 10,* 57–64.

Fairbank, J. A., Gross, R. T., & Keane, T. M. (1983). Treatment of posttraumatic stress disorder: Evaluation of outcome with a behavioral code. *Behavior Modification, 7,* 557–568.

Fairbank, J. A., Hansen, D. J., & Fitterling, J. M. (1991). Patterns of appraisal and coping across different stressor conditions among former prisoners of war with and without posttraumatic stress disorder. *Journal of Consulting and Clinical Psychology, 59,* 274–281.

Foa, E. B., Steketee, G., & Olasov Rothbaum, B. (1989). Behavioral/cognitive conceptualizations of post-traumatic stress disorder. *Behavior Therapy, 20,* 155–176.

Friedman, M. J. (1990). Interrelationships between biological mechanisms and pharmacotherapy of posttraumatic stress disorder (PTSD). In M. E. Wolfe & A. D. Mosnaim (Eds.), *Post-traumatic stress disorder: Etiology, phenomenology, and treatment* (pp. 204–225). American Psychiatric Press.

Gerardi, R. J., Keane, T. M., Cahoon, B. J., & Klauminzer, G. W. (1989, November). *Physiological arousal in Vietnam veterans: Hyperarousal or hyperreactivity?* Paper presented at the annual meeting of the Association for Advancement of Behavior Therapy, Washington, DC.

Gerstley, L. J., Alterman, A. I., McLellan, A. T., & Woody, G. E. (1990). Antisocial personality disorder in patients with substance abuse disorders: A problematic diagnosis? *American Journal of Psychiatry, 147*(2), 173–178.

Goldfried, M. R., & Davison, G. C. (1976). *Clinical behavior therapy.* New York: Holt, Rinehart and Winston.

Goldfried, M., & Robins, C. (1982). On the facilitation of self-efficacy. *Cognitive Therapy & Research, 6,* 361–380.

Green, B. L., Lindy, J. D., Grace, M. C., & Gleser, G. C. (1989). Multiple diagnosis in posttraumatic stress disorder: The role of war stressors. *The Journal of Nervous and Mental Disease, 177*(6), 329–335.

Hodgson, R. J., Stockwell, T. R., & Rankin, H. J. (1979). Can alcohol reduce tension? *Behaviour Research & Therapy, 17,* 459–466.

Jellinek, J. M., & Williams, T. (1984). Post-traumatic stress disorder and substance abuse in Vietnam combat veterans: Treatment problems, strategies, and recommendations. *Journal of Substance Abuse Treatment, 1,* 87–97.

Jellinek, J. M., & Williams, T. (1987). Post-traumatic stress disorder and substance abuse: Treatment problems, strategies, and recommendations. In T. Williams (Ed.), *PTSD: A handbook for clinicians.* Cincinnati: Disabled American Veterans.

Kaplan, R. F., Meyer, R. E., & Stroebel, C. F. (1983). Alcohol dependence and responsivity to an ethanol stimulus as predictors of alcohol consumption. *British Journal of Addiction, 78,* 259–267.

Kaylor, J. A., King, D. W., & King, L. A. (1987). Psychological effects of military service in Vietnam: A meta-analysis. *Psychological Bulletin, 102*(2), 257–271.

Keane, T. M. (1989). Post-traumatic stress disorder: Current status and future directions. *Behavior Therapy, 20,* 149–153.

Keane, T. M., Fairbank, J. A., Caddell, J. M., Zimering, R. T., & Bender, M. E. (1985). A behavioral approach to assessing and treating post-traumatic stress disorder in Vietnam veterans. In C. R. Figley (ed.), *Trauma and its wake* (pp. 257–294). New York: Brunner/Mazel.

Keane, T. M., Fairbank, J. A., Caddell, J. M., & Zimering, R. T. (1989). Implosive (flooding) therapy reduces symptoms of post-traumatic stress disorder in Vietnam combat veterans. *Behavior Therapy, 20,* 245–260.

Keane, T. M., Gerardi, R. J., Lyons, J. A., & Wolfe, J. (1988). The interrelationship of substance abuse and posttraumatic stress disorder. In M. Galanter (Ed.), *Recent Developments in Alcoholism,* Vol. 6 (pp. 27–48). New York: Plenum Publishing.

Keane, T. M., & Kaloupek, D. G. (1982). Imaginal flooding in the treatment of a post-traumatic stress disorder. *Journal of Consulting and Clinical Psychology, 50,* 138–140.

Keane, T. M., Scott, W. O., Chavoya, G. A., Lamparski, D., & Fairbank, J. A. (1985). Social support in Vietnam veterans with post-traumatic stress disorder: A comparative analysis. *Journal of Consulting and Clinical Psychology, 53,* 95–102.

Keane, T. M., & Wolfe, J. (1990). Comorbidity in post-traumatic stress disorder: An analysis of community and clinical studies. *Journal of Applied Social Psychology, 20,* 1776–1788.

Khantzian, E. J. (1985). The self-medication hypothesis of addictive disorders: Focus on heroin and cocaine dependence. *American Journal of Psychiatry, 143,* 1259–1264.

Kilpatrick, D. G. (1990, August). *Violence as a precursor of women's substance abuse: The rest of the drugs-violence story.* Paper presented at the annual meeting of The American Psychological Association, Boston.

Kolb, L. C. (1987). A neuropsychological hypothesis explaining post traumatic stress disorders. *American Journal of Psychiatry, 144,* 989–995.

Kosten, T. R., & Krystal, J. (1988). Biological mechanisms in post-traumatic stress disorder: Relevance for substance abuse. In M. Galanter (Ed.), *Recent developments in alcoholism,* Vol. 6. New York: Plenum Publishing.

Kosten, T. R., Rounsaville, B. J., & Kleber, H. D. (1983). Concurrent validity of the Addiction Severity Index. *Journal of Nervous and Mental Disease, 171,* 606–610.

Kulka, R. A., Schlenger, W. E., Fairbank, J. A., Hough, R. L., Jordan, B. K., Marmar, C. R., & Weiss, D. S. (1990). *Trauma and the Vietnam War generation.* New York: Brunner/Mazel.

Kuhne, A., Nohner, W., & Baraga, E. (1986). Efficacy of chemical dependency treatment as a function of combat in Vietnam. *Journal of Substance Abuse Treatment, 3,* 191–194.

Kushner, M. G., Sher, K. J., & Beitman, B. D. (1990). The relationship between alcohol problems and the anxiety disorders. *The American Journal of Psychiatry, 147,* 685–695.

Laberg, J. C., & Effertsen, B. (1987). Psychophysiological indicators of craving in alcoholics: Effects of cue exposure. *British Journal of Addiction, 82,* 1341–1348.

LaPorte, D. J., McLellan, A. T., O'Brien, C. P., & Marshall, J. R. (1981). Treatment response in psychiatrically impaired drug abusers. *Comprehensive Psychiatry, 22,* 411–419.

Lazarus, R. (1971). *Behavior therapy and beyond.* New York: McGraw-Hill.

Lehmann, L. (1990). Perspectives on PTSD. *National Center for PTSD: A Clinical Newsletter, 1,* 5.

Litt, M. D., Cooney, N. L., Kadden, R. M., & Gaupp, L. (1990). Reactivity to alcohol cues and induced moods in alcoholics. *Addictive Behaviors, 15,* 137–146.

Litz, B. T., Blake, D. D., Gerardi, R. G., & Keane, T. M. (1990). Decision making guidelines for the use of direct therapeutic exposure in the treatment of post-traumatic stress disorder. *Behavior Therapy, 13*(4), 91–93.

Lyons, J. A., & Keane, T. M. (1989). Implosive therapy for the treatment of combat-related PTSD. *Journal of Traumatic Stress, 2*(2), 137–152.

Lyons, J. S., McGovern, M. P. (1989). Use of mental health services by dually diagnosed patients. *Hospital and Community Psychiatry, 40*(10), 1067–1069.

McFarland, R. E. (1985). Post-traumatic stress disorder and concurrent psychiatric illness. *Psychotherapy in Private Practice, 3*(4), 55–58.

McLellan, A. T., Childress, A. R., Griffith, J., & Woody, G. G. (1984). The psychiatrically severe drug abuse patient: Methadone maintenance or therapeutic community? *American Journal of Drug and Alcohol Abuse, 10,* 77–95.

Malloy, P. F., Fairbank, J. A., & Keane, T. M. (1983). Validation of a multimethod assessment of posttraumatic stress disorders in Vietnam veterans. *Journal of Consulting and Clinical Psychology, 51,* 488–494.

Marlatt, G. A., & Gordon, J. R. (1980). Determinants of relapse: Implications for the maintenance of behavior change. In P.O. Davidson & J. Davidson (Eds.), *Behavioral medicine: Changing lifestyles.* New York: Brunner Mazel.

Marlatt, G. A., & Gordon, J. (1985). *Relapse Prevention.* New York: Guilford Press.

Miller, W. R. (1985). Motivation for treatment: A review with special emphasis on alcoholism. *Psychological Bulletin, 98*(1), 84–107.

Moos, R. (1990). *Alcoholism treatment evaluation: Process and outcome.* London: Oxford University Press.

Neff, J. A., & Husiani, B. A. (1982). Life events drinking patterns and depressive symptomatology. *Journal of Studies on Alcohol, 43,* 301–318.

Nezu, A. M., Nezu, C. M., & Perri, M. G. (1989). *Problem-solving therapy for depression: Theory, research, and clinical guidelines.* New York: John Wiley & Sons.

Niaura, R. S., Rohsenow, D. J., Binkoff, J. A., Monti, P. M., Pedraza, M., & Abrams, D. B. (1988). Relevance of cue reactivity to understanding alcohol and smoking relapse. *Journal of Abnormal Psychology, 97,* 133–152.

O'Farrell, T. J., & Langenbucher, J. W. (1985). Alcohol abuse. In M. Hersen (Ed.), *Practice of inpatient behavior therapy: A clinical guide.* Orlando: Grune & Stratton.

Penk, W. E., Peck, R. F., Robinowitz, R., Bell, W., & Little, D. (1988). Coping and defending styles among Vietnam combat veterans seeking treatment for posttraumatic stress disorder and substance use disorder. *Substance Abuse and Posttraumatic Stress Disorder, 6,* 69–88.

Penk, W. E., Robinowitz, R., Roberts, W. R., Patterson, E. T., Dolan, M. P., & Atkins, H. G. (1981). Adjustment differences among male substance abusers varying in degree of combat experience in Vietnam. *Journal of Consulting and Clinical Psychology, 49,* 426–437.

Perconte, S. T., Griger, M. L., & Bellucci, G. (1989). Relapse and rehospitalization rates of veterans two years after treatment for PTSD. *Hospital and Community Psychiatry, 40,* 1072–1073.

Platt, J. J., & Metzger, D. S. (1987). Cognitive interpersonal problem-solving skills and the maintenance of treatment success in heroin addicts. *Psychology of Addictive Behaviors, 1*(1), 5–13.

Platt, J. J., Taube, D. O., Metzger, D. S., & Duome, M. J. (1988). Training in interpersonal problem solving (TIPS). *Journal of Cognitive Psychotherapy: An International Quarterly, 2,* 5–34.

Pomerleau, O. F., Fertig, J., Baker, L., & Cooney, N. (1983). Reactivity to alcohol cues in alcoholics and nonalcoholics: Implications for a stimulus control analysis of drinking. *Addictive Behaviors, 8,* 1–10.

Poulos, C.X., Hinson, R.E., & Siegel, S. (1981). The role of Pavlovian processes in drug tolerance and dependence: Implications for treatment. *Addictive Behaviors, 6,* 205–211.

Prochaska, J., & DiClemente, C. (1983). Stages and processes of self-change of smoking: Toward an integrative model of change. *Journal of Consulting and Clinical Psychology, 51,* 390–395.

Resick, P. A., & Jordan, C. G. (1988). Group stress inoculation training for victims of sexual assault: A therapists manual. In P. A. Keller & Heyman, S. (Eds.), *Innovations in clinical practice: A source book,* Vol. 7. Sarasota, FL: Professional Resource Exchange.

Risse, S. C., Whitter, A., Burke, J., Chen, S., Scurfield, R. M., & Raskand, M. A. (1990). Severe withdrawal symptoms after discontinuation of aprazolam in eight patients with combat-induced post-traumatic stress disorder (PTSD). *Journal of Clinical Psychiatry, 51,* 206–209.

Rosenbaum, M. (1990). A model for research on self-regulation: reducing the schism between behaviorism and general psychology. In G. Eifert & I. M. Evans (Eds.) *Unifying behavior therapy: Contributions of paradigmatic behaviorism.* New York: Springer.

Roth, S., & Cohen, L. J. (1986). Approach, avoidance, and coping with stress. *American Psychologist, 41,* 813–819.

Rounsaville, B. S., Weissman, M. M., Crits-Christoph, K., Wilber, C., Kleber, H. (1982). Diagnosis and symptoms of depression in opiate addicts. *Archives of General Psychiatry, 39,* 151–156.

Rounsaville, B. J., Weissman, M. M., Rosenberger, P. H., Wilber, C. H., & Kleber, H. D. (1979). Detecting depression disorders in drug abusers: A comparison of screening instruments. *Journal of Affective Disorders, 1,* 255–267.

Rychtarik, R. G., Silverman, W. K., Van Landingham, W. P., & Prue, D. M. (1984). Treatment of an incest victim with implosive therapy: A case study. *Behavior Therapy, 15,* 410–420.

Saigh, P. A. (1987a). *In vitro* flooding of an adolescent's posttraumatic stress disorder. *Journal of Clinical Child Psychology, 16,* 147–150.

Saigh, P. A. (1987b). *In vitro* flooding of a childhood posttraumatic stress disorder. *School Psychology Review, 16,* 203–211.

Saunders, B., & Allsop, S. (1987). Relapse: A psychological perspective. *British Journal of Addiction, 82,* 417–429.

Schnitt, J. M., & Nocks, J. J. (1984). Alcoholism treatment of Vietnam veterans with post-traumatic stress disorder (PTSD). *Journal of Substance Abuse Treatment, 1,* 179–189.

Scurfield, R. S. (1991). Treatment of PTSD in the Vietnam combat veteran. In J. Wilson and B. Raphael (Eds.), *The international handbook of traumatic stress syndromes.* New York: Plenum Publishing.

Sierles, F. S., Chen, J. J., McFarland, R. E., & Taylor, M. A. (1983). Posttraumatic stress disorder and concurrent psychiatric illness: A preliminary report. *American Journal of Psychiatry, 140*(9), 1177–1183.

Sierles, F. S., Chen, J. J., Messing, M. L., Besyner, J. K., & Taylor, M. A. (1986). Concurrent psychiatric illness in non-Hispanic outpatients diagnosed as having posttraumatic stress disorder. *The Journal of Nervous and Mental Disease, 174*(3), 171–173.

Spivak, G., Platt, J. J., & Shure, M. B. (1976). *The problem-solving approach to adjustment: A guide to research and intervention.* San Francisco: Jossey-Bass.

Staats, A. W. (1978). *Social behaviorism.* Illinois: Dorsey Press.

Steer, R.A., & Kotzker, E. (1980). Affective changes in male and female methadone patients. *Drug and Alcohol Dependence, 5,* 115–122.

Stockwell, T., Small, P., Hodgson, R. et al. (1984). Alcohol dependence and phobic anxiety states, II: A retrospective study. *British Journal of Psychiatry, 144,* 58–63.

Toland, A.M., & Goetz, K.L. (1988, August). *Dual diagnoses and clinical characteristics of Vietnam veterans with PTSD.* Paper presented at the annual meeting of the American Psychological Association, Atlanta, GA.

VA Health Systems Research & Development. (1987). *Mental Health Services for HSR&D,* Ann Arbor, MI.

Vaillant, G. E. (1980). Natural history of male psychological health, VIII: Antecedents of alcoholism and "orality." *American Journal of Psychiatry, 137,* 181–186.

Volpicelli, J.R. (1987). Uncontrollable events and alcohol drinking. *British Journal of Addiction, 82,* 381–392.

Woody, G. E., McLellan, A. T., Luborsky, L., & O'Brien, C. P. (1985). Sociopathy and psychotherapy outcome. *Archives of General Psychiatry, 42,* 1081–1086.

Chapter 6

A New Model of Posttraumatic Stress Disorder: Implications for the Future

Jennifer C. Jones
David H. Barlow

In 1980, posttraumatic stress disorder (PTSD) was formally acknowledged by the third edition of the Diagnostic and Statistical Manual of Mental Disorders (DSM-III; American Psychiatric Association, 1980) as a definable disorder. Supplanting the term *traumatic neurosis,* the signs and symptoms of PTSD are now described in terms of an anxiety disorder (American Psychiatric Association, 1980, 1987). The separation of PTSD from the theoretical constraints and limitations of the concept of neurosis seems to have produced positive consequences in terms of empirical research. This is consistent with the current emphasis on empirically derived theoretical conceptualizations, testable hypotheses, and data supporting the validity of nosological schema.

The DSM-III-R (American Psychiatric Association, 1987) definition of PTSD includes several behavioral, social, and emotional abnormalities following exposure to a recognizable stressor of sufficient magnitude to evoke stress in almost everyone. Experiences in war, natural disasters, and rape, among others, are thought to meet this qualification. In addition to the diagnostic criteria, DSM-III-R recognizes depression and anxiety as associated features of the disorder. While many of the signs and symptoms have been included on the basis of extensive clinical experience, recent evidence has provided some preliminary empirical support for the inclusion of most symptoms as valid diagnostic criteria based on construct and discriminant validation procedures (e.g., Laufer, Brett, & Gallops, 1985; Pearce, Schauer, Garfield, Ohlde, & Patterson, 1985; Silver & Iacono, 1984; Woolfolk & Grady, 1988). While a full discussion of these validation studies extends well beyond the scope of this chapter, Lyons, Gerardi, Wolfe, and Keane (1988) and Keane, Wolfe, and Taylor (1987) present thorough discussions of these issues.

Nevertheless, PTSD diverges in one important way from other disorders. Specifically, with the exception of organic brain syndromes and substance abuse disorders, PTSD is the only diagnostic category that includes an etiological variable in its criteria—that is, "exposure to a psychologically distressing event that is outside the range of usual human experience" (American Psychiatric Association, 1987, p. 247) and would evoke distress in almost anyone. Thus, PTSD is regarded as a pathological reaction to trauma. This creates the illusion that the etiology of PTSD is known. But if this is the case, why do not all soldiers exposed to combat, all women who have been raped, or all car accident victims develop PTSD? Clearly, conceptualizations are far from complete and in need of further explication.

In response to this void, theories of etiology have emerged from virtually every theoretical persuasion (e.g., information processing, psychodynamic, biological, and behavioral). Many provide a framework useful for understanding certain facets of the disorder. However, most are incomplete and are unable to encompass the constellation of symptoms that comprise the disorder, particularly the reexperiencing phenomena many consider to be the hallmark of PTSD. While many of these models have some initial empirical support, all are lacking in certain respects (see Foy, Osato, Houskamp, & Neumann, this volume; and Jones & Barlow, 1990, for a critical review of these models). Thus, the purpose of this chapter is to discuss briefly our conceptualization of PTSD etiology and maintenance. In addition, we will speculate on possible future directions of PTSD research, particularly with respect to its diagnosis and treatment.

PTSD—A BIOPSYCHOSOCIAL CONCEPTUALIZATION

PTSD is classified as an anxiety disorder, and a considerable body of evidence supports this contention. Primarily this evidence is based on the presence, in individuals with PTSD, of the fundamental components of anxiety in behavioral, cognitive, and physiological response systems. Of course, others disagree with this perspective, arguing instead that the evidence supporting PTSD as an anxiety disorder is weak. Consequently, the classification of PTSD in other categories (e.g., dissociative disorders) would be more appropriate. Nevertheless, we have found consideration of the nature of anxiety and panic and theories of etiology of the anxiety disorders to be useful in developing a more complete understanding of PTSD.

Barlow (1988) has recently described a working model of the origins and process of anxiety (or more specifically, anxious apprehension). He speculates that anxious apprehension may be present and operative in all anxiety disorders. The origins of anxiety involve a core consisting of a biological vulnerability to stress, possibly genetically transmitted, that likely manifests itself across many neurobiological systems. This vulnerability is activated by disruptions of behavior occasioned by negative life events. These stress-produced reactions, at sufficient intensities, may set the occasion for alarm reactions (i.e., fear, panic attack) functionally designed to motivate an individual for immediate action (fight or flight). Whether the alarm is true (rational, as in the presence of realistic dangers or threats) or false (irrational, when no danger is immediately apparent) depends on the nature of the negative event, specifically the degree to which life-threatening danger or challenge is present in the situation. It has been important to our survival that alarms (or other defense emotions) are very quickly and easily associated with contextual events. That is, they are learned. This serves a protective function the next time the threatening context is present. Most alarms, then, are really learned alarms. Such a stressful event, and possibly the alarm also, is experienced as unpredictable (i.e., "It might happen again") and possibly uncontrollable (i.e., "I may not be able to deal effectively with it"). These events may then lead to chronic activation of the process of anxiety just described. It is important to note that the occurrence of alarms is *not* essential to the development of anxiety but may complicate it.

The tendency to focus anxious apprehension on one subject or another (e.g., bodily function, intrusive thoughts, social evaluative concerns) in the absence of real threat also is learned and creates a vulnerability for the context of anxiety. In other words, if one possesses a biological vulnerability to stress manifesting in a labile neurobiological responsiveness and a psychological vulnerability manifesting as a sense of unpredictability or uncontrollability particularly concerning negative life events (including alarms), then one is vulnerable to anxiety. If one possesses a sense of control or mastery, one would be relatively immune to the onset of the anxious apprehension cycle despite one's biological vulnerabilities.

Other moderating variables are thought to be the amount of social support available to the individual as well as whether such support is utilized, and the number and quality of coping skills at the disposal of the individual (which are closely related to one's sense of control).

This complex interaction of biological, psychological, and environmental events is required for the genesis of anxious apprehension (Figure 6.1, taken from Barlow, 1988). Most important are the dual biological and psychological vulnerabilities that must line up correctly. Once this cycle begins, it often becomes self-perpetuating. Thus, many of the factors involved in the development of anxiety also are implicated in its maintenance.

ETIOLOGY AND MAINTENANCE OF PTSD

Figure 6.2 (taken from Barlow, 1988) presents our hypothesized model of the development of PTSD. We propose that variables implicated in the etiology and maintenance of anxiety disorders and anxious apprehension also are involved in PTSD. In fact, the cognitive factors in the feedback cycle of anxious apprehension are crucial to this model. The following sections briefly highlight the role of these variables. A more through discussion can be found in Jones and Barlow (1990) and in Chapter 2 of this book.

Biological Vulnerability

Family and Twin Studies. The notion of biological vulnerability is not new to this field of research. Employing such methodologies as family histories, family studies, and twin studies, a large body of research has demonstrated fairly consistently a familial aggregation in the anxiety disorders. Recently,

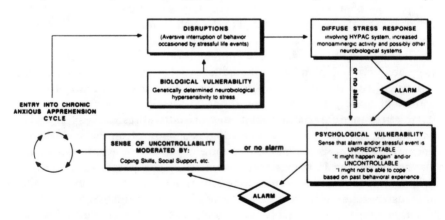

FIGURE 6.1. The origins of anxious apprehension. From *Anxiety and its disorders: The nature and treatment of anxiety and panic* by D. H. Barlow, 1988, New York: Guilford Press. Copyright 1988 by Guilford Press. Reprinted with permission.

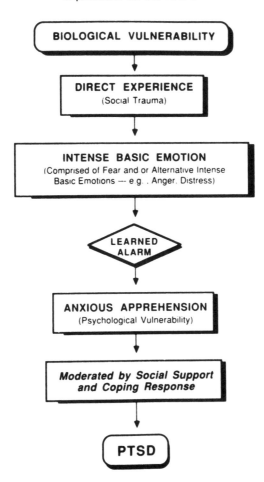

FIGURE 6.2. A model of the etiology of PTSD. From *Anxiety and its disorders: The nature and treatment of anxiety and panic.* by D. H. Barlow, 1988, New York: Guilford Press. Copyright 1988 by Guilford Press. Reprinted with permission.

family history studies of veterans with and without PTSD have appeared (e.g., Davidson, Swartz, Storck, Krishnan, & Hammett, 1985; Foy, Resnick, Sipprelle, & Carroll, 1987; McFarlane, 1988). Results of these studies also have demonstrated the existence of a familial aggregation. These studies, taken together with those examining the familial aggregation of panic disorder and generalized anxiety disorder, provide converging evidence for the hypothesis that a genetic predisposition to certain anxiety disorders may exist. Of course, different subject populations, different diagnostic criteria, different instruments, and different methodologies make it difficult to draw definitive conclusions.

Psychophysiological Studies. If we accept, for the moment, the premise that some genetic component is operative in the etiology of panic disorder and possibly PTSD, the next logical question to ask is, What is inherited? Eysenck (1967; 1981) has suggested that an autonomic lability in response to particular stimuli may be what is genetically transmitted. We postulate that the genetic component may be a predisposition to a diffuse stress responsivity reflected as chronic autonomic overarousal or noradrenergic liability (cf. Barlow, 1988). Again, recent research has supported this hypothesis. For instance, Ehlers, Margraf, and Roth (1987), Gorman, Fyer, Goetz, Askanazi, Liebowitz, Fyer, Kinney, and Klein (1988), and Rapee and Barlow (1990) have reported that panickers regularly exhibit higher resting heart rate than do matched controls. This finding has been extended to include those with combat-related PTSD as well (cf. Blanchard, Kolb, Pallmeyer, & Gerardi, 1982; Blanchard, Kolb, Gerardi, Ryan, & Pallmeyer, 1986; Malloy, Fairbank, & Keane, 1983; Pitman, Orr, Forgue, de Jong & Claiborn, 1987).

While it is likely that increases of heart rate to relevant threat stimuli may simply represent a conditioned emotional response (learned alarm; cf. Kolb, 1987), the results of family history and twin studies suggest that the propensity to *baseline* hyperactivity may be, in part, a genetically transmitted response tendency. This is supported by the relatively consistent finding that combat veterans without PTSD have lower basal heart rate. Similar findings on baseline hyperactivity have been found across the anxiety disorders (Barlow, 1988). Of course, for most of these studies it is not possible to determine the cause-effect relationship of chronic overarousal, since it may be the result of an anxiety disorder. But reports of chronic overarousal predating the development of an anxiety disorder are consistent with a genetic disposition (Barlow, 1988).

Psychological Vulnerability

Similar to biological predispositions, psychological vulnerabilities are thought to mediate the development and maintenance of anxiety disorders. Although still at an early stage in its development, accumulating research, both with animals and humans, is beginning to demonstrate that variables embraced under this rubric play a role in the etiology and maintenance of anxiety disorders. Such variables include prior experience with a sense of control over life events and social support (Barlow, 1988).

The model presented earlier regarding anxious apprehension suggests that the psychological vulnerability may manifest itself in perceptions of unpredictability ("It might happen again") and uncontrollability ("I might not be able to cope"). As such, it is a component important to entrance into the feedback loop of anxiety and the continued cycling through this loop. Furthermore, the sense of uncontrollability may be mediated by such variables as coping skills and social support.

Recent research with PTSD combat veterans has provided some early support for the importance of a sense of control in mediating the development and course of the disorder. For example, Frye and Stockton (1982) found that Vietnam veterans with PTSD had a more external locus of control (i.e., perceptions of no control; Rotter, 1966). Given prior research on this issue, Frye and Stockton (1982) suggested that men with an external locus of control were more susceptible to the unpredictable and uncontrollable nature of their war experiences. Therefore, such individuals may be more vulnerable to the adverse effects of combat.

While this may reflect a consequence of combat rather than an antecedent, it suggests that this variable may influence the way veterans perceived and coped with negative life events after their return to civilian life. If they continued to regard life events as unpredictable and beyond their control, symptoms of PTSD may have developed or become exacerbated. Indeed, recent research by Mikulincer and Solomon (1988) provides some initial support for this hypothesis.

Other studies examining the effects of preexisting emotional disorders on the effects of trauma and subsequent PTSD may also reflect this general psychological (and biological) vulnerability. However, it is important to note that these data provide only very weak support for preexisting vulnerabilities. Nevertheless, they form an interesting point of reference. For instance, Frank, Turner, Stewart, Jacob, and West (1981) found women with a history of depression and suicidal behavior to be more depressed and anxious following a rape. Ruch, Chandler, and Harter (1980) found that rape victims with prior emotional problems were more traumatized at intake and at follow-up. Although PTSD was not examined specifically, these studies suggest that individuals with a history of emotional problems may be more vulnerable to long-term adjustment problems following a trauma.

One could argue that past emotional disorders may simply potentiate PTSD rather than reflect a common diathesis. This seems a possibility, particularly since other researchers have not been able to replicate the finding that past psychiatric history is related to adjustment following a trauma (e.g., Kilpatrick, Veronen, & Best, 1985). Furthermore, no evidence exists that other pretrauma experiences, such as educational history, trouble with authorities, prior substance abuse, or other demographic factors, are related to subsequent PTSD (Foy, Sipprelle, Rueger, & Carroll, 1984; Foy et al., 1987; Penk, Robinowitz, Roberts, Patterson, Dolan, & Atkins, 1981; Roberts, Penk, Gearing, Robinowitz, Dolan, & Patterson, 1982).

Negative Life Events

Negative life events are frequent precursors to the onset of anxiety disorders. For example, recent estimates suggest that approximately 80% or more of patients with panic disorder can clearly recall such an event (cf. Barlow, 1988), although they may not relate this event to an initial panic attack. (It is interesting to note that many PTSD patients fail to associate their current symptoms with the traumatic experiences that ultimately led to the disorder [cf. McFarlane, 1988].) We hypothesize that individuals who are vulnerable to the stress of negative life events may occasionally react to such events in much the same way one reacts to physical threats. That is, they evidence a basic fear response much as they would when confronted with any other threat to their well-being.

Exposure to life events after the development of PTSD may operate to exacerbate or even maintain PTSD symptomatology (as well as symptoms of other emotional disorders). While this hypothesis has not been studied intensively, Green and Berlin (1987) found a positive correlation between PTSD symptoms and current levels of life stress. McFarlane (1988), in his study of bush fire victims, found that individuals with chronic PTSD had more adverse life events both before and after the fire.

Given the small number of studies, results must be interpreted cautiously. However, they provide some initial support for the notions that adverse life events prior to a trauma are associated with posttrauma adjustment and that subsequent adverse life events are associated with continued symptomatology.

Nature of the Stressor

In addition to the presence of a stressor necessary for PTSD and the oft-noted precipitating negative life events in other anxiety disorders, the nature of the stressor is also an important variable. Specifically, events that are perceived as uncontrollable or unpredictable are more aversive and more likely to elicit a "true alarm." This contention has been heavily supported in the literature (cf. Barlow, 1988; Mineka, Gunnar, & Champoux, 1986; Mineka & Kihlstrom, 1978) and is beginning to be examined in the trauma literature (e.g., Ruch et al., 1980; Wirtz & Harrell, 1987b).

The extent and severity of combat exposure consistently has been found to be a powerful antecedent of PTSD symptoms in war veterans (e.g., Foy et al., 1984; Laufer, Frey-Wouters, & Gallops, 1985). Several studies with victims of other traumatic experiences (e.g., rape, natural disasters) also support the importance of stressor severity and subjective appraisal of life threat, although not as consistently as the war veteran data (e.g., Becker, Abel, Skinner, Treacy, & Glasse, 1981; Kilpatrick, Best, Veronen, Amick,

Villeponteaux, & Ruff, 1985). Although neither Becker et al. (1981) nor Kilpatrick et al. (1985) made an attempt to diagnose their victims, their findings do support the hypothesis that stressor severity is a powerful antecedent of emotional problems and PTSD.

Alarms: True, False, and Learned

Although psychological and biological vulnerabilities and the role of negative life events may be similar in the etiology of all anxiety disorders, a distinction has been made between the type of alarm that has been activated. Elsewhere, we have differentiated between true alarms, false alarms, and learned alarms (cf. Barlow, 1988). True alarms are regarded as a fear response that occurs when an individual is faced with a life-threatening event, particularly a severe one. False alarms, although phenomenologically identical, occur in the absence of such an event. Learned alarms are seen as conditioned fear responses to either interoceptive (as in panic disorder) or external (simple phobia) cues.

Panic attacks have been characterized as the activation of a false alarm (or, in some instances, a true alarm) of such intensity (fear) that conditioning to "relevant" stimuli may occur—usually to interoceptive cues. PTSD, on the other hand, may reflect in part the conditioning that occurs upon activation of true alarms (i.e., evocation of fear and accompanying increases in a variety of physiological response systems that would support escape [flight] behavior) under life-threatening conditions. Such a response is adaptive in situations such as combat or rape and is a protective mechanism often necessary for survival.

For patients with PTSD in response to single or repeated true alarms, fear likely has become associated with both internal and external cues associated with the initial event (Kolb, 1987). Thus, perception of stimuli reminiscent of the trauma(s) continues to activate the alarm reaction in the absence of any real danger and is manifested in panic attacks, flashbacks, and other PTSD symptomatology. Consistent with this view is the recent acknowledgment by the DSM-IV PTSD work group that reminders of the trauma can be both internal and external. Research with combat veterans by Blanchard et al. (1982; 1986), Pallmeyer et al. (1986), Pitman et al. (1987), and Malloy et al. (1983) on physiological reactivity to combat stimuli (audio and visual) supports the presence of learned alarms in patients with PTSD. Unfortunately, similar research with victims of other traumas has not been conducted. Finally, the overwhelming support for the relative severity of the stressor as an important variable in PTSD etiology suggests that the true alarm elicited in these individuals is indeed substantial and plays an important role in etiology.

Anxious Apprehension and Reexperiencing

Nevertheless, the presence of learned alarms and other features described, important though they may be, would not be sufficient to account for PTSD. Indeed, much as with other anxiety disorders, the crucial step to pathology would be the development of anxious apprehension about learned alarms. It is only this process, with its strong cognitive components such as distorted processing of information along with marked negative affect, that can account for the downward spiral of symptomatology associated with PTSD. This downward spiral would include the unremitting reexperiencing of learned alarms and associated traumatic memories, the pattern of affective instability associated with alternate numbing and exacerbation of negative emotions, as well as the occasional delayed emotional experience of PTSD symptomatology.

Thus, if the vulnerabilities line up correctly, an individual will experience the overwhelming true alarm and subsequent learned alarms as unpredictable, uncontrollable aversive events. The individual will react to these events with chronic overarousal and additional cognitive symptoms of hypervigilance to trauma-related cues, a hypervigilance commonly observed in PTSD (Kline & Rausch, 1985), accompanied by attention narrowing. Chronic overarousal, characteristic of all anxiety disorders (with the possible exception of some simple phobias), would comprise a negative arousal-based feedback loop perhaps similar to that proposed by Chemtob, Roitblat, Hamada, Carlson, and Twentyman (1988), and Foa, Steketee, and Olasov Rothbaum (1989). Since the original alarm contained many strong arousal-based components, the existing chronic overarousal combined with a hypervigilance to arousal that might signal the beginning of a future alarm would ensure a succession of learned alarms and associated traumatic memories.

It also has been demonstrated in the context of other anxiety disorders that stress of any kind increases the frequency of intrusive thoughts (Parkinson & Rachman, 1981). The chronic overarousal characteristic of anxiety disorders in general, and PTSD in particular, would ensure a steady stream of intrusive thoughts and images, many of which would be trauma related. The hypervigilance and attention narrowing on this threatening and dangerous material (trauma-related intrusive thoughts), which might signal the potential onset of further uncontrollable emotional states, would also play an important role in the downward spiral of negative affect. Therefore, the presence of excessive arousal as well as hypervigilance and attention narrowing on this arousal and any trauma-related intrusive thoughts would paradoxically increase, rather than decease, reexperiencing of the trauma.

Naturally, the tendency for individuals with this process is to avoid emotionally relevant stimuli. For example, individuals with panic disorder will avoid emotional encounters with relatives such as greetings or good-byes, emotional movies such as horror movies, or even soap operas, and sexual relations in an effort to avoid emotionally laden interoceptive stimuli (Barlow, 1988). Individuals with PTSD also experience the well-known and frequently observed emotional blunting in an attempt to avoid the triggering of learned alarms.

In the extreme, attempts to avoid memories of an all-too-real traumatic event may produce the kind of dissociative state occasionally encountered in severe PTSD patients. This provides a phenomenological difference in patients with panic disorder who, for the most part, have no such "real" memories with which to contend. However, some theorists would view this as evidence supporting reclassification of PTSD as a dissociative disorder.

This process of anxiety over learned alarms does not necessarily depend on conscious appraisal and subsequent interpretation of threat. Rather, it is best conceptualized in the Langian sense (Lang, 1984) as a rather diffuse series of propositions stored in memory capable of activation by stimuli similar to only a small number of these propositions. (Once again, for a full explication of the nature of anxious apprehension in this model, see Barlow, 1988.) Nevertheless, what is crucial at this point is activation and focusing of anxious apprehension on emotional alarms and associated trauma-related stimuli. Anxiety in the final analysis contributes substantially to the prediction of who will develop PTSD and who will not. Without the development of anxiety, individuals undergoing severe trauma may occasionally experience a nonclinical learned alarm or flashback to the trauma when encountering triggering stimuli without the overlapping negative affective burden associated with the development and maintenance of PTSD.

FUTURE DIRECTIONS

Diagnostic Issues

When the category of PTSD was introduced into the diagnostic nomenclature, a storm of controversy arose. Primarily this controversy centered on the validity of the category as well as the political issue involving overutilization of the PTSD diagnosis for anyone who had experienced even a mild stressor. Those opposing the inclusion of the disorder in the nomenclature argued that this would become a "wastebasket" category enabling thousands and perhaps millions of individuals to claim disability after experiencing a life stress. In response to this concern, the authors of DSM-III and III-R wrote a very conservative definition of a stressor specifying that it must be outside the range of normal human experience and markedly distressing to almost anybody. This definition precluded any serious consideration of an individual's personal reaction to the stressor that obviously would vary on a dimension of severity. In other words, even the most severe stress does not give rise to a PTSD reaction in everyone and, conversely, more "mild" stressors may elicit full-blown disabling PTSD reactions in some.

In an attempt to rectify this situation, investigators working on DSM-IV criteria are currently experimenting with definitions that take into account one's personal reaction to the stress (see Davidson & Foa, in press, for a review). While this was acknowledged in the DSM-III-R text, it is difficult to put these ideas into a criterion without opening up the category too widely. Therefore, some of the definitions currently under consideration include the following "A" criterion: "The person has experienced, witnessed, or been *confronted with,* an event or events which involve actual or threatened death or injury, or a threat to the physical integrity of oneself or others" (italics added). This criterion would loosen the definition of the stressor by including events that might be within the range of normal human experience, such as being confronted with the death of a loved one, that would still be capable of provoking PTSD in some individuals. On the other hand, one could theoretically "be confronted with" some catastrophe occurring in another part of the country by reading a newspaper and technically qualify for PTSD. Another possibility is to add a criterion specifying one's subjective reaction to the event. An example would be "the person's response involved intense fear, distress, helplessness, or horror." Currently, the committee has proposed that both an objective trauma and a subjective response be present to qualify for the disorder. A final alternative under consideration would be to adopt the somewhat more vague definition proposed for the tenth revision of the International Classification of Diseases (ICD-10), which states "exposure to an exceptional mental or physical stressor either brief or prolonged."

Another difficulty with the current DSM-III-R definition of a stressor is that specifying that the event must be outside the range of normal human experience and markedly distressing to almost anybody implies that we have a ready-made list of such stressors based on normative data. For example, most people would agree that experiencing the ravages of a severe earthquake might qualify, but what about witnessing an automobile accident with mild to moderate injury to others? The subgroup working on PTSD revisions for DSM-IV will be conducting a field trial to collect data on various alternative definitions to test their usefulness.

Another change given serious consideration by the subgroup was to impose a duration of at least 3 months before one could qualify for PTSD. This would eliminate many brief stress reactions that disappear relatively quickly. However, the committee, in its most recent deliberations, opted to drop the minimum duration requirement in an attempt to facilitate early access to treatment for trauma victims. Instead, the committee proposed the use of subtypes to describe duration: acute, chronic, and delayed.

The changes just described represent the more substantive changes under consideration by the DSM-IV authors. On the basis of the extant research, other changes are being proposed. However, many of these involve moving symptoms from one criterion to another, altering the number of symptoms in each category required to make the diagnosis, and subtle changes in wording to reflect the observations of clinicians and researchers.

Another debate within the anxiety disorders work group centers on the placement of PTSD. Currently, PTSD is classified as an anxiety disorder. However, the development of a new grouping of disorders has been proposed. Such a group would hypothetically include all diagnoses related to an identifiable stressor or trauma, adjustment disorders, pathological grief reaction, chronic victimization disorder, and brief reactive dissociative disorders in addition to PTSD in both chronic and acute forms (Davidson & Foa, in press). The rationale underlying this proposal includes the arguments that (1) classification would be based on an etiological variable (i.e., exposure to a know stressor or trauma); and (2) such a category would facilitate research in the field of traumatic stress (cf. Brett, 1990). It would also elevate the status both with respect to the nosological hierarchy and in the perception of the public (Davidson & Foa, in press). Another distinct advantage is that this would be consistent with the organization of stress-related disorders in the tenth edition of the International Classification of Diseases (ICD-10). This category will include acute and chronic PTSD, enduring posttraumatic character changes after catastrophic experiences, and adjustment disorders. Compatability between these systems is a goal.

Despite the validity of these arguments, we would favor the retention of PTSD as an anxiety disorder for several reasons. First, many similarities exist in the etiological and maintaining factors implicated in PTSD (Jones & Barlow, 1990) and the other anxiety disorders (particularly panic disorder). A second reason would be the almost ubiquitous observations that anxiety and avoidance exist across the anxiety disorders and that fear and anxiety are the most prominent and persistent symptoms following exposure to extreme stress (cf. Burgess & Holmstrom, 1974). Finally, retention of PTSD as an anxiety disorder would encourage the continued explosion of research on PTSD that has emerged since its classification as an anxiety disorder. Current theoretical models (e.g., conditioning, information processing) have been derived from theories of anxiety. Similarly, the majority of PTSD treatment modalities involve interventions first developed from the anxiety disorders. Consequently, removal of PTSD from the anxiety disorders may hinder the continued application of these theoretical and treatment models of PTSD. While we have explicated several other reasons for favoring the retention of PTSD as an anxiety disorder, these represent the crux of the argument (Barlow, Brown, Jones, & Prins, 1990).

Treatment of PTSD

Throughout this chapter we have touched briefly on the similarities of PTSD to other anxiety disorders such as panic disorder—particularly in relation to etiology and maintenance. Since consideration of other anxiety disorders has proven useful in this respect, certain aspects of treatment developed for panic disorder also may prove beneficial for PTSD.

Until somewhat recently, behavioral interventions for anxiety primarily involved exposure-based strategies such as systematic desensitization, graduated in vivo exposure, and flooding. Cognitive restructuring strategies were later combined with exposure (Beck & Emery, 1985). However, these strategies tend to emphasize exposure to and restructuring of the catastrophic cognitions associated with the individual's fear or anxiety or external triggers of the fear (alarm) response.

Recently we have developed a working model of the process of anxiety and fear reduction that attempts to highlight what is essential in any therapeutic endeavor directed at anxiety or related emotional disorders (Barlow, 1988). This process is referred to by the rather unoriginal name of affective therapy. The emphasis of this model is on underlying processes at which therapy should be directed rather than specific procedures that might be utilized. Given the very wide agreement that PTSD is an emotional disorder consisting of a variety of unstable, affective responses, including anxiety, depression, and anger, it would seem that this model might be useful. As outlined in this model, there are a number of targets for therapeutic change. Among a number of helpful but not essential targets would be excessive arousal, inappropriate (or catastrophic) cognitions, and the provision of social support. But the essential targets for change in this model would be a sense of uncontrollability and unpredictability, strong action tendencies such as fight or flight associated with inappropriate emotions, and a tendency to focus attention inward, which is a hallmark of negative affective states (see Barlow, 1988, for a full explication). Based on this model, several advances have been made regarding the treatment of panic disorder that may apply to PTSD. Specifically, a treatment containing exposure to the somatic cues associated with the alarm response (i.e., panic attack) has proved useful in eliminating anxiety concerning future panic attacks as well as the panic attacks themselves. In fact, recent data from our center indicate that 87% of patients with panic disorder are panic free at the end of treatment utilizing interoceptive exposure (Barlow, Craske, Cerny, & Klosko, 1989). What is important about this treatment approach is that it attempts to elicit the inappropriate action tendencies in the clinic by reproducing the somatic cues that are so anxiety provoking. At the same time, the patient is provided with a means of managing or controlling these responses associated with the internal or somatic cues of an alarm reaction. Associated components of the treatment, including cognitive restructuring and breathing retraining, are conceptualized as assisting the patient in developing control over these "out of control" internal responses. But it is thought that these coping mechanisms would not be terribly useful in contributing to a new sense of control unless the patient had direct experience with the internal responses themselves, preferably in an office-based setting initially. Nevertheless, more research is necessary to ascertain the essential and nonessential components of treatment. Such treatments are currently in development at our center. It is also possible that other emerging developments in the treatment of anxiety and related emotional disorders may be incorporated successfully into the treatment of PTSD.

Currently, in vivo and imaginal exposure combined with other treatment procedures are quite effective at decreasing and in many instances eliminating the debilitating symptoms of PTSD (e.g., Fairbank, Gross, & Keane, 1983; Keane, Fairbank, Caddell, & Zimering, 1989; Olasov Rothbaum & Foa, this volume). Many of these components are present in the treatment of other anxiety disorders such as panic disorder (Barlow et al., 1989; Klosko, Barlow, Tassinari, & Cerny, 1990). As noted previously, it seems possible that learned alarms may form a substantial part of both panic disorder and PTSD. There is also substantial clinical evidence that a principal component of PTSD is anxiety over unpredictable alarm responses that are manifested in the form of flashbacks or other emotional responses to trauma-related cues, including internal cues. Incorporating treatment procedures for panic disorder directed at these internal interoceptive emotional cues as an additional component of treatment for PTSD may well provide a substantial added benefit.

SUMMARY

Diverse theoretical frameworks from biological to psychodynamic specify a variety of factors as implicated in the etiology and maintenance of PTSD. Evidence exists, some of it quite preliminary, that PTSD develops out of a complex interaction between biological and psychological predispositions, the occurrence of stressful events and alarms, the development of anxiety, and the adequacy of coping strategies and social support. Thus, PTSD shares many features of other anxiety disorders, particularly panic disorder (see Jones & Barlow, 1990, for a full discussion of these similarities).

The model proposed above is derived from an amalgamation of available and diverse research but may prove heuristic in elucidating crucial etiological and maintaining factors in PTSD. Phenomenological similarities with panic disorder are also noteworthy, specifically the presence of anxiety symptomatology (as well as depression in a substantial number of cases), the initial occurrence of emotional alarms that seem to be a discrete fear response (Barlow, 1988), and the association of alarms with a variety of internal and external stimuli. Finally, the avoidance of affect-related stimuli that may set the occasion for another alarm (flashback, panic attack) seems to be another feature common to other anxiety disorders.

Thus, the occurrence of stressful or traumatic events as well as alarms, true or false, in the context of these events are not sufficient for a disorder. Rather, one must also experience chronic emotional distress or anxiety, with its accompanying distortions in the processing of information. This anxiety is focused on the possibility of reexperiencing the intense affect associated with alarms and the internal or external stimuli associated with them. Paradoxically, it is the experience of anxiety, with its associated hypervigilance and attention narrowing, that ensures frequent reexperiencing of emotionally laden material. This suggests that it is useful to consider PTSD as an anxiety disorder and that research into hypothesized etiological and maintaining factors in any anxiety disorder may elucidate underlying mechanisms in PTSD. Moreover, treatment approaches utilized for other anxiety disorders, particularly panic disorder, may prove fruitful for eliminating the debilitating symptoms of PTSD.

REFERENCES

American Psychiatric Association. (1987). *Diagnostic and statistical manual of the mental disorders* (3rd ed., Rev.). Washington, DC: Author.

American Psychiatric Association. (1980). *Diagnostic and statistical manual of the mental disorders* (3rd ed.). Washington, DC: Author.

Barlow, D. H. (1988). *Anxiety and its disorders: The nature and treatment of anxiety and panic.* New York: Guilford Press.

Barlow, D. H., Brown, T. A., Jones, J. C., & Prins, A. (1990). *Commentary on Brett's proposition of PTSD as a stress response disorder.* Paper prepared for review by the DSM-IV PTSD subgroup.

Barlow, D. H., Craske, M. G., Cerny, J. A., & Klosko, J. S. (1989). Behavioral treatment of panic disorder. *Behavior Therapy, 20,* 261–282.

Beck, A. T., & Emery, G. (1985). *Anxiety disorders and phobias: A cognitive perspective.* New York: Basic Books.

Becker, J. V., Abel, G. G., Skinner, L. J., Treacy, E. C., & Glasse, D. (1981). *Rape and incest victims' fears following sexual assault.* Unpublished manuscript.

Blanchard, E. B., Kolb, L. C., Gerardi, R. J., Ryan, P., & Pallmeyer, T. P. (1986). Cardiac response to relevant stimuli as a tool for diagnosing post-traumatic stress disorder in Vietnam veterans. *Behavior Therapy, 17,* 592–606.

Blanchard, E. B., Kolb, L. C., Pallmeyer, T. P., & Gerardi, R. J. (1982). A psychophysiological study of post-traumatic stress disorder in Vietnam veterans. *Psychiatric Quarterly, 54,* 220–229.

Brett, E. A. (1990). *Classification of PTSD in DSM-IV: As an anxiety disorder, dissociative disorder, or stress disorder.* Paper prepared for review by the DSM-IV PTSD workgroup.

Burgess, A. W., & Holmstrom, L. L. (1974). Rape trauma syndrome. *American Journal of Psychiatry, 131,* 981–986.

Chemtob, C., Roitblat, H. C., Hamada, R. S., Carlson, J. G., & Twentyman, C. T. (1988). A cognitive action theory of post-traumatic stress disorder. *Journal of Anxiety Disorders, 2,* 253–275.

Davidson, J., & Foa, E. B. (in press). Diagnostic issues in post-traumatic stress disorder: Considerations for the DSM-IV. *Journal of Abnormal Psychology.*

Davidson, J., Swartz, M., Storck, M., Krishnan, R. R., & Hammett, E. (1985). A diagnostic and family study of posttraumatic stress disorder. *American Journal of Psychiatry, 142,* 90–93.

Ehlers, A., Margraf, J., & Roth, W. T. (1987). Interaction of expectancy and physiological stressors in a laboratory model of panic. In D. Hellhammer & I. Florin (Eds.), *Neuronal control of bodily function—Basic and clinical aspects. II: Psychological and biological approaches to the understanding of human disease.* Gottingen: Hogrefe.

Eysenck, H. J. (Ed.). (1981). *A model for personality.* New York: Springer-Verlag.

Eysenck, H. J. (Ed.). (1967). *The biological basis for personality.* Springfield, IL: Charles C Thomas.

Fairbank, J. A., Gross, R. T., & Keane, T. M. (1983). Treatment of post-traumatic stress disorder: Evaluating outcome with a behavioral code. *Behavior Modification, 7,* 557–567.

Foa, E. B., Steketee, G., & Olasov Rothbaum, B. (1989). Behavioral/cognitive conceptualizations of post-traumatic stress disorder. *Behavior Therapy, 20,* 155–176.

Foy, D. W., Resnick, H. S., Sipprelle, R. C., & Carroll, E. M. (1987). Premilitary, military, and postmilitary factors in the development of combat-related stress disorders. *The Behavior Therapist, 10,* 3–9.

Foy, D. W., Sipprelle, R. C., Rueger, D. B., & Carroll, E. M. (1984). Etiology of posttraumatic stress disorder in Vietnam veterans: Analysis of premilitary, military, and combat exposure influences. *Journal of Consulting and Clinical Psychology, 52,* 79–87.

Frank, E., Turner, S. M., Stewart, B. D., Jacob, M., & West, D. (1981). Past psychiatric symptoms and the response to sexual assault. *Comprehensive Psychiatry, 22,* 479–487.

Frye, J. S., & Stockton, R. A. (1982). Discriminant analysis of posttraumatic stress disorder among a group of Vietnam veterans. *American Journal of Psychiatry, 139,* 52–56.

Gorman, J. M., Fyer, M. R., Goetz, R., Askanazi, J., Liebowitz, M. R., Fyer, A. J., Kinney, J., & Klein, D. F. (1988). Ventilatory physiology of patients with panic disorder. *Archives of General Psychiatry, 45,* 31–39.

Green, M. A., & Berlin, M. A. (1987). Five psychosocial variables related to the existence of post-traumatic stress disorder symptoms. *Journal of Clinical Psychology, 43,* 643–649.

Jones, J. C., & Barlow, D. H. (1990). The etiology of posttraumatic stress disorder. *Clinical Psychology Review, 10,* 299–328.

Keane, T. M., Fairbank, J. A., Caddell, J. M., & Zimering, R. T. (1989). Implosive (flooding) therapy reduces symptoms of PTSD in Vietnam combat veterans. *Behavior Therapy, 20,* 245–260.

Keane, T. M., Wolfe, J. A., & Taylor, K. L. (1987). Post-traumatic stress disorder: Evidence for diagnostic validity and methods of psychological assessment. *Journal of Clinical Psychology, 43,* 32–43.

Kilpatrick, D. G., Best, C. L., Veronen, L. J., Amick, A. E., Villeponteaux, L. A., & Ruff, G. A. (1985). Mental health correlates of criminal victimization: A random community survey. *Journal of Consulting and Clinical Psychology, 53,* 866–873.

Kilpatrick, D. G., Veronen, L. J., & Best, C. L. (1985). Factors predicting psychological distress among rape victims. In C. R. Figley (Ed.), *Trauma and its wake: The study and treatment of post-traumatic stress disorder.* New York: Brunner/Mazel.

Kline, N. A., & Rausch, J. L. (1985). Olfactory precipitants of flashbacks in posttraumatic stress disorder. *Journal of Clinical Psychiatry, 46,* 383–384.

Klosko, J. S., Barlow, D. H., Tassinari, R. B., & Cerny, J. A. (1990). A comparison of alprazolam and cognitive behavior therapy in treatment of panic disorder. *Journal of Consulting and Clinical Psychology, 58,* 77–84.

Kolb, L. C. (1987). A neuropsychological hypothesis explaining posttraumatic stress disorder. *American Journal of Psychiatry, 144,* 989–995.

Lang, P.J. (1985). The cognitive psychophysiology of emotion: Fear and anxiety. In A. H. Tuma and J. D. Maser (Eds). *Anxiety and the anxiety disorders* (pp. 131–170). Hillsdale, N.J.: Lawrence Earlbaum.

Laufer, R. S., Brett, E., & Gallops, M. S. (1985). Dimensions of posttraumatic stress disorder among Vietnam veterans. *Journal of Nervous and Mental Disease, 173,* 538–545.

Laufer, R. S., Frey-Wouters, E., & Gallops, M. S. (1985). Traumatic stressors in the Vietnam war and post-traumatic stress disorders. In C. R. Figley (Ed.), *Trauma and its wake: The study and treatment of post-traumatic stress disorder.* New York: Brunner/Mazel.

Lyons, J. A,. Gerardi, R. J., Wolfe, J., & Keane, T. M. (1988). Multidimensional assessment of combat-related PTSD: Phenomenological, psychometric, and psychophysiological considerations. *Journal of Traumatic Stress, 1,* 373–394.

Malloy, P. F., Fairbank, J. A., & Keane, T. M. (1983). Validation of a multimethod assessment of posttraumatic stress disorders in Vietnam veterans. *Journal of Consulting and Clinical Psychology, 51,* 488–494.

McFarlane, A. C. (1988). Posttraumatic morbidity of a disaster: A study of cases presenting for psychiatric treatment. *The Journal of Nervous and Mental Disease, 174,* 4–14.

Mikulincer, M., & Solomon, Z. (1988). Attributional style and combat-related posttraumatic stress disorder. *Journal of Abnormal Psychology, 97,* 308–313.

Mineka, S., Gunnar, M., & Champoux, M. (1986). Control and early socioemotional development: Infant rhesus monkeys reared in controllable versus uncontrollable environments. *Child Development, 57,* 1241–1256.

Mineka, S., & Kihlstrom, J. F. (1978). Unpredictable and uncontrollable events: A new perspective on experimental neurosis. *Journal of Abnormal Psychology, 87,* 256–271.

Pallmeyer, T. P., Blanchard, E. B., & Kolb, L. C. (1986). The psychophysiology of combat-induced post-traumatic stress disorder in Vietnam veterans. *Behaviour Research and Therapy, 24,* 645–652.

Parkinson, L., & Rachman, S. (1981). The nature of intrusive thoughts. *Advances in Behaviour Research and Therapy, 2,* 101–110.

Pearce, K. A., Schauer, A. H., Garfield, N. J., Ohlde, C. O., & Patterson, T. W. (1985). A study of post traumatic stress disorder in Vietnam veterans. *Journal of Clinical Psychology, 41,* 9–14.

Penk, W. E., Robinowitz, R., Roberts, W. R., Patterson, E. T., Dolan, M. P., & Atkins, H. G. (1981). Adjustment differences among male substance abusers varying in degree of combat experience in Vietnam. *Journal of Consulting and Clinical Psychology, 49,* 426–437.

Pitman, R. K., Orr, S. P., Forgue, D. F., de Jong, J. B., & Claiborn, J. M. (1987). Psychophysiologic assessment of posttraumatic stress disorder imagery in Vietnam combat veterans. *Archives of General Psychiatry, 44,* 970–975.

Rapee, R. M., & Barlow, D. H. (1990). The assessment of panic disorder. In P. McReynolds, J. C. Rosen, & G. Chelune (Eds.), *Advances in psychological assessment,* Vol. 7. New York: Plenum Publishing.

Roberts, W. R., Penk, W. E., Gearing, M. L., Robinowitz, R., Dolan, M. P., & Patterson, E. T. (1982). Interpersonal problems of Vietnam combat veterans with symptoms of posttraumatic stress disorder. *Journal of Abnormal Psychology, 91,* 444–450.

Rotter, J. B. (1966). Generalized expectancies and internal versus external control of reinforcement. *Psychological Monograph, 80,* 1–28.

Ruch, L. O., Chandler, S. M., & Harter, R. A. (1980). Life change and rape impact. *Journal of Health and Social Behavior, 21,* 248–260.

Silver, S. M., & Iacono, C. U. (1984). Factor analytic support for DSM-III's post-traumatic stress disorder for Vietnam veterans. *Journal of Clinical Psychology, 40,* 5–14.

Wirtz, P. W., & Harrell, A. V. (1987b). The effects of threatening versus nonthreatening previous life events on levels of fear in rape victims. *Violence and Victims, 2,* 89–98.

Woolfolk, R. L., & Grady, D. A. (1988). Combat-related posttraumatic stress disorder: Patterns of symptomatology in help-seeking Vietnam veterans. *The Journal of Nervous and Mental Disease, 176,* 107–111.

Author Index

Subject Index

ABOUT THE EDITOR

Philip A. Saigh, Ph.D., is a Professor and Head of the Doctoral Program in School Psychology at the Graduate Center of the City University of New York. He previously (1977–1986) was a member of the faculty at the American University of Beirut. His research and clinical interests involve the epidemiology, assessment, and treatment of posttraumatic stress disorder. Dr. Saigh currently sits on the editorial boards of the *Journal of Consulting and Clinical Psychology, Comportement Humain: Psychologie, Éducation, Médicine, et Thérapie Comportementales, School Psychology Quarterly, Handicap e Disabilita di Apprendimento,* and the *International Journal of Special Education.* He is a Fellow of the American Psychological Association and a member of the American Psychiatric Association's committee for revising the PTSD classification in the DSM-IV.

ABOUT THE CONTRIBUTORS

Francis R. Abueg received his Ph.D. in clinical psychology from the State University of New York at Binghamton in 1986. Following his graduation, he took a position as research clinical psychologist at the Palo Alto VA Medical Center. In 1987, he co-founded the first inpatient PTSD-substance abuse program in the Department of Veterans Affairs. In 1988, he helped the Menlo Park site obtain funding as one of four sites of the National Center for PTSD, where he is currently Associate Director for Research. He also serves as a member of the clinical faculty at Stanford Medical School.

David H. Barlow, Ph.D., is Distinguished Professor in the Department of Psychology at the State University of New York at Albany. Dr. Barlow is Co-Director of the Center for Stress and Anxiety Disorders, and Director of the Phobia and Anxiety Disorders Clinic and Sexuality Research Program at SUNY-Albany. He is past President of the Association for Advancement of Behavior Therapy, past Associate Editor of the *Journal of Consulting and Clinical Psychology,* and past Editor of the *Journal of Applied Behavior Analysis,* and *Behavior Therapy.* Dr. Barlow has published over 200 articles and chapters and nine books, mostly in the areas of anxiety disorders, sexual problems, and clinical research methodology.

John A. Fairbank received his Ph.D. from Auburn University in 1980 and is Senior Clinical Research Psychologist at Research Triangle Institute, Research Triangle Park, North Carolina. In addition to publishing over 25 scientific journal articles and book chapters on the nature, assessment and treatment of PTSD, Dr. Fairbank has recently co-authored two books, *Trauma and the Vietnam Generation* (1990) and *The National Vietnam Veterans Readjustment Study: Tables of Findings and Technical Appendices* (1990). He has been the recipient of research grants from the National Institute of Mental Health and the Department of Veterans Affairs, and is currently a consulting editor for *Psychological Assessment: A Journal of Consulting and Clinical Psychology.*

Edna B. Foa, Ph.D., is a Professor of Psychology and Director of the Center for the Treatment and Study of Anxiety at the Medical College of Pennsylvania. She is an internationally renowned authority on the psychopathology and treatment of anxiety and one of the leading experts on obsessive-compulsive disorder and posttraumatic stress disorder. Dr. Foa has published several books and over one hundred articles or chapters.

David W. Foy, Ph.D., is a Professor of Psychology in the Graduate School of Psychology, Fuller Theological Seminary. He also holds a part-time position in the Psychology Service at the West Los Angeles VA Medical Center, Brentwood Division. His primary research interests involve etiological factors in the development of trauma-related distress and victimization, including cross-trauma comparisons between combat, sexual assault, and domestic violence.

Robert J. Gerardi, Ph.D., State University of New York at Albany, is a Clinical Research Psychologist at the National Center for PTSD in the psychology service of the Boston VA Medical Center, and Assistant Professor in Psychiatry at Tufts University School of Medicine. His research interests are psychophysiological parameters of PTSD and implosive therapy for PTSD.

Beth M. Houskamp received her Ph.D. in clinical psychology from the Graduate School of Psychology, Fuller Theological Seminary in 1990. She is currently a Postdoctoral Research Fellow at the Neuropsychiatric Institute, University of California at Los Angeles. Her clinical and research interests focus on assessment and treatment of trauma related distress in children, adults, and families.

Jennifer C. Jones received her Ph.D. in 1990 from the State University of New York at Albany. She is currently a Clinical Research Scientist at the Phobia and Anxiety Disorders Clinic affiliated with the State University of New York at Albany. Her clinical and research interests include behavioral assessment and treatment of panic disorders, mixed anxiety-depression, and male sexual dysfunction.

Terence M. Keane, Director of the National Center for PTSD in Boston, is also Chief of the Psychology Service at the Boston VA Medical Center and Outpatient Clinic. A Professor of Psychiatry (Psychology) at Tufts University School of Medicine, Dr. Keane's clinical and research interests are in traumatic stress disorders. He is a Fellow of the American Psychological Association and is a member of the editorial board of the *Journal of Abnormal Psychology* and *Journal of Traumatic Stress.*

Brett T. Litz, Ph.D., State University of New York at Binghamton, is a Clinical Research Psychologist at the National Center for PTSD-Behavioral Sciences Division, Boston VA Medical Center and Assistant Professor in Psychiatry at Tufts University School of Medicine. His research interests are information processing in PTSD and the psychological assessment of PTSD.

Debra A. Neumann is currently an advanced graduate student in the clinical psychology doctoral program at Fuller Theological Seminary. Her clinical and research interests include women's issues and sexual assault.

Sheryl S. Osato received her Ph.D. in clinical psychology from the University of Hawaii in 1986. Her research interests have included the evaluation, treatment, and conceptualization of PTSD. A second interest area focuses on gerontology, particularly neuropsychological assessment of older adults. She is currently Director of Geropsychology Services at the West Los Angeles VA Medical Center, Brentwood Division, and is affiliated with the UCLA Neuropsychiatric Institute and Fuller Graduate School of Psychology.

Walter E. Penk, Ph.D., is Director of Psychology for the Department of Mental Health in the Commonwealth of Massachusetts and a Research Associate in the National Center for PTSD, VA Medical Center, Boston. He serves on the faculties of Harvard Medical School, University of Massachusetts Medical School, Tufts University School of Medicine, and Boston University. He is a Diplomate in Clinical Psychology and a Fellow in the American Psychological Association. His research interests are in diagnosis and treatment of severe and persistent mental disorders accompanied by addictions and adjustment to combat and civilian traumas.

Barbara Olasov Rothbaum received her Ph.D. in clinical psychology from the University of Georgia in 1986 and is currently an Assistant Professor at Emory University School of Medicine. Her research interests include posttraumatic stress disorder, obsessive-compulsive disorder, trichotillomania, and premenstrual syndrome.

Psychology Practitioner Guidebooks

Editors
Arnold P. Goldstein, Syracuse University
Leonard Krasner, Stanford University & SUNY at Stony Brook
Sol L. Garfield, Washington University in St. Louis

William L. Golden, E. Thomas Dowd & Fred Friedberg—
HYPNOTHERAPY: A Modern Approach

Patricia Lacks—BEHAVIORAL TREATMENT FOR PERSISTENT INSOMNIA

Arnold P. Goldstein & Harold Keller—AGGRESSIVE BEHAVIOR:
Assessment and Intervention

C. Eugene Walker, Barbara L. Bonner & Keith L. Kaufman—
THE PHYSICALLY AND SEXUALLY ABUSED CHILD: Evaluation
and Treatment

Robert E. Becker, Richard G. Heimberg & Alan S. Bellack—SOCIAL
SKILLS TRAINING TREATMENT FOR DEPRESSION

Richard F. Dangel & Richard A. Polster—TEACHING CHILD
MANAGEMENT SKILLS

Albert Ellis, John F. McInerney, Raymond DiGiuseppe &
Raymond J. Yeager—RATIONAL-EMOTIVE THERAPY WITH
ALCOHOLICS AND SUBSTANCE ABUSERS

Johnny L. Matson & Thomas H. Ollendick—ENHANCING CHILDREN'S
SOCIAL SKILLS: Assessment and Training

Edward B. Blanchard, John E. Martin & Patricia M. Dubbert—NON-DRUG
TREATMENTS FOR ESSENTIAL HYPERTENSION

Samuel M. Turner & Deborah C. Beidel—TREATING OBSESSIVE-
COMPULSIVE DISORDER

Alice W. Pope, Susan M. McHale & W. Edward Craighead—SELF-
ESTEEM ENHANCEMENT WITH CHILDREN AND ADOLESCENTS

Jean E. Rhodes & Leonard A. Jason—PREVENTING SUBSTANCE
ABUSE AMONG CHILDREN AND ADOLESCENTS

Gerald D. Oster, Janice E. Caro, Daniel R. Eagen & Margaret A. Lillo—
ASSESSING ADOLESCENTS

Robin C. Winkler, Dirck W. Brown, Margaret van Keppel & Amy
Blanchard—CLINICAL PRACTICE IN ADOPTION

Roger Poppen—BEHAVIORAL RELAXATION TRAINING AND
ASSESSMENT

Michael D. LeBow—ADULT OBESITY THERAPY

Robert Paul Liberman, William J. DeRisi & Kim T. Mueser—SOCIAL
SKILLS TRAINING FOR PSYCHIATRIC PATIENTS

Johnny L. Matson—TREATING DEPRESSION IN CHILDREN AND
ADOLESCENTS

Sol L. Garfield—THE PRACTICE OF BRIEF PSYCHOTHERAPY

Arnold P. Goldstein, Barry Glick, Mary Jane Irwin, Claudia Pask-McCartney
& Ibrahim Rubama—REDUCING DELINQUENCY: Intervention in
the Community

Albert Ellis, Joyce L. Sichel, Raymond J. Yeager, Dominic J. DiMattia,
& Raymond DiGiuseppe—RATIONAL-EMOTIVE COUPLES THERAPY

Clive R. Hollin—COGNITIVE-BEHAVIORAL INTERVENTIONS WITH
YOUNG OFFENDERS

Margaret P. Korb, Jeffrey Gorrell & Vernon Van De Riet—GESTALT
THERAPY: Practice and Theory, Second Edition

Donald A. Williamson—ASSESSMENT OF EATING DISORDERS:
Obesity, Anorexia and Bulimia Nervosa

J. Kevin Thompson—BODY IMAGE DISTURBANCE: Assessment and Treatment

William J. Fremouw, Maria de Perczel & Thomas E. Ellis—SUICIDE RISK: Assessment and Response Guidelines

Arthur M. Horne & Thomas V. Sayger—TREATING CONDUCT AND OPPOSITIONAL DEFIANT DISORDERS IN CHILDREN

Richard A. Dershimer—COUNSELING THE BEREAVED

Eldon Tunks & Anthony Bellissimo—BEHAVIORAL MEDICINE: Concepts and Procedures

Alan Poling, Kenneth D. Gadow & James Cleary—DRUG THERAPY FOR BEHAVIOR DISORDERS: An Introduction

Ira Daniel Turkat—THE PERSONALITY DISORDERS: A Psychological Approach to Clinical Management

Karen S. Calhoun & Beverly M. Atkeson—TREATMENT OF RAPE VICTIMS: Facilitating Psychosocial Adjustment

Manuel Ramirez III—PSYCHOTHERAPY AND COUNSELING WITH MINORITIES: A Cognitive Approach to Individual and Cultural Differences

Martin Lakin—COPING WITH ETHICAL DILEMMAS IN PSYCHOTHERAPY

Ricks Warren & George D. Zgourides—ANXIETY DISORDERS: A Rational-Emotive Perspective

Emil J. Chiauzzi—PREVENTING RELAPSE IN THE ADDICTIONS: A Biopsychosocial Approach

Matthew R. Sanders & Mark R. Dadds—BEHAVIORAL FAMILY INTERVENTION

Philip C. Kendall—ANXIETY DISORDERS IN YOUTH: Cognitive-Behavioral Interventions

William L. Golden, Wayne D. Gersh & David M. Robbins—PSYCHOLOGICAL TREATMENT OF CANCER PATIENTS: A Cognitive-Behavioral Approach

Jane Close Conoley & Collie W. Conoley—SCHOOL CONSULTATION: Practice and Training, Second Edition

Philip A. Saigh—POSTTRAUMATIC STRESS DISORDER: A Behavioral Approach to Assessment and Treatment